T0366360

Transformational Strategy

Facilitation of ToP Participatory Planning

Bill Staples

iUniverse, Inc.
Bloomington

Transformational Strategy
Facilitation of ToP Participatory Planning

iUniverse books may be ordered through booksellers or by contacting:

iUniverse
1663 Liberty Drive
Bloomington, IN 47403
www.iuniverse.com
1-800-Authors (1-800-288-4677)

ISBN: 978-1-4759-6839-2 (sc)
ISBN: 978-1-4759-6840-8 (ebk)

Printed in the United States of America

iUniverse rev. date: 01/18/2013

Contents

Part A. Transformation by Participation

Part B. Transparent Method

Part C. Four Transformational Phases of the Spiral Process in Planning

Part D. Embedding Transformation with Enhanced ToP Methods

List of Figures

Preface

by John L. Epps

Often something extraordinary happens in a ToP® Strategic Planning workshop. Of course, effective strategies are developed and plans for their implementation are crafted, but many planning processes can achieve those results. The "happening" I've observed transforms the group of participants: they become a team with ownership of, and commitment to, what they've created together. There is often an enthusiasm, sometimes even excitement, about getting started.

It would be arrogant to suggest that the ToP process "causes" these responses, but it would be far too modest to suggest that it has nothing to do with the transformation. The ToP strategic planning process was designed to provide occasions for that transformation to happen.

I witnessed this happening in working with a petroleum refinery that was having labor difficulties. The senior managers decided to engage in ToP strategic planning to involve all members of the plant in a series of workshops. They warned us, the facilitators, that most personnel would not speak up since they were Asians and we were Westerners. After the senior managers' workshop, one manager looked in on a staff workshop and was astounded at what he saw: not only were people contributing actively and enthusiastically, their analysis was virtually identical to that of the senior managers in terms of vision and contradictions. The upshot of this program was that 70 improvement projects were completed over the next three years, and the staff morale index had climbed from less than 30% to over 90%.

Finding ways to occasion this "extraordinary happening" in groups is increasingly important. The happening indicates a recovery of meaning in work. Few maladies are more widespread today than the perception that work is meaningless—boring, trivial, routine, and insignificant—though it consumes half of one's waking hours. People devise numerous ways to contend with this ennui, ranging from arguing for increased benefits to job-hopping to apathy. The popular remedy is to achieve a "work-life balance" as if work were not part of life.

The present workforce increasingly demands more from work than good pay and other benefits. Generation Y seems to have as part of its DNA the quest for meaningful work. Elsewhere I have chronicled the journey of meaning at work; here it is enough to say that ToP Strategic Planning provides ample occasions for group members to find that their hopes and dreams are shared, that their obstacles are doorways to a positive future, and that their efforts together can make a difference. Work becomes an adventure in building the future. It has meaning.

In this book, Bill Staples provides a thorough account of the Technology of Participation Strategic Planning Process. He includes both the background and the practical methods, so readers can gain an appreciation of what it entails and what it can produce. The latter portion of the book contains detailed procedures for each step. The book is a very useful reference and supplement to hands-on training, but should not attempt to replace it. Until one experiences this extraordinary happening firsthand, attempts to occasion it are likely to be ineffective. Once one has that experience, the facilitator will find the book is a valuable guide to an incredible journey.

— John Epps
Kuala Lumpur
August, 2012

Foreword

by Larry Philbrook

I remember meeting Bill Staples in India 35 years ago, when both of us were young and exploring what it meant to be facilitators in a community context. We had no idea how facilitation work would grow around the globe. We and our colleagues in ICA India were inventing community-based planning processes that enabled communities to essentially make their own decisions, a simple process at the core but with transformational underpinnings. It was seen as strategic planning, but it was strategic thinking that challenged communities to soar beyond the plan, searching for systemic self-reliant transformation.

Bill went back to Canada and I moved on too, eventually to Taipei, Taiwan. The Taiwanese easily integrated the same processes into their own communities and lives and I saw the same thing going on in other parts of the world. For the past twenty years in southeast Asia I have been able to practice the same strategic planning, thinking and transformation within the Taipei business community, which is well linked to the private sector on every other continent. It has been an amazing journey!

I was very pleased when Bill told me three years ago he was going to document our global work on participatory strategic planning. It is hard to believe it has been more than twenty years since *Winning through Participation* was published. Taking on the description of the ensuing transformation and expansion of the past forty years is a momentous task, as you will see when you read the book. Our work has evolved as we incorporated learning and insight from communities and organizations and from diverse cultures and individuals. Capturing the complexity of the story and the scope of the work took a lot of reflection and energy, as Bill pursued colleagues around the world for their insights and stories and integrated them with his own experiences.

Bill is the latest of his colleagues at ICA Associates and ICA Canada to take on a writing task. They have been willing and disciplined enough to support each other as they explore and share major elements of our common practice. In each case they based their writing on their own expansion and application of our work while reaching out to the global community to include the work of others, providing access to much of ICA's global learning. In fact their work Is so wellknown that last week in China I was asked if ICA is a Canadian organization since so many of our books are written there. I said absolutely yes; ICA is Canadian, and Chilean, and British, and Kenyan and Zimbabwean and many other nationalities. ICA is a worldwide community with each part contributing its bit to the mosaic.

To write this particular book was a challenge because the scope of our strategy work has been vast. ICA and strategic planning have been synonymous for more than 30 years. From planning groups, large and small, to transforming from the personal and systemic; from New Orleans after Katrina to global boardrooms and small community-based NGOs; the work has been diverse and yet quite simple. How do we help this group or person think through their past and present, explore their future, discern their systemic contradiction, and then decide and act on their resulting commitments?

The method has been the same yet always evolving. In the East people tell me it is a western method; in the West they tell me it must be from the East. My reply is, this is a human method developed through practice with 1000 communities and organizations. In this book Bill has documented many sources which fed our learning and thinking, and important practices added by many groups and ToP facilitators. This is a living methodology. As facilitators we are in a constant dialogue of creation, yet if you go into a ToP planning process anywhere in the world today you will experience a sense of the familiar.

In facilitator training, my context is: Prepare for every step; write every procedure; then when you walk into the group, be present and love them as they are. The process will flow from that marriage of deep preparation and deep presence. This book represents that type of preparation.

Bill, resolute, focused and disciplined, grounded in reality and yet willing to dream with his vast global experience, is the ideal one to sketch out this work. So Bill, I thank you for your own deep preparation and presence which shows through your integration of ICA's creative facilitation process.

Introduction

A large ICA network developed the planning methods in Laura Spencer's *Winning through Participation: Meeting the Challenge of Corporate Change With the Technology of Participation.* Laura spoke directly to the corporate world when she and her colleagues coined the term "ToP Technology of Participation®" to bring a unifying perspective to those values and approaches that:

- Bring together a wide range of perspectives, resulting in a comprehensive strategic plan
- Accomplish in a short time what would have taken weeks or even months using traditional planning methods
- Produce action plans that get done
- Generate commitment and team spirit, resulting in quick, effective implementation
- Follow up with strategic reviews that keep plans on track as circumstances change.

She showed how ToP processes and methods enabled companies to be much more effective in what we might call the productivity paradigm, with examples from McDonald's Corporation, Hughes Tool Company, Sun Chemical, Nichii Department Store, and others in the private sector.

Today, however, a sea change has swept over our world. Society is becoming more interested in participatory management and facilitative leadership, and participation means much more than productivity and accomplishments. The bar is higher for participation, communication, ethical behavior, stakeholder relations, organizational culture, and social responsibility than ever before. The internet and global media have produced a quantum leap in connectivity. The globalization of everything from markets to community-based development has wired us all more closely together and we are far more aware and attuned to what is happening than we ever were. We're a knowledge-based society rather than a world based on production. Ideas are the currency of the day. Crises and large-scale collapses in finance, international relations, or failed states are requiring us to come up with new ways of being together in this interdependent world.

Also, since that time, at least 100,000 people have taken ToP courses and there are master ToP practitioners and trainers in 30 countries. Using ToP methods, the Asian Development Bank accelerated micronutrient food fortification in seven countries; the City of Toronto unanimously passed a unique five-pillar policy on drug use; the Inuvik Hospital quickly moved from one site to another within a few days, with no disruption to patient care; Great Eastern Life Assurance Co. Ltd. won an award for people-oriented management; the cities of Cedar Rapids and New Orleans planned for flood recovery and rebuilding; the 100 Valleys Project in Peru reversed the decline of agricultural production; the African Foundation for Development in London developed new and sustainable partners; the Il Ngwesi Maasai community in Kenya tested 90% of its population for HIV/AIDS.

This is a small sample from hundreds of stories reported by ToP practitioners. Equally important, those organizations experienced benefits beyond the realization of goals. Employees became directly involved in planning and problem solving tasks. They took new roles, animating and inspiring project teams and departments. These organizations retained employees by involving them in serious initiatives to improve everything from policy to operations. The surge of commitment created by using ToP methods ignites the energy, enthusiasm, and creativity essential to any organization's success and sustainability in today's complex environment.

ICA created ToP methods to provide leaders and facilitators with approaches adaptable to the unique specifics of any situation. Many deeply divided groups in society have experienced reconciliation, as sophisticated ToP methods enabled them to focus on common visions of the future, rather than factional differences. ToP practitioners have worked with United Nations organizations, civil society organizations, scores of national and state governments, hundreds of corporations and companies, and innumerable regional authorities and non-profit associations.

Our intensified awareness and closeness is extending our sense of empathy beyond all known boundaries. With the world in our living room, we cannot avoid forming closer bonds, seeking new solutions, and calling for new levels of ethical behavior and transparency. People want deeper and more meaningful engagement. We are beckoned to step beyond functional, production-oriented ways of thinking, organizing, and acting—to move into deeper and more meaningful engagement that integrates new value sets and operating modes. Beyond mere progressive change, we are all together rewriting the book on how to be human, how to be an organization, and how to make the transformation.

The world used to cry out for participative management that linked values to a management style of the future. Now, however, the world needs facilitative leadership—the ability to lead social, organizational, and corporate transformation in a way that engages everybody in it together. ToP methods go far beyond the old productivity paradigm, and actually help organizations make this leap. In the 1980s, few books explained how to translate participative management from theory into reality. So *Winning through Participation* was written to bridge that gap. Today, as facilitative leadership is taking root in organizations around the world this book, *Transformational Strategy: Facilitation of ToP Participatory Planning,* shows substantial ways to put that concept into practice.

Transformational energy

From their earliest efforts, practitioners of ToP methods discovered they were getting much more than just solid plans and positive results. Something was happening to the people in the organizations. There was a sparkle in the eye, a lightness in the step, and a degree of commitment that was delightfully new and seemed almost magical. People in the organization would notice a real difference, but be at a loss to explain what it was. Clearly some kind of transformational energy was at work. What is the transformational capacity of ToP methods? Different ToP practitioners might answer that question in their own unique way, but here is what I have seen.

It happens first at a very personal level. Participants say their voices are heard and their ideas treated with respect. They understand how their practical decisions affect the direction of the organization or community. They know how to have a positive effect on their own future. They have deeper respect for others in the organization. They understand their situation better, because they have integrated the perspectives of others with their own. They talk about assuming greater responsibility for the whole organization, because they have participated in determining what is necessary. They want to expand their personal capacities in ways they have not used before.

Second, they see a change in other people. They notice people listening more carefully, being less fearful of new situations, and building up the confidence that comes with accomplishing goals as a team. They notice colleagues trying out creative, innovative solutions to previously insoluble problems. They recognize that the group as a whole is demonstrating values, exhibiting behaviors, and generating results. Everyone is taking more interest in their work.

Third, they talk about the positive impact that the organization is having on its intended stakeholders or on society. They mention how the organization has a new story about its role, and how that story is being acted upon. They refer to a new courage in the organization's ability to act, and how this courage is not simply vested in the leadership at the top, but is imbedded throughout the organization. It seems that the old riddle of "What comes first … personal transformation? Or social transformation?" has been solved. They occur simultaneously, with a feedback loop from one to the other.

Strategic thinking

This book is about strategic thinking. But as Henry Mintzberg, McGill University professor of Management Studies, says, "Strategic planning is not strategic thinking." Mintzberg draws a distinction between strategic planning (or the systematic programming of pre-identified strategies), and strategic thinking, which seeks innovation and imagines new futures that lead to the formation of core strategies.

Strategic thinking is concretely grounded in reality, and deals with the real specifics of the situation. It is not a detached analysis, but emerges from deep within the actual workings of an organization and its world. It is indicative in that it deals with the way things are, rather than assumptions about the way things ought to be in a perfect universe. It is practical, aimed at real results, and at making a substantial impact.

The facilitation of participative strategic thinking is complex because it requires cooperation in creating and guiding a journey of innovation. Participative strategic thinking is focused on determining intentions. It is positive in that the whole thinking process is oriented toward making good things happen. It ensures that both creative and critical thinking are incorporated into strategy. It is intuitive and imaginative.

Strategies of transformation involve dealing with contradiction. ICA has brought a unique gift to the practice of strategy development and of transformation through its understanding of contradiction. No one else comes close to ICA's ability to ground that concept in philosophy, psychology, change theory, and planning methodology—so that transformation, not productivity, is the result of strategy. ToP participatory strategic planning offers that unique gift, which has benefitted organizations and communities the world over.

It will take the entire book to explain, illustrate, and illuminate the power that contradiction gives to strategies of transformation. Contradiction is derived from a synthesis between a positive image of an intended future (which is one's mission, purpose, values and vision), and an analysis of the real and complex current situation that one finds oneself in. It requires real courage to stare into the hard cold reality of the present situation while figuring out how to bring about a new future. The ToP orientation keeps the big picture in mind. It takes a whole systems perspective, and draws meaning from the complex relationships.

Part A, Transformation by Participation, illustrates how the Technology of Participation has guided large and small-scale transformation in adapting to a wide variety of situations. Brief stories show how the methods have helped resolve problems associated with the diversification of populations, responding to natural disasters, building ecological and sustainability movements, forming communities of interest and practice, or enhancing the quality of life and social change in general. Examples are included of specific organizations, communities, and companies. This section also includes a history of the development of the ToP approach, and its foundations in philosophy and the social sciences.

Part B, Transparent Method, illuminates the mental models, theory, methods, and tools that make ToP participatory planning so dynamic and powerful. It also shows the framework of participation that envelops the ToP participatory strategic planning process, and how it guides a transformation from its early stages through the entire process.

Part C, Participatory Strategy: The Spiral Process, goes deeply into the theory, practice, and application of the key parts of ToP participatory strategic planning that have occasioned transformation in communities, organizations, businesses and governments over the past three decades. This section includes specific examples and expanded procedures for those who have taken the ToP Participatory strategic planning course, and who need additional help in their specific situation.

Part D, Enhanced Methods and Tools, demonstrates the variations that add a higher level of intention to transformation, and therefore make it more seamless. This section also includes documentation of live examples of participatory strategic planning processes, and detailed procedures for some of the tools mentioned earlier in the book.

ToP practitioner's dilemma

Dependent on fundraising to fund their charitable activities, many of the 34 ICA offices around the world found a new source of self-support by marketing to many types of clients the planning methods they had developed. Their clients included dozens of civil society and United Nations organizations, scores of national and state governments, hundreds of corporations and companies, and innumerable regional authorities and non-profit associations. Leaders of all these groups wanted solid, measurable results from their investment. ToP methods demonstrated again and again that they delivered results.

By the mid 1990s there were over a thousand ToP practitioners around the world, many of whom would call themselves part- or full-time facilitators. At the time, the landscape was beginning to shift. Founders of the newly forming profession were beginning to consider the very nature of facilitation, and one of its most basic tenets was that of neutrality. As facilitators, ToP practitioners knew they could always play a neutral role with participants, but as agents of transformation there was still the question of whether they could really be neutral.

Professional facilitators debate this possibility of being a neutral presence and at the same time being a conscious agent of transformation. A transformational process used by an agent is heavily dependent on the values and philosophy of that agent, but those values and philosophy may not be shared by the client group and participants. Does one knowingly use a transformational process that shifts the client or participants in the direction of one's own values, or does one try to remain neutral knowing that the client's values may be the main dysfunction within the group?

This tension exposes the central dilemma of the ToP practitioner. On-the-ground evidence from 35 years of practice by hundreds of master ToP practitioners shows that the methods are indeed transformational—as they were designed to be. Therefore, the ToP practitioner can remain simply a professional facilitator, and use the methods as neutral planning and productivity tools—just as many clients want. On the other hand, the facilitator can admit to a transformational intent, use the methods at their full power … and take the consequences. Typically, the consequence is that the client is happier afterwards. However, if you talk about the potential for transformation beforehand, it can cause a degree of nervousness in clients. As more and more ToP practitioners and certified facilitators become passionate enough about the potential for positive change in society they talk about it with the client in advance. When they don't mention it, they are in a similar position to a master architect who doesn't mention his or her qualifications when renovating a neighbor's garage. Selecting a master ToP practitioner to create a plan to increase productivity is somewhat akin to selecting a Ferrari to drive to the convenience store for milk. A reasonable question for every ToP practitioner is "When do I want to facilitate just what the client wants, and when do I want to ask about transforming their situation?"

Consequently, while this book is primarily about the transformational aspects of ToP methods and how contradictions are at the core of the transformation, it can also be used by facilitators who want to know how to guide and facilitate the participatory development of an effective strategic plan.

Part A

Transformation by Participation

1

Social transformation
through ToP methods

Participation is often assumed. Most people, however, have only the vaguest understandings about the ways to make it happen.
—Terry Bergdall, ToP practitioner, Chicago, Illinois

Transformation is happening all around us all the time. It is no news to anyone that we are experiencing massive economic, scientific, technological, political, social and cultural changes that together conspire to take us far beyond business as usual. Our institutions and conventions are under intense scrutiny from all directions. People are looking at our world and their own situations quite differently from how they did even 20 years ago. Indeed, we are living through several earth-shaking shifts that are rewriting our story of who we are in the world. The speed and manner in which this is happening make it more clearly visible to some people and less obvious to others. However, not being aware of it does not mean that it is not happening. When a hurricane flattens a forest, it makes a sound—even if no one is there to hear it.

People today feel genuinely empowered to see fresh opportunities, to step onto the stage of history, and take an active part in directing it the way they want their world to go. It is the premise of the Technology of Participation (ToP®) that within any social grouping, participation by its stakeholders in analysis, planning, decision-making, and implementation is fundamental to transformation. This does not mean that participation is the only way to occasion transformation, but effective participation can empower people to consciously decide about what change is necessary, rather than have it "happen" to them. ToP participatory planning can leverage significant change, generate commitment and build powerful momentum.

ToP participatory approaches have proven to be particularly effective in certain areas. In some cases up to 40 years of documentation is available to verify the obvious transformational effects, especially in such settings as these:

- Areas where population size and demographics are changing at a rapid pace.
- Situations in which natural disasters require concerted effort by many organizations.
- Groups developing and implementing corporate social responsibility for the environment.
- Movements for engaging local people in various types of social change.
- Efforts to improve the quality of life for employees of for-profit enterprises.
- Communities of interest seeking to generate commitment and action.

Before we examine the details of the methods, let's look at some examples from the experiences of ToP practitioners from across the world.

Empowering diverse and migrating populations

External pressures can rapidly shift the density and demographics of a population, a market, or a region, creating requirements for new services where none were needed before. The world's megacities are now home to a multitude of new immigrant populations, each requiring support and services in their own language, with their own ethno-cultural understanding and style. In order to accommodate the changing demographics even though there is no one template for delivering services to such a diverse public, organizations working in these situations inevitably undergo transformations in the way they deliver their services.

Toronto had over 90 different settlement organizations serving national, ethnic, or language groups from African countries. Since there were so many, and the complexity of working with all the individual settlement organizations was so great, one government department, which was constantly being petitioned for funds, wanted all 90 to form an umbrella organization. ToP methods engaged all the organizations in developing an operational model for the umbrella organization.

Government, private sector, and community organizations around the world are being required to make staffing changes to keep up with the change and segmentation of populations in both their clientele and their internal staff. Some police departments have to provide on-the-spot-translation for as many as 30 languages. Shifts in values, policies, working styles, and behaviors generally require a major transformation of an organization.

From California:

I work within the City of Fremont's Human Services Department (HSD), in the Aging and Family Services Division. HSD received a grant from the Robert Wood Johnson Foundation to develop a community strategic plan for the older adults in our area. The communities of Fremont, Newark, and Union City are very diverse, and there is no one majority population. Over 120 languages are spoken in area schools. Many older adults in the area are unable to speak English. HSD was challenged, in that we had to bring the multiple ethnic communities together to develop an overall strategic plan. It was at this point that one of our staff stated that she had participated in a facilitation that involved a "sticky wall." She was impressed by the consensus the facilitation had produced. HSD staff took the Group Facilitation Training course and hired Jane Stallman, a ToP facilitator. Subsequently, we conducted 14 focus groups in 9 languages and dialects, and then we held two very large open community dialogues. The core leadership team used the methods to develop a five-year community strategic plan for older adults, which is currently being implemented through our partnership with the Tri-City Elder Coalition, called Pathways to Positive Aging, with further funding provided by the Robert Wood Johnson Foundation. HSD continues to use the ToP approach because it is effective. It works amazingly well within our diverse community, and has helped a variety of start-up nonprofits achieve success. What keeps us going is the fact that it works so well, and it generates excitement throughout the community.
—Raymond Grimm, ToP practitioner, Fremont, USA

From Nepal:

Devda community is not a very old village. Twenty years ago people migrated from the mountains southward to the forest and created the village. It had no services, infrastructure, nor organization of any kind, and no NGOs operated in the village. There were about 50,000 people, and one specific site near the edge of the village had around 6,000 people. Most of them had no real awareness of themselves as an actual community, or of any leadership within their boundaries. About 40 people decided to take part of a participatory strategic plan, including some of the key people within the village. The planning session was a major event, building environmental, social, cultural, and personal awareness. For the first few months after the plan not much was done, but soon heavy implementation of the strategies began. They launched a community market every Monday morning, which had an immediate positive impact, as people began to sell their products including chickens and goats. A one kilometer road was built from the outer sector of the village to the market, with beautification including directional signs. Then they installed four acres of drip irrigation to increase the crop potential of about 200 families. Cultural development occurred as people explored their inner capacity and creative capacity.
—Tatwa Timsina, ToP practitioner, Kathmandu, Nepal

From Bangladesh:

Ghoramara community of 2,000 people in Chandpur, Bangladesh, was a landless community under the government shelter project, in which only land and plots were given, but no health infrastructure or schools. The leadership was distrusted, because they did not share information with the population. The community did not know what to do, had no clear goals, and did not know their own potential and assets. After a participatory strategic plan and a set of action plans two years later, the men and women are working together to start and run a preschool and a primary school with books, and a school building is under construction. Older students are gaining skills and are involved in the projects. The adults have installed tube wells and are now much more self-reliant.
—Aziz Rahman, ToP practitioner, Dhaka, Bangladesh

From the UK:

AFFORD, the African Foundation for Development, is a UK-based diaspora organization that works with other diaspora organizations in the UK, linking them to development efforts in Africa. In 2002, amidst many conflicting priorities, they were uncertain about which possibilities to focus on in developing coalitions and partnerships in the UK. ICA:UK facilitated a strategic planning event for the entire board, staff, and stakeholders. Participants got a taste of how a participatory approach works, and understood firsthand how all ideas could be included and drawn upon to produce a coherent product that was both agreed on and owned by the participants. The AFFORD staff recognized that they wanted to use these particular processes in their day-to-day work and relationship building. One board member said "If not for that planning process, I believe I might have given up volunteering for AFFORD some time ago. I gave up all the other organizations I used to serve, because their processes were not sufficiently participatory and inclusive for me."

The event has also had a bearing on who they are attracting as an organization, who they work with, and the relationship they have with their partners. AFFORD is more confident in promoting participation and training African facilitators to manage workshops at conferences. Sixty young Africans were trained for the annual African Diaspora and Development Days. They have been taught to listen, not to fear disagreement, and to build consensus. The planning event also changed the criteria by which they choose their partners: If they don't see any commitment toward participation, they won't engage with them. Information Officer Onyekachi Wambu said, "ICA techniques and ideas have had, I would say, a big impact on AFFORD. From my own perspective it has shaped the way I approach meetings and seek to build consensus for actions."
—Jonathan Dudding, ToP practitioner, London, UK

Responding to natural disasters

Hurricanes, earthquakes and tsunamis devastate entire regions, leaving little or no infrastructure in their wake. People have to organize quickly to get things done, in spite of the trauma. ToP methods can organize people quickly and empower them to act. Any organization that intends to be successful over the long term is routinely required to work on risk management or emergency plans. The "millennium bug" was a new phenomenon for many organizations at the end of the last century, which required participation by many minds in thinking through the various scenarios and build adequate responses. In the last decade, emergency planning had to be carried out many times for a host of reasons. Since no single individual can calculate all the variables, many perspectives must be involved. Large organizations must consider the prospect of a sudden shift in communication, leadership, and delivery. In places where such natural disasters have actually occurred, front line staff must take on new responsibility and respond immediately, without instruction or training, and usually with inadequate resources. ToP planning and implementation can help them be ready.

In the past few years, on every continent, media reports have riveted our attention on natural disasters. It has been easy to see that the capacity to respond proactively is a hallmark of the best organized efforts. ToP methods were used in the earthquake zones of mountainous Peru, after Hurricane Katrina in New Orleans, after the tsunami in Japan, and in many other places to galvanize the efforts of dozens of organizations that collaborated in transformative efforts to organize leadership as quickly as possible after the event.

From New Orleans, USA:

> *Local residents in the Holy Cross Neighborhood Association in New Orleans determined to become a model community following the destruction of Hurricane Katrina. In hurricane recovery groups across New Orleans there is a preference for participatory interactive meetings and participatory modes of decision making of all kinds.*
> *—Jean Watts, ToP practitioner, New Orleans*

From Chincha, Peru:

> *On August 15, 2007, the city of Chincha was struck by an 8.0 earthquake, and most of the residents lost their homes. To be able to relocate the people back onto their properties, the rubble had to be removed—the ruins of what used to be their homes only a week earlier. The Little Houses for Christmas campaign was initiated to build 1,650 provisional but secure houses, and also to strengthen the soup kitchens that had sprung up in this time of need. To*

be able to build that many houses in three months, a team had to catalyze a broad initiative on the part of the local people. The area was divided into 30 sectors, with the support of the mayor of the city, Mr. Jose Navarra. Two representatives from each sector voluntarily lead the campaign to facilitate the work in their sector, forming team of five families to build the houses. Due to the speed and low cost of the project, the campaign was repeated in another 30 sectors, and a record 1,800 more homes were built in just two and a half months.
—Gloria Santos, ToP practitioner, Chincha

Sustaining ecology movements

In the past two decades there has been a groundswell of interest in solving, or at least moving toward solving environmental problems. The demonstrated unsustainability of current consumption practices has caught everyone in the ethical dilemma, between the demand for economic growth and the need to conserve resources. It now takes very little in the way of organizational leadership to get a whole company thinking how to "reuse, reduce, and recycle." For anything more than that, a more sophisticated whole-systems approach is needed. People are actually ready to implement this change, but most have not given thought to the feedback loops between the resource, production, and distribution systems within a company, or the more subtle political and cultural shifts that are needed.

Corporate social responsibility (CSR) is now taught in many universities and colleges to corporate leaders, which indicates executives' interest in driving internal organizational transformation down to the level of personal values, and not simply trying to mandate it from the senior level. ToP methods have been used to help universities develop their CSR curriculum, and to develop and implement socially responsible practices and policies in companies, governments, and in civil society. Many environmental groups and municipalities similarly use ToP methods to engage stakeholders and citizens in the creation of strategies leading toward long-term sustainability.

From Minneapolis, USA:

The Department of Natural Resources is very big in the State of Minnesota, which is blanketed with nature trails that are used by skiers, bikers, hikers, horseback riders, snowmobilers, and recreational vehicles. The department was heavily involved in ToP participatory strategic planning because so many user groups use the same trails, and some of them, especially the horseback riders and the cyclists, were in regular conflict—causing difficulties for the other groups. We used ToP planning with a large number of focus groups, followed by one large participatory roll-up planning session. As a result a new organization formed that jointly represented the interests of the users to the department and the legislature. They had never worked

together before, but the formation of that group, a direct result of their experience of ToP methods, was a high point for all of them.
—Sue Laxdall, ToP practitioner, Minneapolis

From Toronto, Canada:

In 2005, after using collaborative processes to draft a new Endangered Species Act in Ontario, the ministry in charge hired the same consultants to facilitate an extremely diverse group of stakeholders to create a policy framework to deal with all future occurrences of conflicts between humans and wildlife. The manager overseeing the project felt anxious initially, but years later praised the process as "the benchmark" in her mind, of how public policy needs to be created collaboratively with stakeholders. Sixty passionate stakeholders, whose perspectives ranged from animal rights activists to trappers, met with a few bureaucrats from related government ministries for two whole days. The ToP participatory strategic planning process was slightly adapted to fit their purposes: "vision" was called "ultimate outcomes," so that it could be used eventually for impact evaluation. Sessions on values and criteria in decision-making were added. The facilitator ensured that participants invested substantial time into building consensus on the kinds of outcomes they all really wanted to see. The group struggled with the workshop, because it was the first time most of them had worked together on anything, and as lobbyist and advocates, they were unaccustomed to listening to one another. The unedited strategies became official government policy, and were put to use by a diverse advisory group convened to pre-think the most difficult conflicts in the province. Today, they give their ideas to the ministry using the policy framework as their primary communication tool. The advisory group members learned to trust each other as they built the policy framework, paving the way for respectful cooperation on other potentially contentious issues. Subsequent ministers can take their advice seriously because of the depth of consultation and commitment behind it.
—John Miller, ToP practitioner, Toronto

Networking communities of interest and practice

Communities of interest and practice form new types of relationships, and expand them right around the world. These include professional associations like doctors, nurses, acupuncturists, and organizational development professionals, groups working within an industry, very large companies or unions, and rights-based groups that want to promote or advocate for their cause. Although the internet has provided rapid data-sharing and information tools that broadly support these communities, these same web-based tools are open to manipulation, and can be used for unacceptable and even criminal behavior. While data and information can be shared over the internet, real wisdom is created as a result of deep reflection, critical thinking, and synthesis, which is spurred by inclusive dialogue and challenging conversation. Although not exclusively the realm of ToP methods, the creation of new wisdom and knowledge is the domain in which the ToP approach excels in generating fresh analysis that leads to new insights.

While the ToP approach generates critical reflection and inclusive dialogue, it also creates commitment with action. The approach is biased towards action, and many communities of practice have been launched and empowered through participatory workshops and strategic planning. Every ToP method, tool, and process leads to the point of generating commitment and anticipating action. Although data gathering, analysis, problem solving, and story creation are particularly strong within the ToP suite of methods, there is also a conscious movement toward resolution and getting things done.

From Oakland, USA:

> *I saw the methods used when I was the manager of OD, Training and Development at Lockheed SkunkWorks in the '70s. I was impressed with how the methods helped form the new leadership team. Later as an independent consultant, I wanted to bring facilitation skills into the schools, and looked for a reasonably priced, practical facilitation course that could help increase the ability of those in the school system to work collaboratively and productively. Someone suggested that I talk to Beret Griffith. When I did, I realized that she and the consultant who worked with us at Lockheed were talking about the same methods. At that point I decided to take the courses and become a trainer in the methods. I now use them with all my clients.*
> *—Jane Stallman, ToP practitioner, Oakland*

From Phoenix, USA:

> *The American Academy of Medical Acupuncture used ToP methods to establish the association, then again ten years later to deal with incredible growth, and again ten years later to transition to a new leadership team. Each time they were willing to gather the insights and perspectives of their whole membership.*
> *—Marilyn Oyler, ToP practitioner, Phoenix*

Enhancing the quality of work life

In the private sector, what begins as a campaign to increase productivity can sometimes turn into a large-scale transformation of values. The need for increased productivity can lead to the requirement for immediate problem solving, and then to the need for front-line creativity and responsibility. This taste of creativity and responsibility can subsequently increase the capacity for inquiry, dialogue, and aspects of personal growth. In several large insurance companies, directors who went looking for real gains in productivity were surprised by the renewed trust, open dialogue, and creativity that came with it. For anyone who knows this field, productivity is an actual by-product of trust, dialogue, and creativity. So managers should not be surprised that wanting "bottom-line productivity" will drive them to truly engage staff in developing solutions, and that renewed levels of trust and dialogue, along with many other quality-of-life indicators, and even staff retention, will occur.

ToP methods have always produced both types of results—increased productivity, and increased quality of work life with staff retention, so organizations sometimes put their whole staff through ToP training. While ToP trainers and practitioners often speak the language of productivity to clients, they are quite clear that the real benefit is a happier, more respectful workplace.

It is common knowledge that the twentieth-century habit of creating a conventional hierarchical structure and organizational chart conditions its members toward straightforward behaviors of accountability. Some unsophisticated leaders may think that a simple change in the organizational chart will occasion a transformation. Many organizations are finding that conventional reporting and decision-making structures have outlived their usefulness, and that those conventional structures can end up blocking the effective operation of the organization. Consultants sometimes propose enterprise "cluster models" and "matrix models" as the new hierarchy, but then staff raise questions like "Which boss will resolve my competing priorities?" Just as Linux is one native operating system for the collaborative nature of the internet, the ToP approach is a native operating system for matrix and cluster organizations with participatory values. Healthy patterns of behavior and dialogue become the norm when the ToP approach is applied throughout an organization. Old-style managers newly arriving at a ToP-trained workplace may try their command and control behaviors, and be quickly corrected by staff: "We talk about things to solve problems around here!"

From a manufacturing plant in Hyderabad, India:

In India, a major US personal products company was suffering great difficulty with unrestrained union "gangsters," as productivity fell in their Mumbai plant. Senior management understood the situation and invited us to facilitate a participatory strategic planning event with them. After two and a half days, they were able to begin to take some measures to make changes.

The real story, however, was the planning event we did for a handful of managers who were opening up their new plant outside of Hyderabad in the south, where they wanted to

do everything "right." We did the usual process with those managers, and heard no more about the company for three or four years. Then on a visit to Hyderabad, I arranged to visit the plant. It was astonishing! All the production workers were young women who worked in close-knit teams, rotated the production-line jobs, depending on how stressful a particular job was compared to others—in other words, with care and respect for each other. I was told that the year after this small plant began production with 40 to 50 workers (compared to several hundred in Mumbai), it was responsible for 40% of the company's profit in India.
—*Richard West, ToP practitioner, Taipei, Taiwan*

From an American bank:

The executive team, including the president, of the finance and banking system of a US bank engaged in participatory strategic planning. After the first planning session, follow-up planning with the three business units determined their business plans, bottom lines, and actions plans to create the plans on how the goals and priorities of the larger division could be met. The meetings included finance officers, legal experts, and treasurers, who would determine whether a goal or an action plan could be done or not, depending on various legal or other reasons. Employees could see their own ideas and suggestions in the plans. The whole project took three years.
—*Eunice Shankland, ToP practitioner, Fairfax, USA*

The vanguard of social change

Small groups of people have always been at the vanguard of social change in society. Change often happens first at the grassroots level. People become aware of a problem causing innocent suffering in a sector of a population, and they want to change things to help those people. At root, we are a compassionate species. Social change agents see transformation as necessary for society, and they do not shy away from the personal difficulties it may cause them. They encourage others to stand up for themselves. One can find such people in every part of society. The more hopeless things become, the stronger these people tend to be. You can find them dealing with issues around drug use, homelessness, inequities in employment, or trying to change public policy.

Social change agents have always known that the best way to empower people is to have them participate in the decisions that affect them. You will find them in urban neighborhoods and rural areas in dozens of countries, in communities in Kenya and in neighborhoods throughout Toronto, working on initiatives to provide low-cost housing, working with victims of HIV/AIDS, or working with youth to provide alternatives to gang peer pressure.

From a village in India:

The ToP facilitation seed got planted in me during my year with the Maliwada Village Human Development Project in 1976 in India. Witnessing the impact of the planning week on the population awakened me to the power of ToP facilitation. However, it wasn't until six years later that facilitation became a regular part of what I do even today. What keeps me going today is the story of what happened in Maliwada. Facilitation process that engenders people's authentic participation switches them on to their own innate power of effectiveness.
—Kevin Balm, ToP practitioner, Bangkok, Thailand

From Guatemala:

I am still using the ToP approach because I see the life transformations in people just like me, just as when I encountered it for the first time in Santiago when I was 20. I used this methodology first as a volunteer for a long time with no financial benefit, but now I can use it for my own sustainability.
—Joaguina Rodriguez Ruz, ToP practitioner, Guatemala City, Guatemala

From New Orleans, Louisiana:

In early 1997, I saw a great mentor facilitator, Jean Watts, at work in a community forum at a local university. I sensed that something very different was producing the energy I saw unleashed in the room. I went up to her and told her I didn't know what it was she was doing, but that I wanted to learn how to do it!! And that was the start of my ToP life-changing journey.
—Erness Wright-Irvin, ToP practitioner, New Orleans, USA

In all of the large societal transformations mentioned above, the foundational ToP values of comprehensiveness, affirmation, responsibility, and courage are evident in the facilitators. More interesting, however, is that the disciplined application of ToP methods actually helps develop these qualities in facilitators. For this reason ToP practitioners are generally sensitive to the comprehensive needs of society. They stand in affirmation rather than in judgment of those needs. They act responsibly in complex situations, and they demonstrate courage tempered by pragmatism.

ToP transformation in organizations

Since private, public, non-profit, and local organizations are at the locus of many participatory endeavors, most ToP practitioners operate at an organizational level. Although some practitioners specialize in one type of organization rather than another, there is almost always a multidisciplinary quality to their work. Created in response to multi-sector and multi-stakeholder situations, ToP methodologies are perfectly suited to complex environments.

Throughout the book, numerous references clearly demonstrate the range of potential application of ToP methods to organizations. These case studies illustrate the theory behind the methods and demonstrate ToP facilitation practice. In the following section you will find several examples of the results and outcomes of ToP participatory planning. Full case studies start on page 99 and documentation of the strategic plans on page 243 but here are some briefer examples of the results and outcomes of the ToP participatory plan.

Transformation during a ToP planning weekend

The administrator of a national board of a professional organization called to ask about long range planning. The board wanted to formalize its 36,000 member organization which was currently an unincorporated group under the umbrella of another organization. After phone interviews with half of the board members I fine-tuned a weekend agenda for a participatory strategic planning process to be held a month later in a location that everyone could fly to from across the country.

The session in the hotel banquet room started on Friday night. The board discussed their last fifteen years and the most important trends driving change in the field of health care. They projected forward to describe what the organization would look like in five years. By the end of the evening the board members knew where they had come from, what society wanted from them, and had drafted a consensus on the long range vision of the organization. They were pleased with all this agreement on the first night.

On Saturday morning the board members engaged in dialogue about what was holding them back as an organization, getting clear on unhelpful patterns of personal and group behaviours that needed to be changed. It was a very frank discussion with soul searching, breakthrough insight and a collective sigh of relief. After a long break they discussed dozens of ideas on how to move ahead, finally agreeing on several strategies that would overcome their organization's inertia and forge a new direction. During the lunch hour people were pensive, personally processing the decisions they had just made.

After lunch they considered several mechanisms for the organization's structure, but decided to put that off until Sunday morning. For the rest of the afternoon they focused on designing a set of solid, measurable goals that would focus all the strategies to engage the wider membership in the new directions. By dinner time, they had a complete timeline of goals and some implementation steps for each strategy. Their dinner together at a fine restaurant was celebratory and their conversation about potential future board members was lively and enthusiastic.

On Sunday morning, the board picked up on their Saturday conversation about mechanisms, and decided on an organizational structure that would directly implement the strategies and goals with decision making mechanisms to match, and with personal assignments to the committees and task forces. They spent an hour listing and prioritizing all the people and partners to contact, and drafted a case for support to send to potential funders.

After a short lunch they held a brief official business meeting and several of them left for the airport.

Three years later, the organization had transformed itself into a major player in the health field, with a leadership role at most policy tables, with research capacity that proved its value within the entire field, and a new set of competencies and certification for its membership. The executive administrator reported that the board had implemented almost all of its strategic plans, so they asked for another cycle of ToP strategic planning, but this time with many important successes under their belt and a renewed sense of confidence. (See page 244 for detailed results.)

Regional economic development

A newly amalgamated city in Atlantic Canada and its surrounding rural area used ToP participatory strategic planning to launch over a dozen action teams in such areas as tourism, industrial research, information technology, youth development, and leadership reform. The city considered using a traditional consulting firm to give it "a bankable plan" that could be used with provincial and federal governments for funding, but decided that they wanted the "citizen teams in action" that ToP methods would launch. The new participatory plan heralded a transformation from a century-old resource economy to a new tourism and technology economy.

Area hospital

A hospital in Ontario, Canada was mandated to transform itself into an area health center, shifting from treating illness and accidents to becoming a cradle-to-grave wellness center for an entire population. A secondary shift involved moving from being a hospital with a religious affiliation to becoming a public institution. With the CEO reporting changes even seven years after their five-year plan, it is clear that the three-day ToP participatory strategic planning event started the entire effort on a solid footing.

International NGO

A small 12-employee department within a Canadian federal government-owned corporation was being spun off into a non-governmental organization. The aspirations of the NGO were of global proportions, and ToP strategic planning was used to launch the transformation. For several years a ToP practitioner occasionally assisted with certain strategies. Today the organization is an international NGO with offices on three continents, and it positively impacts the lives of 200 million children annually.

Information technology department

The information technology branches of four government departments each used ToP participatory strategic planning to focus their individual long-range plans. A larger matrix enterprise within the government then merged all four branches into one, using the ToP methods to transform the four separate IT branches into one larger cluster organization serving all four departments at once. A smaller core hardware group further used the methods to develop strategies and goals to get ahead of the exponential change in communication technologies.

Industry association

An industry association was comprised of competitive companies within the same industry. The association had a mandate to support the industry as a whole and be proactive about government legislation that affected them all. By conducting ToP participatory strategic planning, they created a long-range plan that would benefit all the members, in spite of the intense competition for clients that existed amongst them. The plan launched several new initiatives and hiring practices within the association.

From an international bank:

The CEO of a major national bank in southeast Asia wanted to involve his management staff from across the country in innovative and creative thinking about the operations of the bank. Specifically, he wanted to ensure that major board decisions benefitted from the thinking of the managers who were the direct link to front-line operations.

In the 1990s the national bank hired a new CEO to run a cluster of 18 branches across the country. The CEO had experienced ToP methods earlier in a job with another organization, and they had impressed him in helping to renew his earlier passion about being an economist. After becoming the CEO of this national bank, he asked ToP practitioners to facilitate a num-

ber of planning sessions in order to involve a wide spectrum of people in developing strategies for the bank.

Over a seven-year period, 12 participatory strategic planning sessions were facilitated with both branch managers and specific departments, such as trade finance and new business marketing. The CEO opened each session with a talk about why the participatory planning was important. A secretariat documented each session, and after reading through the documentation, the CEO gave a closing speech to affirm the participants' work, to let them know what he thought was exciting in their document, and to let them know what the board was thinking about bank strategies. The ToP work also involved training team leaders who assisted with the planning sessions.

Interviews with the client were held over a period of years. The CEO indicated that whatever changes the bank was planning to undertake, it became much easier to make the changes because people had already come to the table with ideas similar to what the board was contemplating. Over time, the style of the main branch shifted from primarily a top-down, to a collaborative, participatory approach and culture.

One of the important values in this planning was that it had been blessed by the higher levels, and therefore was taken quite seriously throughout the organization.
—Ann Epps, ToP practitioner, Kuala Lumpur, Malaysia

2
The power of
participatory decision making

The reasons for using participatory approaches continue to grow as society changes in this information-oriented age. Nonetheless, some individuals have a vested interested in keeping stakeholders out of the loop of planning and decision making. Here are some of the reasons for and against a participatory approach to planning.

Arguments against participatory decision making

In earlier times throughout history, only a handful of people had the required knowledge or information to make decisions that affected large numbers of people. Representative democracy is predicated upon a majority authorizing and empowering a small minority to make decisions on behalf of the majority, who then abide by those decisions. This was essential when most people did not have the ability or the means to know about public choices or policy, but that is not generally the case now. In many nations and organizations, people have access to even more information than they can handle, and they know or can know enough to help make decisions. Because of the ubiquity of media and the internet, many people have no choice but to know. A fundamental reason for keeping people out of the decision making loop has largely disappeared.

Nonetheless, people are kept out of decision making because foreknowledge of the potential choices might give them the opportunity to take advantage of a situation for their own profit rather than the common good. This potentially unfair advantage is most visible in the unveiling of a government budget, or in the stock market, banking industry, and in regulations around information sharing. While this possibility is used as an argument for keeping people out of the decision-making loop, it is also an argument for making timely and accurate information available to everyone.

Some make the argument that if people are given information and choices, they will react emotionally or illogically to the information and arrive at ill-considered decisions. One hears about this in relation to emergency planning, to disaster situations, and in some political affairs. However, this reasoning is somewhat of a smoke-screen because it works both ways. If one fears people will act emotionally and irresponsibly when they are informed of any given detail, the same fear exists when people find out that they have not been properly informed.

Arguments for participation

Respect for people

A major reason for engaging people in decision making is that it signals respect for them, based on the understanding that all human beings should be respected and appreciated regardless of who they are. In and of itself, this respect for the basic dignity of all human beings is a compelling reason for participatory approaches to decision making.

> This approach really encourages all voices to be heard and included, and opens peoples' eyes to the power in building consensus. I always hear positive, encouraging feedback after leading sessions with ToP methods. I find the system to have a very natural progression.
> —Inez Bush, ToP practitioner, Culver City, USA

Growth of leadership

As people practice participatory decision making, they grow as individuals. They recognize more clearly the basic fallacy of simplistic answers, and they become more open to seeing the impact of their decisions on other stakeholders. The more they practice participatory decision making, the more they are able to help when crucial recommendations are needed in the future—ready and open to the ambiguity they will be asked to traverse.

> People are expecting to participate versus being passive, and enjoy the new level of leadership that this brings.
> —Elizabeth Phillips, ToP practitioner, Sacramento, USA

Enhanced communication

To be able to give opinions so others will listen, people who participate in decision making have to listen to others, understand, and communicate clearly. Enhancing people's capacity to communicate is important for numerous reasons, including enabling them to find workable solutions to problems and encouraging common action toward agreed upon goals. People who communicate well with a common vocabulary and methodology do not have to argue over procedure nearly as much; they can get right to work.

> Team members' collaborative patterns become more transparent and consistent. The conversations between them are more focused and effective.
> —Wenjun Du, ToP practitioner, Shanghai, China

Better understanding

When people participate in decision making, they gain a better understanding of the forces at play and who will be affected in various ways. With this enhanced understanding, they are able to suggest better ways of implementing their plans.

> They appreciate one another more than before, they work from what is, rather than what should have been. They listen and support one another.
> —Richard Maguire, ToP practitioner, Wentworthville, Australia

Better options and recommendations

There is no question that different people see things from different perspectives. Exploring those perspectives and the options that emanate from them provides additional options and recommendations not previously considered. Some of those options are very likely to be better.

> Participants realize that they possess—within their own collaborative group—the ability to be successful at their goals, once they are clearly articulated, shared and revisited regularly via application of ToP inclusive participation methods.
> —Erness Wright-Irvin, ToP practitioner, New Orleans, USA

Quicker implementation

The point of making decisions is to get them implemented. Some decisions will have broad implications for a large number of the people who will have to implement them. However, when people have participated in the decision making, they have already started to consider the implications for themselves and for the potential implementation.

> *People say they understand better, are surprised that expected arguments don't happen, and are delighted at how fast people get into action—how much is achieved in such a short time.*
> —*Marilyn Doyle, ToP practitioner, Macclesfield, UK*

More innovation

In the foreword of *Winning through Participation*, Rosabeth Moss Kanter said that the involvement of more people in a planning process, especially a mixture of people with different perspectives, generates new insights into problems and encourages a fresh look at opportunities. The cross-fertilization from a group bringing diverse backgrounds to a planning task can sometimes result in breakthrough strategies.

> *The stated sense of the senior managers and leaders of the diverse businesses within a family-owned group in India is that ToP methods are their route to excellence as a world class organization. Managers of another company, a conventional consulting and training company in Bangkok, feel that facilitation methods in general and ToP methods in particular will be their competitive advantage.*
> — *Kevin Balm, ToP practitioner, Bangkok, Thailand*

Flexible implementation

The implementation experience often brings in new data, and the external or internal situation can change quickly. But when people have participated in prior decisions, they are better able to flex to the situation, because they have a better grip on the larger strategy, and are not simply stuck in what they were told they were supposed to do.

> *More leaders are actively seeking the participation of "line level" staff than they were a decade ago. There is more willingness to engage the many types of internal and external stakeholder groups in planning and implementation processes.*
> — *Darin Harris, ToP practitioner, Madison, USA*

Better risk management

When people participate in decisions, they are better attuned to the risks involved because they are more likely to discern conditions that can evolve into a risk or potential threat. Sometimes the only people who know about a particular risk are those who are at the front end of implementation.

Back in the mid-1990s, I was a "policy analyst" who found out that giving people answers to questions wasn't nearly as useful as helping them ask and answer powerful questions. Growing into the role as a facilitator and organizational development consultant was natural in my field of complex problem solving. Because engaging many stakeholders, taking ideas from many sources, and understanding another person's perspective were constantly feeding back to me as the way to address complex problems, I learned how constructive futures can be built through full, engaged participation.
— Darin Harris, ToP practitioner, Madison, USA

Positive role modeling

Involving people in decision making embodies those types of generally positive leadership behaviors that lead to trust, commitment, and personal growth.

ToP methods fit totally with my own personal philosophy of profound respect and inclusive participation. I am always inspired by what a group of people can accomplish when they are working together effectively, and my work allows me to feel I am contributing positively to the world. Each group that I work with is trying to do something positive. I contribute a little piece to their success, and that is what keeps me going and loving what I do.
—Penny McDaniel, ToP practitioner, Denver, USA

Increased ownership

In *The Change Masters*, Rosabeth Moss Kanter said that participation in decision making gets greater commitment—and ability—to implement decisions and strategies. When people participate in a planning process, they are more likely to be committed to the plans, because they have talked them through, because the plans reflect their own thinking, and because the group has developed consensus. While this is common sense it took scores of social science studies to convince some managers of its obvious truth.

Several levels of impact on an organization

Some clients already know the type of impact they want from the planning, while others may have only a vague impression of what the result might be. The ToP practitioner can design the following outcomes or impacts on the organization. These impacts are arranged in order of difficulty.

1. Enhancing or changing current operating structures

The plan might lead to a shift or a new emphasis conducting normal operations. For instance, strategies might emphasize practical training even though some training activities are already in existence. Implementation of these types of strategies may involve a simple reshuffling of some workloads or resources. ToP action planning can be used for the immediate implementation of strategies of this nature. If the implementation team is very small, it can be very helpful to prioritize the strategies first.

2. Creating new initiatives

The final plan may call for a brand new focus in a new area that is markedly different from the normal areas of operation. Strategies implemented for this purpose are added to the workload normally carried out within the organization. For instance, a strategy might call for the creation of a new research area or product line. Gearing up for this new focus could require new activities that have never been done before by the organization, and which they currently do not have the capacity to initiate internally.

3. Formalizing organizational structural change

The client may need a plan that is significant enough to require some substantial changes in organizational structure and reporting relationships. For example, a strategy could be to gather all the communication functions operating throughout the organization at many levels and in several areas of work into one cohesive area of responsibility.

4. Transforming whole systems

Some clients may be looking for a major transition of their entire organization, with a completely new focus and new modes of operation. This need for transformation can happen during organizational mergers, break-ups, or periods of accelerated growth. If this is the case, the strategies call for transition planning, and the organization's new vision often highlights dramatic changes in mandate.

5. Supporting value-based, behavioral changes

Sometimes, rather than shifting what is done, a major shift is needed in how things are done. This occurs, for instance, when a new set of values are to guide all operations of an organization, or when a new accountability framework and new measures are to be embedded throughout the system, or when an the organization decides to operate in an entirely new way.

Any of the five levels of impact above can also require people within the organization to make personal life changes. During periods of personal transition (such as in career, health, or relationships), a person can develop strategies that keep them from making "the same ol' mistakes." The behavior changes are more sweeping than changes to specific activities and may require the development of a personal vision and an understanding of the root causes of difficulties in their personal lives. The development of strategies within that context can be very powerful for encouraging sustained changes in life.

Five years ago, I came into contact with ToP facilitation when I participated in a conversation conducted by a ToP facilitator, Tamyra Freeman. Tamyra did not tell us what method was being used, only about the topic being discussed. I was struck by the flow of conversation, and later I became friends with Tamyra. Curious to learn more, I decided to pursue certification in ToP methods through Ann and John Epps in Kuala Lumpur, and eventually became a ToP trainer. What always amazes me is the simplicity yet complexity of the methods. When I first experienced the method, it looked very simple. Yet, when I started to use it as a facilitator, I began to see the subtle nuances. I've also felt the spirit of facilitation through using the methods. I'm starting to see the multi-layers of each method, and there is still so much to learn. I find I learn something new each time I use the method and whenever I observe different ToP facilitators. There is a lot of versatility and depth that I enjoy learning. Being connected with ToP facilitators in Asia and the larger ToP community in other parts of the world enables me to feel it's more than just methods. I am also part of a social change movement.
—Anita Yap, ToP practitioner, Singapore

3

The history and evolution of the technology of participation

ToP® participatory planning is a work in progress. For several decades the methods have continued to evolve, based on the experience of testing and integrating of many theories and practices. For the most part testing and integration have taken place simultaneously around the world by sharing experiences through formal and informal networks.

Milestones in its evolution

While ToP practitioners have pulled in new insight and wisdom along the way, clients have received the benefits of the participatory planning and any resulting transformation. Here are some of the basic milestones in the evolution of the methods.

Mid-1960s — Imaginal education theory is developed and tested throughout the sixties by the Ecumenical Institute, primarily in community development work in Chicago's West Side. This theory is core to the ToP methodology because it links self-image to personal behavior.

1968 to 1971 — Detailed project planning and implementation in the crucible of hundreds of community action campaigns in the late sixties and early seventies lead to ToP action planning. The ICA Summer Research Assembly in Chicago in 1970 focused research on implementation and tactical systems.

1971 to 1972 — Social analysis screens are developed during further ICA summer research assemblies in Chicago and in research by ICA offices in the Americas, Asia, Australia, Latin America, and Europe. The research combines mass participation with systems change theory. In 1972 the social process triangles are created as a way to understand and analyze social systems.

1973 to 1974 — Think tanks are convened in Chicago by ICA Dean Joseph Wesley Mathews to integrate previous study into a formal methodology and to project its use for the next 20 years. This effort results in a formal methodology called LENS ("Living Effectively in the New Society" or "Leadership Effectiveness and New Strategy") and a similar method called Community Forum, with detailed participant and facilitator manuals. ToP approach is rooted in both methodologies.

1975 to 1981 — Application of LENS and community forum in hundreds of organizations and communities around the world. With the earlier project planning and implementation methods, an explosion of social transformation initiatives occur in many countries across all sectors of society.

1977 to 1982 — The community consultation process is used in several dozen communities around the world to launch large-scale community development. The community consult process links an analysis framework including the social process triangles to ToP participatory strategic planning with specific emphasis on implementation.

1981 to 1984 — Large-scale documentation of thousands of community transformation initiatives results in the study of innovations in ICA analytic tools, LENS, community forums, project planning, action planning, and implementation. A milestone is the publication of "Sharing Approaches that Work," among other documents.

1985 to 1990 — The publication of many books by current and former ICA staff begins to codify the intellectual property. Continued research and integration includes the application of insights from David Bohm, Peter Senge, Harrison Owen, David Cooperrider, Jean Houston, Howard Gardiner, and many others. In 1986 Laura Spencer gets the approach named as ToP® Technology of Participation® and publishes a book about it, *Winning through Participation.*

1990 to 1994 — Participation by ToP practitioners and ICA staff in founding the International Association of Facilitators in the US in 1994. Many members of the ICA global network develop training curriculum, independently and collaboratively, for many ToP methods including participatory strategic planning with an eye to training a new generation of facilitators in ToP methods.

1994 to 2000 — ToP training of thousands of facilitators worldwide helps embed ToP values and practices into the newly emerging profession of facilitation. ICA or ToP facilitators host and sponsor several International Association of Facilitators conferences in Oakland, Toronto and Minneapolis in North America and in other cities internationally.

2000 to 2006 — Competencies needed for ToP facilitation are developed by the ICA global network to bring discipline into the theory and practice of applying the methods to facilitate individual, organizational, and social transformation. The Certified ToP Facilitator (CTF or CToPF) designation is created and is backed up by curriculum, practice and testing.

2006–2011 — Ongoing experimentation makes ToP methods available for online facilitation. ToP theory and methods are slowly being infused into university and college curricula. The number of facilitators and trainers continue to grow.

Roots of early ToP methods in social science theory

Much of the current literature on strategic planning was written after the formal development of the ToP approach in the early seventies. And since ToP methods were being used for mass implementation of social change outside academia, it was not included in most of the dialogue among writers and academicians in the 1970s and 1980s. Before the '70s, however, the precursors to ToP participatory strategic planning were being derived from pioneering theorists in social psychology, organizational development, and other social science fields. Among these leaders were Victor Frankl, Kenneth Boulding, Alex Osborne, Norman R. F. Maier, Kurt Lewin, Muzafer Sherif, Fritz and Laura Perls, Mao Zedong, and many others.

In 1945 psychiatrist Victor Frankl wrote *Man's Search for Meaning*, which was formative to the ToP approach, and elevated the understanding of planning. Early ToP founders and practitioners never saw participatory strategic planning merely as a way to increase productivity or efficiency, or even as a better way of getting things done, but rather as a way for people to take control of their lives and to transform the external situation in which they found themselves, as well as their interior story. Having survived the Nazi Auschwitz concentration camp, Frankl wrote:

> *Man's search for meaning is the primary motivation in his life and not a "secondary rationalization" of instinctual drives. This meaning is unique and specific in that it must and can be fulfilled by him alone; only then does it achieve a significance which will satisfy his own will to meaning... Man, however, is able to live and even to die for the sake of his ideals and values.*

The search for meaning and the development of a personal and group story is a very strong component in ToP participatory strategic planning.

In 1956 economist Kenneth L. Boulding, a co-founder of General Systems Theory, wrote *The Image: Knowledge and Life in Society*. This small book was revolutionary for Joe Mathews and other originators of the ToP approach. It linked images, values, and behaviors into a coherent whole and gave rise to ICA's imaginal education. Boulding's imaginal education insights can be summed up in the following theory:

1. Everyone operates out of images.
2. Images govern behavior.
3. Messages shape images.
4. Images can be changed.
5. Changed images change behavior.

This elegant theory is at the core of ToP methods, and links all of the specific procedures used in the methods to transform and empower the behavior of all the participants.

Alex Osborne, in 1957, published a set of procedures to separate creative processes from judgmental processes, for a more open generation of ideas in problem solving. "Brainstorming," as it quickly became known, is now widely used in all forms of planning, including ToP planning. While research by F. M. Jablin and D. R. Seibold (in 1978) and then by B. Mullen (in 1991) questioned the efficacy of group interaction over nominal or individual brainstorming, ToP methods used both types of brainstorming with great success since its origin.

In 1967, Norman R. F. Maier wrote "Greater Sum Total of Knowledge and Information" for the American Psychological Association. In discussing the intellectual potential of group thinking, he wrote:

> There is more information in a group than in any of its members. Thus problems that require the utilization of knowledge should give groups an advantage over individuals. Even if one member of the group (e.g., the leader) knows much more than anyone else, the limited unique knowledge of lesser-informed individuals could serve to fill in some gaps in knowledge. For example, a skilled machinist might contribute to an engineer's problem solving, and an ordinary workman might supply information on how a new machine might be received by workers.

While this is self-evident today after several decades, to the originators of LENS and community forums participating in think tanks in 1970–74, this was another revolutionary idea that matched their common sense, reinforced their philosophy of the unlimited human potential of every human, to integrate into their methods.

Kurt Z. Lewin's field theory, and specifically force field analysis, is used widely in most strategic planning as well in ToP methods. In the late 1940s Lewin started the Tavistock Institute in the National Training Labs in Bethel, Maine, out of which T-groups and sensitivity training arose. Regarding the application of field theory to ToP methods, when a group creates a vision together, a force-field analysis identifies the forces that are driving that vision into being and the forces that are restraining the vision from becoming a reality. After valencing, or prioritizing these forces, the group has two possible responses. They can increase the influence of the driving forces, or they can decrease the influence of the restraining forces. Lewin noted that a scientific look at nature shows that the most energy-efficient way of moving toward one's vision is to decrease the restraining forces. From the laws of physics, there is a reaction to every action. If driving forces increase, restraining forces increase as well. This understanding aligns with the ToP understanding of contradictional thinking, in which strategies are primarily directed at dealing with contradictions to reduce the powers of blockages and mitigate or alleviate those restraining forces.

In 1936, the Turkish psychologist Muzafer Sherif published *The Psychology of Social Norms*, which contained a systematic theoretical analysis of the concept of social norms and an experimental investigation of the origin of social norms among groups of people. This research is important in demonstrating that getting many people together to create a plan can be superior to getting an expert to create the plan. Sherif found, "When the individual, in whom a range and a norm within that range are first developed in the individual situation, is put into a group situation, together with other individuals who also come into the situation with their own ranges and norms established in their own individual sessions, the ranges and norms tend to converge." Adding even more power to his observation, Sherif noted, "When a member of a group faces the same situation subsequently alone, after once the range and norm of his group have been established, he perceives the situation in terms of the range and norm that he brings from the [group] situation." The ToP corollary is that participatory planning is a good way to prepare individuals and groups to handle new situations that arise after the planning process is over.

Fritz and Laura Perls's gestalt school of psychotherapy played an important role in the development of the ToP approach. ToP practitioners must develop the ability to suspend judgment, to treat all data as equivalent, and to enable people to collectively develop a new "big picture" that incorporates the viewpoints of all the participants, especially in the clustering (gestalt) stage of the consensus workshop method. The competence of a ToP practitioner in helping a group with a "gestalt shift" looms large in the transformational potential of ToP participatory strategic planning, and especially in contradictional analysis.

Eastern philosophy, and especially the *Tao Te Ching*, was important in the development of the ToP body of knowledge because of the emphasis on balance and tension within systems. Mao

Zedong updated some of that philosophy in the attempt to transform a Chinese agrarian, feudal patchwork into a twentieth-century nation-state. His theory about contradictional analysis contributed indirectly to the ToP approach. From his 1937 paper "On Contradiction":

> The universality or absoluteness of contradiction has a twofold meaning. One is that contradiction exists in the process of development of all things, and the other is that in the process of development of each thing a movement of opposites exists from beginning to end. Engels said, "Motion itself is a contradiction." Lenin defined the law of the unity of opposites as "the recognition (discovery) of the contradictory, mutually exclusive, opposite tendencies in all phenomena and processes of nature (including mind and society)." Are these ideas correct? Yes, they are. The interdependence of the contradictory aspects present in all things and the struggle between these aspects determine the life of all things and push their development forward. There is nothing that does not contain contradiction, without contradiction nothing would exist.

Any failings of communism do not negate the value of contradictional analysis, just as the failings of banks do not negate the value of free market theory.

Emphasizing the essential free will of human beings to direct their own course of affairs, existentialist philosophers from Kierkegaard to Bonhoeffer all played an important part in the philosophy that gave rise to ToP methods. R. Brian Stanfield describes the influence of these thinkers in detail in *The Courage to Lead* as does John Epps in *Bending History, Selected talks of Joseph W. Mathews*, Volumes I and II.

More recent contributions integrated into the body of practice

The three-day LENS and one-day Community Forum methodologies, used extensively between 1975 and 1985 in campaigns involving hundreds communities and organizations, were essentially merged and enhanced to create the five-day community consult process that generated enormous energy for sustainable community development. Even though this primary breakthrough methodology remained the same for several years, teams of practitioners brought many innovations to the process. During this period, the initial stages of an overall planning framework (page 45) of ToP participatory strategic planning were added. The final implementation stage was already widely practiced, well before the present ToP terminology was developed. During this decade, ICA participatory planning could refer to any part of the community forum, LENS or community consult methods—all used with somewhat different audiences and for different purposes.

During the 1980s and 1990s, several new facilitation theories were making an appearance in both practice and in the literature. Some ToP practitioners integrated these new theories into their ToP practice, while others kept them separate. In many cases, the main insights of the new theories were already inherent in the ToP approach, but the literature and interchange brought a new degree of consciousness and discipline to practices within the ToP body of knowledge.

Open Space

In 1985, organizational consultant Harrison Owen coined the term Open Space Technology (OST) to describe a new way to enable self-organizing systems of large groups. He developed the approach when he found that conversation during the coffee breaks in conferences was more lively than during the formal sessions. Open Space was further developed over the course of several years and is contining right to the present. Although ToP practitioners had used a somewhat similar process, called the marketplace method, since the early 1980s, there was no attempt to coordinate best practices across disparate practitioners. However, Open Space was suggested as a useful organizing principle during a 1988 global ICA conference in Mexico, in which Harrison Owen participated. ICA immediately recognized that Open Space could sometimes add value to the ToP participatory strategic planning process, especially between the phases of strategy development and implementation. In essence, after some general strategies have been developed, people can "vote with their feet" about the implementation activities in which they wish to engage.

Appreciative Inquiry

In 1980, David L. Cooperrider and Suresh Srivastva began their research into Appreciative Inquiry leading to Cooperrider's doctoral thesis in 1986, *Appreciative Inquiry: Toward a Methodology for Understanding and Enhancing Organizational Innovation*. From 1982 to 1984, ICA was involved in a campaign called "Sharing Approaches That Work," which was like a global appreciative inquiry into community development projects and organizations around the world. This culminated in a large conference in New Delhi called the International Exposition of Rural Development, which published the results. Some ToP practitioners recognized the full power of Appreciative Inquiry when Cooperrider and Tojo Thatchenkery held a series of interview sessions using the methods at ICA staff headquarters in Chicago and in Brussels at an international staff gathering. The ToP historical scan, in which a group looks back at events in its history and builds a common meaningful story together, has a similar impact to Appreciative Inquiry. A ToP historical scan, followed by a ToP long-range practical visioning workshop, can give power and depth to a planning process, similar to that of the integration of Appreciative Inquiry into the process.

Total Quality Management

W. Edwards Deming developed the practice of Total Quality Management, and brought about a transformation of team practice and continuous learning within the private sector in North

America. Teamwork has always been an essential hallmark of the ToP approach, and drive toward continuous learning has its greatest impact during the implementation stages of ToP participatory planning, with the plan review and mid-course corrections that occur during phase IV of the participatory strategic planning framework. Because it is the source of the continuous improvement that is at the core of quality, stopping, reflecting, and affirming what went wrong during the implementation of a plan is just as important as affirming what went right.

Future Search
The Future Search approach, as developed by Marvin Weisbord, Sandra Janoff and others, has similarities to several elements of ToP participatory strategic planning. Future search is a constant reminder to ToP practitioners that the greater the diversity in the room, the more profound will be the results. The future search approach inspired a greater emphasis in ToP practice on involving all participants in creating their own story and developing their own sets of commitments. This emphasis has been a conscious assumption of ToP participatory planning since its development in the Fifth City neighborhood of Chicago's West Side in the 1960s and '70s.

Widening the range of stakeholders
Henry Mintzberg, in his books on management and with his theory on organizational forms, commented extensively on strategy and compared many models of strategic planning. An important insight mirroring that of ToP practitioners is the necessity for widening the scope of stakeholders in the planning cycle. The ToP framework-building tool is one such method for ensuring a wide range of stakeholders, as is the social process diagnostic system. In 1994, Mintzberg wrote *The Rise and Fall of Strategic Planning: Reconceiving the Roles for Planning, Plans, and Planners*, which highlighted the drawbacks of academic analysis in planning.

Asset-Based Community Development
In 1993, as an antidote to those who focused primarily on deficiencies and problem analysis in community development, John McKnight and Jody Kretzmann wrote about Asset-Based Community Development in *Building Community from the Inside Out*. Even earlier, a similar shift toward building on local peoples' strengths is seen in Terry Bergdall's *Methods for Active Participation*, and in Robert Chamber's *Rapid Rural Appraisal* and later in *Participatory Rural Appraisal*. They all view community development as a glass half full rather than half empty. All of these efforts lent academic credibility to approaches like the community consult method, which built on local wisdom and which was eventually formalized in the ToP methods.

Systems thinking
Peter Senge's 1990 book, *The Fifth Discipline*, promoted the value and practice of systems thinking throughout society. The four other disciplines of personal mastery, mental models, build-

ing shared vision, and team learning were already deeply embedded into ToP practice, but the fifth discipline of systems thinking prodded ToP practitioners to look back to the original global systems analysis that generated the ToP approach in the first place, and to use a holistic analysis with every client. The social process triangles developed by 1,000 ICA staff in the early 1970s, is the gold standard of systems thinking, and has many applications at every stage of the ToP participatory strategic planning process.

Strategy development

From the business world, Michael Porter has written a number of classic books on business strategy, including *The Competitive Advantage of Nations* and *Competitive Strategy.* He stresses the importance of three different strategies, especially segmentation, cost leadership, and differentiation. Countering this approach, C. K. Prahalad, and Gary Hamel have noted how quickly competitive positions can be overturned, requiring all businesses to focus on their core competencies. ToP practitioners have paid heed to all these warnings, and generally avoid the traps of developing certain "types" of strategies as does, for instance, the Balanced Scorecard. ToP methods place energy and priority on developing "insight" and "breakthrough," in the areas that are determined by the analysis.

Root cause analysis

Root cause analysis, which has evolved over several centuries, can be linked to a large number of social scientists and consultants, including David Kellogg Lewis, Eliyahu Goldratt, Kaoru Ishikawa, Charles Kepner and Benjamin Tregoe, Russ Ackoff, and the Total Quality Management movement. ToP contradiction analysis goes deeply into root causes and determines what type of responsibility is in the hands of the participants for problems and solutions. *The Groan Zone*, described in Sam Kaner's Facilitator's *Guide to Participatory Decision Making*, can sometimes mirror the experience of contradiction analysis. Because of its complexity, it has always been difficult to explain contradiction analysis to clients. Those who do decide to do it comment on the participant ownership of the problem and solutions.

Graphic facilitation

David Sibbet's lifelong work on the visual components of planning and thinking has reminded practitioners to include metaphor and visual learning in their participatory strategic planning. Visuals and metaphors, which are valuable when creating stories during a ToP historical scan, are especially empowering during the action planning stage of strategic planning. They also help keep motivation high during the implementation phase.

Scenario creation

Peter Schwartz, Paul Schoemaker, and Royal Dutch Shell all developed long-range scenario planning as a strategic planning tool. The thinking skills used in scenario creation help generate strategic thinking that can straddle many possible futures and increase flexibility within the organization. ToP practitioners also use long-range projection into the future to generate visionary and strategic thinking by participants. Although Royal Dutch Shell has formalized scenario creation more fully, long-range projection is essential to ToP historical scan and ToP trend analysis.

ToP participatory strategic planning and its ICA precursors (LENS, community forums, and community consults) did not originate as planning methodologies. Instead, they were developed as an intention of ICA staff to spark campaigns of "awakenment" and "engagement" on several continents. Joseph Wesley Mathews convened dozens of conferences and think tanks in Chicago in the late 1960s and early 1970s with social activists, community development practitioners, and business people on how to inspire masses of people to engage themselves in new forms of social responsibility. Mathews' context for most of these think tanks was that

> … the emergence of a global consciousness in today's civilization is of greater consequence than the industrial revolution of the eighteenth-century and the development of agrarian societies in the distant past. Every human being has unlimited potential to create on a global scale a new social vehicle and a new religious mode.

ToP practitioners

"ToP practitioners" are facilitators, trainers, change agents, educators, community developers, and many others who consciously integrate ToP methods into their jobs, consulting and training practices. By 2012 about a hundred and fifty people had become "Certified ToP Facilitators" with the CTF designation. In some nations certified facilitators have gone on to become ToP trainers. In other nations ToP trainers were active long before certification existed.

ToP practitioners are respectful of the organizational cultures in which they work, as a direct outgrowth of the roots of the methods in the Institute of Cultural Affairs. Master ToP practitioners recognize the power of a participatory organizational culture, and generally have no difficulty championing such a transition or transformation within the culture of an organization. They are lucid about the personal drives and limitations of the members of the organization, accept the difficulties as well as the potentials inherent in the transformation. They are able to stand in the tension between freedom as an outside agent and their responsibility to the client.

In the middle to late 1970s, communities using ToP approaches ranged from urban neighborhoods in Chicago, Toronto, Calcutta, London, Nairobi, and Berlin, to agricultural communities across North and South America, to settlements in India, Africa, Australia, Malaysia, Korea, and other countries. About 1300 ICA volunteers engaged these communities in various transformative community development activities.

ICA staff created partnerships with other non-profit, government, and quasi-government groups including social service agencies, hospitals, schools, housing co-ops, food banks, and any number of language-specific service groups. Since these other groups were also working for the benefit of the community, they regularly took part in many of the planning sessions, and they began to use ICA or ToP methodologies in their own organizations. Until the late 1980s, new people learned ToP methods by working in a kind of apprenticeship with more experienced lead facilitators.

ICA staff facilitators eventually moved on to other initiatives or developed their own independent practices. But almost all remained deeply affected by their experiences in community work, and came away with inspiring stories of team effort and of individual transformation. Some of these stories are found in *Sharing Approaches that Work, Stories from the Field, Creating Community, Methods for Active Participation*, and other books by ICA staff.

As Laura Spencer described in *Winning through Participation*, various ICA facilitators began using their skills in fee-for-service consultations with such clients as McDonald's, Massey Ferguson, Boeing, Vazir Sultan Tobacco, Bata Corporation, and Tata Industries. These companies hired ICA facilitators to enable participative planning in areas like new product development, teamwork, and organizational culture. Still other ICA teams used the same methods and processes in hospitals and other large institutions, such as national NGOs and government agencies. *Participation Works* by Jim Troxel, and *Beyond Prince and Merchant* by John Burbidge detail these and other efforts. The values were the same for all clients—public or private institutions, communities or voluntary organizations—the essential planning process, respect toward participants, the careful listening, and the need for impartiality.

After seeing the methods in action, participants often joined the organization as volunteers or staff. Volunteers with little or no experience matured into master ToP practitioners. John Telford's story is typical. He joined ICA in 1972, and spent the next 15 years learning ToP methods as part of his on-the-job training. Today he uses ToP methods with a wide variety of clients in varied situations—with community organizations, government agencies, large and small groups—in Australia as well as other countries, such as Timor Leste.

Marilyn Oyler attended summer training at ICA as a college student in 1965. After completing her degree she returned to join the staff in 1966, and worked as a volunteer or paid staff member for the next 40 years. She, John Oyler, and six other associates have formed Partners in Participation, to continue offering ToP training and facilitation services. Marilyn maintains, "The continued effectiveness of the ToP methods keeps me going!"

Terry Bergdall's first conscious engagement as a facilitator was during Town Meeting '76, an ICA-initiated series of daylong community meetings held in every county across the USA. He has been doing professional facilitation ever since, and his work now takes on many dimensions. One facet is facilitating participatory monitoring and evaluation exercises for development programs around the world. Enabling people to deal with their real situations, and becoming excited and energized as they do, is one of the things that "keeps me going."

Like Terry, the late Sandra True, a health care professional and ToP practitioner in New York, also had her first experience of facilitation in a 1976 town meeting in the south side of Chicago. What impressed her was the inclusive participation and the ability to engage many people in a rational process moving toward a fresh consensus.

Twenty-year-old Joaquina Rodriguez Ruz encountered ToP methods for the first time in Santiago, Chile. Struck by how it transformed people's lives, she has continued to use this methodology ever since.

From 1985 through the early 1990s there was an explosion of creativity in the use of ToP methods. With many people facilitating developmental and transformational activities in different countries, the methods were adapted to local cultures, client bases, and the abilities of the facilitators, while they incorporated the creativity of others they worked with. Many volunteer staff found their own personal areas of passion and expertise, and became consultants, teachers, trainers, professionals, professors, or facilitators in particular areas.

From the mid-1980s to the mid-1990s, many ICA facilitators became trainers and created curriculum for teaching participatory methods and processes effectively. Laura Spencer led a group of people to write ICA's first major publication, *Winning through Participation*, and the term "Technology of Participation," or ToP, entered the ICA's facilitation lexicon. This more systematized training revolutionized the facilitation practice, because for the first time people outside the organization could understand and practice ICA methods without one-on-one coaching or mentoring from ICA facilitators. Because of this book, many ICA and other facilitators began to refer to a whole suite of original ICA processes and tools as ToP methods.

It was also in this period that ICA facilitators began to recognize the value and rigour of other types of facilitation and integrate other approaches into their facilitation practices. In 1994, 73 people banded together as charter members of the new International Association of Facilitators

(IAF). Eighteen years later, this organization is the main face of the profession of facilitation, with regular conferences around the world, a certification process for facilitators, a bi-annual association journal, and numerous opportunities for networking.

Adoption of ToP methods has varied from country to country. ICA USA branded ToP and trademarked the ToP technology and developed a ToP curriculum that spread rapidly to other ICAs around the world. Marilyn Oyler of ICA Phoenix and a large ICA team created courses and standards, resulting in a very large network of ToP trainers. An estimated 60,000 people have taken basic ToP courses across the USA alone. The ToP Network is a registered organization in the USA, and no one actually knows the extent of the facilitation that emanates from these facilitators and trainers.

Emphasizing the explicitly transformational methods, and training facilitators and trainers in great depth, ICA Canada took the route of developing a robust curriculum of all the ICA and ToP methods. It assigned Duncan Holmes to assemble ICA Associates Inc., a for-profit facilitation and training company that supports the charity. Principal Jo Nelson guided the Canadian team in developing ToP competencies and ToP certification. As of 2011, ICA Canada and ICA Associates Inc. have trained over 20,000 Canadians in ToP methods.

For many years, ICA UK sent volunteers overseas as social change agents to ICA community development projects, and then later supported volunteers to go to projects of their choice. A team led by Martin Gilbraith and Jonathan Dudding created curriculum to prepare people for the transformation they would encounter in their work overseas. ICA UK also created a ToP trainer and facilitator group through its network of associates. Four thousand people have taken ToP training in the UK.

Long a part of the ToP branding effort, ICA Australia supports a faculty of ToP trainers, facilitators, and consultants who have developed a facilitative leadership curriculum. Kevin Balm is one such individual in a large Australian network that facilitates major projects around South and Southeast Asia, and convenes public ToP courses throughout Australia.

ICA Taiwan colleagues Larry Philbrook, Dick and Gail West have championed ways to utilize ToP in organizational and community change processes and began a ToP certification in English and Chinese in 2000. This work has led them to be an incubator of private and non-profit firms, including Open Quest Technology with Laura Hsu, Shawn Chung, and Jorie Wu and others, to make ToP, along with many other methods, especially Open Space and Appreciative Inquiry, available to the Greater China community.

In Malaysia, John and Ann Epps were invited by local partners to help establish LENS International, named after the ICA LENS method, one of the precursors to ToP methods. They hold courses through Malaysia, Singapore, and other countries in the region.

Shizuyo Sato and Wayne Ellsworth of ICA Japan have facilitated ToP participatory strategic planning with hundreds of Japanese companies and organizations. Some very large companies have embedded ToP participatory values throughout their entire organization. ICA Japan supports social and economic development projects in many countries.

ICA Peru has always been heavily involved in community development. Ken and Alison Hamje, Julio Aguirre and a large group of development practitioners have innovated ToP methods to handle the extreme emphasis on implementation that is needed in isolated communities in mountainous regions.

Eduardo Christianson, Anna Marie Urrutia and Isabel de la Maza of ICA Chile have modified ToP methods for facilitators with physical disabilities and for use in communities and organizations supporting populations with disabilities. Gerd Luders and Amanda Urrutia have translated ToP books into Spanish.

ICA Nepal conducts ToP training on a regular basis. Tatwa Timsina's team has incorporated ToP methods into its widespread human development activities and projects in five regions of Nepal.

ICA India has continued to use ToP methods in village development in Maharashtra state for decades. Shankar Jadhav and partners operate the Environment Education Centre for this purpose near Pune, but many other practitioners work independently.

Kanbay International has been an innovative user of ToP methods. John and Thea Patterson, Raymond Spencer, Cyprian D'Souza, Betty Pesek, Dileep Nath—some of them ICA staff—formed a high tech company to make use of the extraordinary capacity of Indian programmers in the global technology market. ToP philosophy, values and methods were imbedded into the operation of the company and helped its meteoric rise to becoming a major player in IT service to the financial sector.

This very partial listing could be expanded with innovations in many other countries. ToP approaches, for instance, have launched community responses to the HIV/Aids pandemic in a number of African nations, while in Bosnia Herzegovina they have spawned legislative initiatives.

Altogether, more than 100,000 people have taken ToP training since 1990. It is likely that 5% of these course graduates have taken advanced training, such as in ToP participatory strategic planning. From a 2008 survey of 150 advanced practitioners primarily in the USA, conducted by Jim Wiegel, ToP methods are widely used for team building, problem solving, and productivity initiatives, an average of at least 30 days per year per practitioner. In particular, almost all advanced practitioners use ToP participatory strategic planning.

Part B

Transparent Method

4

The spiral process
of ToP

ToP participatory strategic planning is like a glass container that shows everything going on inside. It is not a backroom method accessible to only a few privileged individuals. The method itself is transparent, visible and out front, where everyone can both participate in it and see it in operation. Participants are aware of being empowered by the planning method but they are not distracted by the mechanics of how that happens.

ToP transparency empowers every person who participates in the process. The ToP approach harnesses the latent potential that exists in every person in a group. Because it makes use of a very natural thinking process, it seems and feels effortless. First, ToP participatory strategic planning clears away extraneous ideas and agendas that cloud group decisions, and then it focuses everyone in the group on their own commitment to the transformation needed to move everyone ahead into the future. At the very core of this transformation is the understanding of the contradiction between what exists now and what we want to exist in the future, and of the inherent tension that exists between them.

Found in the mental models, methodology, philosophy, and values that nurture transformation within a group, the understanding of contradiction is fundamental for all ToP practitioners. Section B delves into each aspect in some detail, while exploring the underlying process that creates the energy for the transformation. It presents an overall framework that guides the use of tools and methods so that they apply to the situation and the cohesiveness of the group.

Participants experience transparency when strategy emerges seamlessly from the group itself, without being imposed from outside. Even though they may initially follow a series of steps, those steps soon become instinctive and emerge as part of a natural thought process that operates at both the individual and the group level.

Participants quickly realize that the ToP approach comes from a different paradigm from many other planning methods—one where everyone is assumed to have wisdom to communicate, where everyone is responsible for the outcome, and where the empowerment they experience during the process models the empowerment to implement the final results. From this perspective, what happens to a group while doing the planning is just as important as what the group produces. This can be communicated to participants early on in the process by talking about some of the practical assumptions of the ToP approach:

- Everyone knows something that the group needs; everyone has a piece of the puzzle.
- The members of the group or organization have something in common, a purpose for being, perhaps a mission, some objectives, individual beliefs, or some operational values.
- People who have a hand in the implementation are well suited to participate in the planning.
- Decision-makers will be involved in, or at least aware of, the planning so that it has a genuine possibility of implementation.

When someone decides that a group will do ToP participatory strategic planning, it is a commitment to a substantial reality check. To develop a practical vision of the future, a group has to be bold enough to consider a range of future possibilities. To discern the contradictions that are blocking that vision, the group has to be willing to look at its true situation and see the ways in which its vision is being negated. This is tantamount to admitting that something has to change… and it starts here! To formulate strategic directions, the group must tap into creativity and risk. To forge action plans, the group needs each person's commitment to put wheels under the new directions through precise deeds and timelined assignments.

"Humankind cannot bear very much reality," T. S. Eliot reminds us of the evasive characteristics of human consciousness when confronted with overwhelming possibility or creaturely limitations. Some groups do not feel permission to hope and dream about the future. Others shy away from looking at real contradictions, obstacles, or learning from negative experiences. Still others revel in clarifying all the blocks they face, but they pull up short when it is time to create strategies to deal with those blocks. Then again, some groups and individuals seem noncommittal in the first three phases, but suddenly take interest in the action planning when decisions about real action are made. There is nothing abnormal in these types of responses and, in the hands of a ToP practitioner, the whole process feels seamless to the group. Practitioner Susan Fertig-Dykes puts it this way: "People who thought they wouldn't like the use of facilitation sometimes suddenly discover they didn't realize it was in use in situations where they were participating, and since it worked, they now see its usefulness."

The spiral as an imaginal tool describing how ToP works

The spiral image was developed in the mid-1970s to describe the flow through key parts of the ToP process and is not related to Wilber and Beck's *Spiral Dynamics*. ICA first used it in the "spiral curriculum" they developed in the 1960s. The spiral in Figure 1 is an image-based tool that describes the deepening through several phases during ToP participatory strategic planning.

Spiral mood line
A spiral reflects the changing internal experience of people who participate in the planning process. Motivating images of the future vision pull people forward, while a deep analysis of the underlying obstacles pulls them down into the contradictions. Their mood picks up as they develop strategies and feel a forward surge of power and momentum with the goals and timelines of action planning. When they implement their action plans, the central values of the mission represented at the centre of the image spin outward, involving other stakeholders.

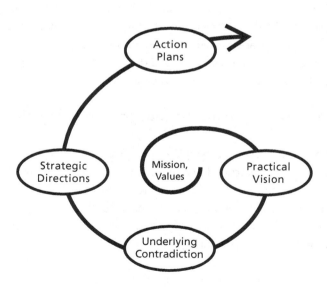

FIGURE 1. The spiral participatory planning process

Snowballing participation

Participatory strategic planning can be done with a small group of people. The strategies and action plans often call for the participation of a larger group in further rounds of strategic planning in the future. Participation grows like a snowball gathering size and momentum as it rolls down a hill.

Infinite fractal spirals

Fractal geometry describes a similar pattern of macro and micro relationships. When large-scale strategic planning creates objectives for the organization or community, some of those objectives can become the object of another round of smaller scale strategic plans. A regional health strategic plan might call for consultations on upgraded infrastructure, which might require its own strategic plan. The infrastructure plan might call for the development of a fundraising foundation that needs its own strategic plan. The spiral process can grow like a fractal into ever greater detail, even to the level of problem solving for small practical steps.

Rollup spirals

Several small departments can work on their own strategic plans, while the entire organization can roll up all the plans into one large planning process. Or many neighbourhoods might do separate participatory strategic planning or community forums, and then the city can roll up the results into one strategic plan that has strong neighbourhood buy-in.

The spiral inward

Vision, contradictions, strategies, and action plans all emanate from the mission and values at the centre of the spiral. While the planning process drives outward into more and more participation, the mission and values are reinforced at the centre. The spiral moves inward because those people participating in the outer discussion and dialogue to create the plans become more personally grounded in the values that drive the organization.

The spiral as a mental model for the thought process of planning

A natural thinking process occurs in people during problem solving and strategy development. This natural process can be described in a mental model or cognitive model of planning. While ToP technology makes the mental model explicit in groups, it generally operates relatively unconsciously in each of our minds. However, people who know the pattern will recognize vision, contradiction, and strategy almost immediately in individual problem solving. Here is a simple example of this mental model in personal problem solving.

I'm a young guy who likes to party with my buddies. My apartment is party central. My sports accomplishments and the parties should make me popular with girls, but it hasn't worked. A good buddy told me that this wasn't going to happen until I stopped being sloppy. I didn't believe him. But then a girl broke up with me and I later heard she called my place a pig pen. I guess I'll have to keep the place clean in spite of the parties, and do laundry more often.

Vision, contradiction and strategy is obvious in this young man's thinking. Contradictions and even simple blockages give rise to solutions, as in the following example.

I dream of delicious home-grown salads, which motivates me to have vegetable planters on my back porch. A squirrel keeps nosing around trying to dig up the planter but I cannot stay around all day scaring it away. A strategy might be to make the plants inaccessible and put some chicken wire over the top. A different strategy is to scare the squirrel with a little wind propeller and some tin plates. I think I'll put chile powder on the soil and make the garden unpalatable.

This mental model of vision, contradiction, strategy and action plan describes how people often make everyday decisions, especially when they are being deliberate about it. Here is another example.

I wanted to live nearer the core of the city, but in a new house rather than an old one. I was really lucky to find an empty lot on which to build. I could clearly imagine a beautiful new two-storey house with a cool interior. Was my strategy to build the new house? No. Was my action plan to buy bricks and wood to build the house? No. This is because there were several blocks in my way: an old shoulder injury, a large tree halfway down the lot that the neighbours all wanted to keep, and complex city building regulations. My strategy was to get expert architectural advice to incorporate the tree into the architectural drawings, which would handle both the tree and the permit blockages, and to hire a contractor, which would save my shoulder. With those two strategies in place, I now had lots of small actions to take, including going to the bank to fill out loan forms.

The vision of "a beautiful new house" does not lead to a simple strategy of "building the new house." We automatically engage in complex thought processes to arrive at a workable strategy. The four-stage thinking process describes those thought processes.

When making plans for oneself, the thinking process is intuitive and the planning almost automatic. When more than one person is doing the planning, each one needs to understand each others' reasoning, or they may end up with entirely different strategies. For instance, a spouse might well have a different idea of what "a beautiful new house" actually looks like. Even if there is agreement on the vision of the house, the spouse might not understand the city regulations about large trees in the yard, or might not understand the aggravation a weak shoulder can get from construction. Even after the issues and obstacles are clarified, the spouse may have a different strategy, such as hiring a relative to do the work rather than a contractor, or becoming your own contractor and subcontracting tradespeople to do the work. The action plans in this case might require studying by-laws, researching sources, and learning the proper order for establishing the heating, plumbing, and electrical systems.

The spiral process as a common discipline for the participants

The more people are involved in the planning process, the more important it is to be disciplined in using the spiral. Each member of the group could create an entirely different action plan based on their own understanding of the vision, contradictions, and strategies. Every person could have a different vision of what the future needs to look like. Even with a common vision, each person might have a very different idea of what the blockages are. Moreover, even if everyone clearly understands the blockages, each person could still create an entirely different set of strategies. To generate a common plan with everyone committed to it, group members need to discuss together the vision, the blockages, and the strategies; then they need to build an action plan based on those common strategies.

The need for disciplined thinking has an important corollary. If the purpose of participatory strategic planning is to engage people in the planning, *then engage as many people as possible in one phase of the thinking process before moving on the next.*

Before moving on to discover the underlying blocks, guide the whole group in creating a vision together. Then help the whole group obtain clarity on the underlying blocks or contradictions before moving on to develop strategies. Develop strategies together before moving on to create action plans. It doesn't matter that some people may want to jump ahead too quickly, or that they may become frustrated because they want the action planning done "right now." Since there is so much less confusion when the phases of thinking are considered in their natural order, the effort is worth any momentary aggravation. Reaching agreement at the early levels will circumvent expensive future arguments during the implementation.

What happens when this disciplined thought process is not practiced during participatory strategic planning? People get confused. Consider the following conversation of eight people all talking about getting new office space. Confusion reigns because there is no logical model to their conversation. No heed is paid to the order of thinking, and problems occur.

Pradeep: Let's continue our conversation from last month about new offices. I think we have all agreed that we are envisioning a new office that is accessible by most of our clients. *(Pradeep is trying to get clarity on the vision.)*

Calistha: That's right. I've already begun checking the parking situation in some of the downtown office towers. We'll have to have handicapped parking for many of our clients. *(Calistha just jumped to the tactical action planning level of thinking.)*

Aziz: While I do agree that accessibility is important, the real problem is that our clients mainly live in the suburbs and won't go downtown. Many don't drive anyway. Why think about downtown parking? *(Aziz is thinking about the blocks to client accessibility.)*

Kyla: What we really need for accessibility is a client transportation strategy, not an office relocation strategy. *(Kyla is trying to generate strategies for Aziz's blocks.)*

Crispin: Just a moment! Our conversation about new offices was supposed to be about empowering and giving dignity to our clients by having more appealing office space. *(Crispin is exploring another dimension of the vision.)*

Jane: That's right! We need a client-centred empowerment strategy. It's what I've been thinking all along. *(Jane just tried to convert a vision into a strategy!)*

Bob: What about the fact that our client base now has 10 different languages? That is surely an issue we need to address. *(Bob has just uncovered a blockage to empowerment, and maybe even to accessibility.)*

Bhimrao: That's OK. I have a team ready to translate all our brochures, and also a funding proposal in to the government to pay for it. *(Bhimrao has just come up with an action plan for Bob's blockage.)*

This confusing dialogue contains two examples each of visionary thinking, contradictional thinking, strategic thinking, and tactical thinking. Since there is no discipline in their thought process, they will continue to jump around and have difficulty understanding each other.

By focusing on visionary thinking first, followed by contradictional, strategic, and then tactical thinking, the confusion turns into a focused plan.

What is our future vision of our office space? What do we want to see in place?

Pradeep: I think we have all agreed that we are envisioning a new office that is accessible by most of our clients.

Crispin: And it's not just about the location of the office. It's all about the dignity of our clients no matter where they live. So, it's about office accessibility and the environment of empowerment that we create within it.

What is blocking this vision from becoming a reality?

Aziz: A major block is that our clients live in the suburbs, don't have cars, and are isolated.

Bob: Not only that, but our clients now speak 10 different languages; so even when they get here, they still have some problems.

What are the approaches or strategies that could deal with these blocks and move us ahead?

Jane: Get a nice office central to the suburbs with a multi-language reception capacity.

Kyla: Also, we need some sort of a client transportation strategy.

What action plans will be needed to implement these strategies?

Bhimrao: I'll figure out the multilingual reception idea, get our brochures translated, and create a funding proposal to shop around.

Calistha: I'll look into various transportation modes and subsidies that apply to our clients, and client car-pooling from our database of the postal codes of our clients.

Pradeep: I'll check online for central suburban realtors. Looks like we can move pretty quickly.

While this conversation is simplistic, it illustrates the clarity achieved when a disciplined thinking process is used.

5
The dynamic method within transformation

With ToP methods, people are able to look at whole systems, rather than just band-aid solutions that deal with symptoms.
—Heidi Kolbe, ToP practitioner, Sacramento, USA

ToP participatory strategic planning is not a static set of steps and procedures to apply to a situation. While it's possible to use the questions in a formulaic way just following the steps, a practitioner may not understand why or how any transformation is occurring. Static use of ToP methods is like pushing a small model car with a stick. The car only goes where you push it; there is no energy in the movement, no mystique in the destination. On the other hand, when the rubber band inside the model car is wound tight, a tension drives the little model on its own energy and takes it where it will. Similarly, tensions within the ToP methods provide energy that propels a group forward.

The tensions that make the method dynamic are not within the method itself, but rather within and between the individuals in the group. ToP participatory strategic planning uses deeply human natural drives to create the energy to move ahead. These deep human drives can be described in philosophical terms, in life stances, and in sociological terms. They can also be used to understand and give form to personal, group, and social transformation.

A transformational stance makes the methods work

Early connections found in the philosophy explore the relationship between objectivity and subjectivity, and the transformations that exist between them. Another early foundation is the nature of unlimited human potential found in the existential philosophy foreshadowed by Søren Kierkegaard and Friedrich Nietzsche, establishing the basis for willing transformation. Paul Tillich's *Systematic Theology* includes important contributions on personal transformation. Ethics, contextual ethics, and indicative ethics are all rich grounds where Kant and Bonhoeffer describe the tensions between the internal world of the individual and the world of external relationships, and between freedom and obligation. *The Courage to Lead,* by Brian Stanfield, describes these in detail.

Central to transformation is the concept of **contradiction**. Explanations of contradiction range from the pedantic "A logical incompatibility between two or more propositions," in Wikipedia, to the rarefied "In the process of development of a thing, a movement of opposites exists from beginning to end," by Mao Zedong. The most useful description of contradiction for understanding ToP methods is the conscious naming of the tension between current reality and the desired future state. Conscious awareness is paramount: you must be conscious of the actual details of your current reality and how those details differ from those envisioned in the future state. You must be especially conscious of the tension that exists between the present and future, especially of the drives that are pulling you toward the future state, and of the opposite drives that are maintaining the inertia of the current reality. Then, to ensure that you understand the real contradiction, you must consciously put a name on that tension. Racism and slavery were not only unjust; they were genuine contradictions that attempted to hold back a new world of freedom and opportunity by maintaining an old world of class domination.

ICA core principles can be described in terms of life stances that have allowed staff and volunteers to stand in the midst of very difficult situations and be transformed by those situations. ToP methods not only transform the situations where they are used, they also help the people who use them to grow. There are four such life stances. They are:
- Disciplined lucidity and being comprehensive.
- Continual affirmation.
- Inclusive responsibility, being ethical: freedom and obedience.
- Courageous style: pro-, dis- and trans-establishment style.

Disciplined lucidity and being comprehensive

Being comprehensive ensures that you do not succumb, for instance, to a CEO's simplistic vision of high profit margins, while the rest of the management team wants harmonious relationships with a union, and the staff wants safe working conditions. As the facilitator you may have no problem with expressions of a soaring and wonderful desired future, but you may have to force some participants to revise their vision if it is only so much "pie in the sky." Consultants who are not interested in participation will tend to ask a CEO what he or she wants to see and then recommend a course of action. ToP practitioners, however, engage all the participants in comprehensive thinking. Everyone experiences the increase in motivation and effectiveness that comes from including all of the stakeholders in thinking about their desired future.

To engage participants in an illuminating dialogue about contradictions, to be lucid about what is driving the group toward this new future, and to ascertain what the actual limitations are, you need to understand the limits and possibilities inherent in the group's situation.

To help participants safely discuss the tensions between their current reality and the future, you want more than just a clear head. You must be lucid about the games people play to avoid seeing and taking responsibility for their own situations. Who, for instance, really wants to admit that their health problems are a result of overeating caused by stressful dysfunctions within the family? It is much easier to blame it on the prevalence of junk food and the media, thus throwing up an element of obfuscation. You are taking a big chance if you rely on moments of blinding insight, which may or may not occur during a facilitation event. You must constantly practice disciplined lucidity, deeply examining many elements of everyday life and asking hard personal questions of yourself, and thus not be afraid to ask difficult questions in the midst of strategic planning.

Continual affirmation

> Deeper reflection generates more shared insights and understandings; space to talk about feelings leads to more appreciation of each other; methods leave people with a greater sense of unity and diversity.
> —Helen Ritchie, ToP practitioner, Whaingaroa, New Zealand

Blocks impede a group from moving toward its vision of the future. People are generally unaware of the most deep-seated blockages, which are typically invisible or submerged like the nine-tenths of an iceberg that rip out the bottom of a ship. Significant blockages remain unacknowledged, as in the story of the "emperor's new clothes." While all the adults are fawning over how beautiful the clothes are, a child asks, "Mother, why does the emperor have no clothes on?" It can take an innocent or otherwise neutral party to bring out the inescapable truth. When truth is outed it may intrude on the illusion of some participants: a very unwelcome intrusion for some. Although you may not understand the full importance of what is revealed in the moment, sometimes you are the only one who can ask the question that leads a participant to "state the obvious" or "speak the unspeakable." Then, even if it is taboo, painful, or a sacred cow, you must ask the difficult question about why the issue should be more thoroughly investigated. You already know that the conversation will be unsettling, and unpleasant, or at the very least uncomfortable.

Regardless of who or what the truth might expose, or what secret or entrenched behaviours might be revealed, you must affirm that truth in order for the entire group to move forward. Although you may not know the origin of the elephant in the middle of the room, the participants must affirm that its existence was probably part of a pattern that was necessary and possibly helpful at some earlier time. For example, the managers of one non-profit were in despair because they had no power to send their volunteers to the countries that needed them most. Each year the director told them "The board wants volunteers in country A and B, and that's where we are sending them." This created trust issues and stress between the director and the managers, leading to the despair. As they discussed this painful predicament the director admitted that the board was reacting to the sole funder of the organization to determine the locations. It became utterly clear to them that sole source funding was blocking them from controlling their own staffing. Despite the pain of their own distrust, an affirmation of the truth included the acknowledgment that this funding source had made it possible to keep the agency alive for many years and it was the genuine source of all the past good work. With consummate clarity, the managers and director created strategies to develop several new revenue sources, which would give them and the board new options for their programming.

If, even inadvertently, you recoil in judgement from a client truth or want to lecture participants about their participation in it, you will become ineffectual. Some participants will hide the rest of the situation. Some will side with you or try to win you over to a particular point of view. Affirmation is a stance required by all ToP practitioners; it releases the group to explore hard truths and intrusions in depth so that they can actually be dealt with. What you are affirming is that those behaviours, sometimes obvious and sometimes secretive, that no one is proud of and that are now roadblocks to moving ahead, were once the very behaviours that served the group and got them this far.

Continual affirmation, before and after the experience of intrusion, is a basic stance toward life, explicitly seen in the style of ToP practitioners. Participants remark on it. Affirmation allows clients to trust ToP practitioners to help them with their most troubling situations. It plays out at every stage of an engagement with a client; if a facilitator is not able to practice affirmation continually, she will not get the significant results they need and become frustrated by the methods. Affirmation is essential whatever the situation: in tribal villages in India, in UN-convened sessions in New York, in preschools in Whitby, and in boardrooms in Taipei. If you cannot practice continual affirmation, you may have difficulty remaining a practitioner. ToP practitioners know that they have their own "bubbles of illusions about life" that will be burst on occasion, and they need to experience affirmation as well.

Inclusive responsibility

As a Human Ecologist, I have focused and formalized ToP methods for planning and designing 'green' schemes with organizations, cities, counties, design professionals and neighborhoods in North Carolina. People need to think in an integrated manner and ToP methods work well to do that. Groups can "scheme" better with methodologies that allow for both rational and intuitive thinking. ToP methods help guide people's thinking to combine both natural and human systems.
—Elaine Stover, ToP practitioner, Greensboro, USA

Naming the contradiction bursts illusions about the current situation and blows the door to the future wide open. No longer held hostage by blaming someone else for their current problems, the group is free to move forward, step through, and take inclusive responsibility for their own situation. Inclusive responsibility is the life stance of making decisions based on personal freedom from what the past has been and in personal obligation to what the future could be. Responsibility flows from the freedom to be fully obligated to whatever and whomever one chooses. As Brian Stanfield describes it, responsibility is a "tension between being 100% free and 100% obligated."

Freedom

Moving through the door opened by a contradiction is an exercise in freedom. Einstein's familiar quote applies directly to strategic thinkers who do not allow themselves to be fettered by boxes or rules: "You can't solve a problem from the same consciousness that created it. You must learn to see the world anew." An old rule or policy might actually be the source of a problem. As one executive explained, "If our financial policy is that any unspent budget at the end of the fiscal year is returned to treasury and expenses will be reduced by that amount next year, how will we ever save up enough money to purchase multi-year equipment?" A facilitator has to prompt a group to think freely when they have named a contradiction, in order to define a strategy. If some people in the group say that they don't have the freedom to do what they want and that they can only do what they are told, the facilitator has to find ways to demonstrate their ability to think freely and create innovative options. You must be prepared with numerous examples of how freedom is inherent in every situation. If necessary, you may have to check with the client in advance to find out exactly how far that inherent freedom to think can honestly become freedom to act.

Obligation

Participants have obligations that emanate from their current reality and new obligations that come from the desired future they have helped to define. Obligations may take the form of roles or lines of authority, or they may be less explicit, such as unstated values or norms of behaviour. Occasionally, obligations are laws, regulations, and mandates that must be fulfilled, and sometimes they are of the participants' own making.

You can help participants become clear about their own obligations as well as those of the other participants. For instance, unclarity about the distinct obligations of public health inspectors and public health nurses can create problems between them. Public health inspectors might say, "We are mandated to ensure that restaurants are safe and free of disease, and we are obliged through legislation to visit every restaurant,"—an obligation that informs the strategies of a public health department. Public health nurses in the same organization point out, "We are mandated to make sure that kids do not experience violence at home, but there is no legislated requirement on home visits unless we receive a complaint." These two public health department groups need to know and understand the obligations of each other if they are to engage in a dialogue about support staff levels.

Tension

The recognition of the tension between freedom and obligation is an important stance of ToP practitioners. This is a major reason why ToP participatory strategic planning results in eminently feasible plans and why participants feel immediately empowered to implement the plans. A ToP practitioner ensures that the participants have looked at their obligations, alternatives, and implications, and that they have freely chosen the course of action, knowing who is responsible for implementation and who is empowered to do each part. While a consultant might recommend a course of action, a ToP practitioner guides the group to decide a course of action that they themselves will follow through on. This tension between freedom and obedience creates the energy to move implementation forward immediately.

You could listen to clients and participants for examples of freedom and obligation, and sometimes point out the tension. When person A advises person B, "You should try this approach," you might ground the point of responsibility by asking person A, "Excellent. Now what specific part of that approach would fall within your range of responsibilities or would you be free to work on?" This dialogue strikes a balance in the creation of strategy, which needs to be rooted in responsibility or nothing will come of it.

This tension between freedom and obedience is inherent in the ToP practitioner's stance and style. It is reflected in the capacity of a practitioner either to let go so that the client can implement the plan, or to commit to help implement the plan if that is the responsible thing to do. For instance, in a community development setting, you might lead the meeting in a decision to dig latrines, and then stay the next day to help dig the latrines. On the other hand, you might let go and move on to lead a meeting about the village box factory!

Courageous style

> When I started this work, it was not called facilitation. I worked with community groups in the U.S. asking their opinions and working with them to develop community plans or to imple-ment plans created by the communities. In the early days, it was energizing and frustrating. It was much later that I realized that the only way to be sure of the consensus was to wait and see what happened that represented the consensus. I remember a workshop in 1977, in a village in India called Nandapur. It was a simple brainstorm of actions to do on a visit to the nearby city to try to find support for community health and community income-generating projects. The reason it stands out in my memory is that I had no idea what to do. I had just arrived in India and was completely lost, but here I was standing in front of the room asking the questions. Later I was complimented, since I seemed so neutral and open to everyone's ideas. It's not very hard when you don't have a clue what to do. Every day since, I am remind-ed that my task with every group is to return to that place and that style.
> —Larry Philbrook, ToP practitioner, Taipei, Taiwan

ToP participatory planning is about commitment and people doing what they say they will do. If they say a proposal needs to be written, it needs to get done. If they say a brochure needs to be designed, it needs to get done. Other people need that work done so that they can also do theirs. The final essence of a participatory plan is this: everyone knows what needs to be done and they can depend on everyone else to do their part to be sure that the goals are reached. ToP practitioners model this stance through a courageous style.

Every participant knows that when planning is over and implementation begins, old comfort-able patterns of behaviour will have to change. Instead of working alone on your computer—like you prefer—you actually have to get to know those three other collaborative partners who are part of the action plan. Instead of taking your regular 2:30 coffee break with Karen, you have to attend the meeting every Tuesday at 2:30 pm with Bob and Pradip. Because getting your work done on time depends on them being done on time. And even though you know they will react badly, you might have to suggest that your slow colleagues be done on time. When implement-ing a plan you are opening yourself up to new risks.

It takes courage to create a participatory plan and courage to implement it. Other people will depend on you. Things will impede your progress, causing difficulties for you and others.

Proactive leadership comes into play because difficulties may have to be solved alone. Since the plan depends on others, you may have to give occasional encouragement and you may have to troubleshoot. New structures of engagement and new behaviour patterns can be both scary and risky for some.

Courageous style is inherent for the ToP practitioner as well. In spite of all your best planning, you may arrive to find problem after problem with the venue and equipment; however, that's no excuse for not providing a superlative experience for all those who gave their time to participate. You never honestly know if all the right people will show up for any given session; therefore, you sometimes have to demonstrate your own courage and, with some people missing, go ahead with the session anyway. You may have to stand up and take a leadership role in front of a large group of people who you don't know, in a place you have never been, after a poor night's sleep in a strange hotel. All of these things take courage and resilience. The participants will fully expect that you know what you are doing and where you are taking them. Those participants see your style and they take courage from it.

You will step into the planning process, especially into contradictional analysis, with no idea where the planning will truly end up. As Brian Stanfield puts it, "One lives in that nether-world between the no-longer and the not-yet." However, with the knowledge, and indeed the certainty, that the group has everything it needs to be able to plan for the future and move into it, you can operate out of a courageous style that generates courage for transformation in others.

The four life stances of lucidity, affirmation, responsibility, and courage operate not only in working through the contradictions, but also within each of the phases of the spiral process. Developing a vision takes courage. Forging strategy requires lucidity. Creating goals and action plans requires freedom and obedience.

"We are, each of us," as Stanfield continues so eloquently, "driven and limited by life's possibilities, open to its intrusion and affirmation, in complete freedom and obedience, which is responsibility, standing and acting in the ambiguity of the no-longer and the not-yet." ToP facilitators know this about themselves at their essence; they also know that this is true for each individual in the room and for the whole group.

The whole systems approach to planning

ToP participatory strategic planning represents a whole systems approach to transformation. ICA's earlier analysis of social processes led to important links in understanding between the spiral process and transformation.

During the early 1970s, the Institute of Cultural Affairs conducted a comprehensive study and analysis of societal dynamics, ranging across history and cultures. Visually distilling the results into a triangular format illuminated how economic, political, and cultural dimensions of any human society or community interact with each other. These **social process triangles** (see Figure 2) are holographic in that the interactions between economy, polity, and culture are shown visually to operate at all levels, macro and micro, of human community. Because of its comprehensivity, the social process triangles are a useful tool to analyze whole systems. Tensions between economic, political, and cultural drives within a society or a group create imbalances that dramatically affect the everyday lives of people.

The triangular form models a recursive pattern of the drives operating within any social system: foundational or sustaining drives (economic), ordering or organizing drives (political), and mean-ing-giving or significating drives (cultural). The triangular form repeats itself in a Koestler holonic pattern and predates Wilber's holonics by a decade. There is a corresponding implicit patterning of foundational, ordering, and meaning-giving drivers at every level of the triangles.

Visioning and comprehensive thinking

The spectacular array of social description generated by the triangles ensures inclusive vision-ing. The social process triangles can help a group be comprehensive in its practical visioning.

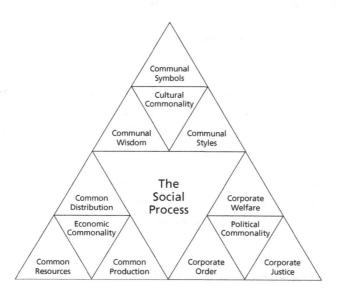

FIGURE 2. Social process triangles

Participants in a group can be asked to use a poster of the triangles on the wall as a screen for thinking about their own vision of the future. The triangles are one background tool to ensure that a group is comprehensive in its visioning. They are especially helpful with community or large scale societal visioning. Variants have emerged, such as the Corporate Process Triangles that use language more familiar to the private sector. The *dynamics screen triangles*, in Priscilla Wilson's book *The Facilitative Way*, have further descriptions that make them even more useful in general organizational settings.

Contradictions and Tensional Imbalances

The social process triangles are broken down into a series of levels, so that each level represents the increasing complexity and detail of societal functions. The three major triangles—economic, political and cultural—are level 1. Each major triangle is broken down into three smaller triangles. Each level 2 triangle is further broken down into three more triangles, and so on, down to level 5. The intention is that each set of three triangles at any level can describe a balanced state in society, a sort of ideal. In real life, there are always imbalances and these imbalances are revealed when doing contradictional analysis during the ToP strategic planning process. The social process triangles provide a helpful tool for analyzing these imbalances.

For example, in the economic triangle, the three level 2 triangles are resources, production, and distribution. The ideal economic life of a community can be described as a balanced state of its resources, production, and distribution systems. For instance, a small farming community might grow its own resources, produce its own food, and distribute it around. An imbalance occurs when any one dimension becomes too strong or too weak. For example, an imbalance occurs if the farming community only grows the food and then sends it all away to be processed before bringing it back again for distribution. A different imbalance exists if the community grows all of its own food and processes much of it and sells it to distributors, but since there are no stores in the village, people have to drive 20 miles away to get to the stores to buy what they themselves produce.

An imbalance occurs when one of the triangles dominates the others. A dominant resource system is a logging town with no secondary industry and few stores. A dominant production system is a factory town with none of its own resources and few shopping opportunities. A dominant distribution system is a mall town with mall jobs, which outside people travel to for shopping but leave immediately because there is nothing else to keep them there, no resources in the town, and no production of any sort. All three examples describe an imbalance and are thus not particularly balanced economic systems.

Another example is large imbalances in the political dimension. A large factory pumping out 500 refrigerators a day is a system dominated by order. So is a police state. A town weighed down by overregulation and bureaucracy has an imbalance in the justice dimension (not only the courts). Welfare dominates an extremely large commune where everyone helps each other out, but otherwise does what they want. There is generally great tension between the two most dominant triangles. That tension is like a power struggle between the two, which robs attention from the third or smallest triangle and collapses it.

An understanding of imbalances in a social system provides extremely good clues to contradiction analysis within that system. One such example can be seen in city budgetary struggles between the police (an institution of order) and the departments of human resources and council (generally institutions of equity and justice). The losers in this battle are likely housing, health, education, and elder care (representing institutions of welfare.) It matters little whether a citizen has a strong vision of housing and nutrition for all if there is a power struggle between the ordering dynamics represented by the police and the justice dynamics represented by council and bureaucracy. Welfare dynamics suffer and individual needs are forgotten in the squabble.

In the triangles in Figure 3, economic processes (especially production processes) are dominant; they create tension with the political processes (especially order processes). In a real world situ-

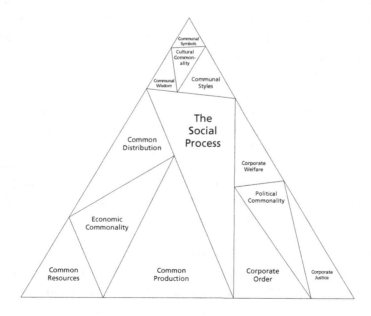

FIGURE 3. Social process imbalances

ation, this imbalance might appear as a supercharged industrial production system attempting to control the social system through a weaker bureaucracy. It might be a well established farm production system attempting to maintain control of migrant workers using a police force. In the meantime, cultural institutions, mores, and traditional wisdom are slowly being squeezed out and replaced by a production and consumption mentality.

Strategy and pressure points

A comprehensive analysis of vision and a thorough analysis of issues and tensional polarities generates a set of highly leveraged strategies. However, if one attempts to redress an imbalance by paying more attention to either of the two bigger triangles, the basic problem will likely be compounded. Putting time, energy, and resources into the collapsed triangle is a better strategy. On the surface, this approach might seem like betting on the smallest in a three-horse race. Better analogies are strengthening a cracked leg of a three-legged stool, tightening the loose string of a guitar, or moving some people over to the empty side of a lifeboat.

Many high tech software firms and newer mining firms have found that doing well financially (foundational is strongest) and having a well-organized workplace (ordering is strong) still does not save them from absenteeism, lateness, and morale problems. Trying to solve this by rewarding the strongest performers with bigger individual bonuses can cause backstabbing and internal competition, while creating more workplace rules just increases resentment in the ranks and worsens the morale. However, placing energy in the cultural dimension with new learning options, more staff social interaction, and a better understanding of how the company is helping society, can create positive change.

In communities around the world where religious convictions and values are very strong (meaning-giving is strongest), and the local politics mirror the religious conviction (order is strong), there is often an appalling abuse of the powerless and of minority populations. Trying to impose ethical values or holding public meetings just sets off worse clashes and retribution. However, investing energy into the economic sector through micro-credit, skills training, and bartering systems has changed the lives of millions for the better. Again, the indirect strategy of putting energy where the social process is the weakest pays off.

When, as a ToP practitioner, you engage clients in an analysis of imbalances in their own organization or community, focusing attention on the small imbalanced triangle will provide good insight into useful strategy. When planning in an extremely well-organized company with an economic powerhouse, raise questions of how to energize the values, story, and succession of the company. When working in a community with a great self-story and history, with numerous icons and heroes, where culture and tradition drive the political institutions, consider asking questions about new economic activity. When working with a non-profit organization with a great story and stable funding, consider asking questions about the welfare of the staff and of the decision-making processes within the organization.

Priscilla Wilson's *dynamics screen triangle* in Figure 4 illustrates some areas in the social process where creating strategy will leverage results, especially within the private sector. Focusing on servicing a market niche has made many people wealthy. However, doing your own analysis is an option well worth considering.

FIGURE 4. Dynamics screen triangle

Senior ToP practitioners often use the social process triangles for large analyses of social dynamics. They have even used the analysis to help them decide which organizations, companies, or sectors of society they will put their time and energy into.

Organizational transformation and the organizational journey map

The *organizational journey map* is a tool developed by ICA to help people in an organization gain quick insight into their own journey of transformation and to develop strategies to guide that transformation. The map incorporates the spiral process without explicitly referring to it or using its language.

The organizational journey map consists of four concentric squares divided into eight sectors, as shown in Figure 5. The squares represent four stages in the evolution of many organizations from the inner square, the hierarchical organization, to the outermost square, the learning organization. The sectors focus on eight different aspects of an organization across the stages: skills, leadership, structure, preoccupation, mission context, worker, communication, and values. These eight aspects represent some of the economic, political, and cultural elements of the organization.

Rather than merely pinpointing the level of an organization, the map provides a simple analytic tool that reflects the complexity of a multifaceted organization. The map works well with the spiral process.

1. *Current reality*

   Participants are asked to consider how the organization currently operates. Each person is given eight red dots and asked to plot them (where the organization is) onto the eight aspects (across the triangles). Group reflection on the distribution of the red dots reveals insight into the current reality of the organization.

2. *Visionary thinking*

   Participants are asked to think about the kind of organization that they would like to see in the future. Each person is given eight green dots, one for each sector, and is asked to plot their own vision for each of the eight aspects of the organization. Again, group reflection on the distribution of the green dots shows what participants want the organization to evolve into.

3. *Contradictional thinking*

   Further conversation about the differences between the current state and the future vision can reveal some contradictions.

4. *Strategic thinking*

   Conversations in small teams and the whole group discuss instances where people have seen elements of an evolved organization operating within their current organization. They consider how to promote and expand these elements within the organization.

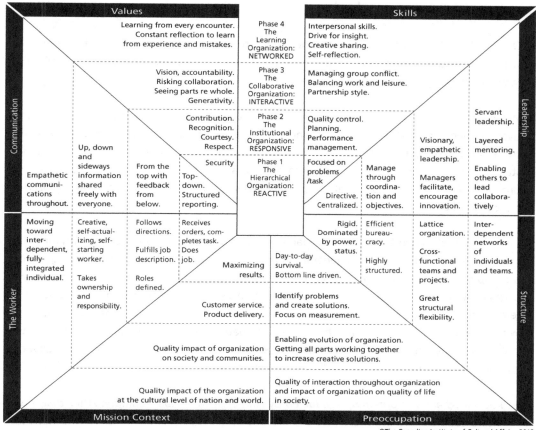

FIGURE 5. Organizational journey map

5. Tactical thinking

Further conversations discuss relevant indicators of the readiness to make the shift to the new and what tasks would be required to make the change.

While not showing the full complexity of the organizational journey map, this illustration demonstrates how the spiral process works naturally, even without an explicit understanding by the participants or even the facilitator.

Consensus workshop method

One method that is indispensable for the ToP participatory planning process is the **consensus workshop method**. *The Workshop Book: From Individual Creativity to Group Action,* by R. Brian Stanfield, fully explores this method.

While strategic planning does not require the consensus workshop method, the transformative experience of ToP participatory planning is almost impossible to achieve without it. The consensus workshop method can lead a large group of people through a "gestalt shift in understanding" in just three hours. The ability to occasion such a shift is part of the transformational property of ToP participatory strategic planning. The size of the group—from half a dozen to several hundred—does not matter.

With the consensus workshop method a large group of people can enter a session with their own individual ideas and leave with a general consensus on several major ideas. In a visioning session, a group can create a concrete practical picture of the future based on what everyone says. In a contradictions session, a large group of people can walk into a session with gripes, issues, problems, and constraints, and leave the room with a full analysis of the root causes of entrenchment within the organization and realize how they participate in that entrenchment. The design of the consensus workshop method takes a group of people with no ideas about strategy to a full set of strategies and approaches to which they are all committed.

I attended a ToP programme conducted by Ann Epps from Kuala Lumpur. After that, I was interested in exploring more and started out by observing workshops. Then I met Joan Firkins, who brought me into the ToP faculty in Australia where I continued to attend more workshops. Around this time, I started to use the consensus workshop and focused conversation methods with clients and had good results. My participants develop great clarity about what they want to do. I find it exciting to experience how ToP methods can create safe and supported environments for various types of people and groups to work.
—Cynthia Lau, ToP practitioner, Singapore

I was involved in experimenting with what is now the consensus workshop and the focused conversation methods in the sixties while on the faculty of the Ecumenical Institute and ICA, before these methods were packaged as the ToP technology, and just continued using them. They work. They change the lives of individuals and deepen the experience they have while in a group.
—Jean Watts, ToP practitioner, New Orleans, USA

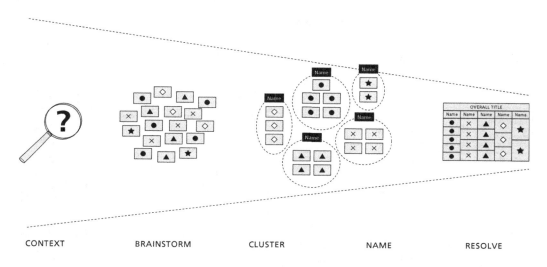

CONTEXT   BRAINSTORM   CLUSTER   NAME   RESOLVE

FIGURE 6. Consensus workshop method flow

As shown in Figure 6, the main steps of the consensus workhop method are:

1. *Context*—Consider and discuss a single, open-ended focus question that becomes the object of the workshop.
2. *Brainstorm*—Individually and then in small groups, develop 25 to 100 ideas and short answers to the focus question.
3. *Cluster*—Determine the main patterns of thought in the group by clustering all the answers to the focus question.
4. *Name*—Create names for each cluster that represent the pattern of thought and consensus of the group.
5. *Resolve*—Discuss the use of the final results and decide on the next steps.

In Figure 7 you can see the result of a consensus workshop with 10 board members of a national association. The small cards represent the brainstorming of the 10 people. The large cards state a consensus on seven major points of agreement on their practical vision, particularly on the results they want to see within five years.

The four phases of the spiral process use the consensus workshop method in slightly different ways. This book contains a variation of the method used for each of the four phases.

What can we do to help our team function effectively?

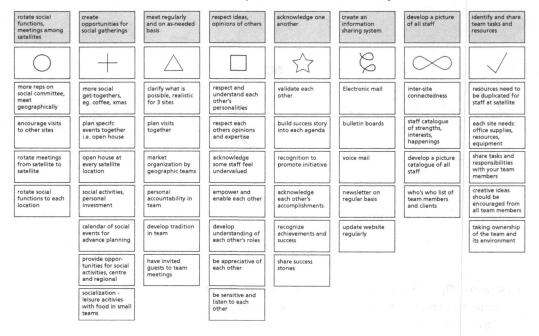

rotate social functions, meetings among satellites	create opportunities for social gatherings	meet regularly and on as-needed basis	respect ideas, opinions of others	acknowledge one another	create an information sharing system	develop a picture of all staff	identify and share team tasks and resources
○	+	△	□	☆	ჰ	∞	✓
more reps on social committee, meet geographically	more social get-togethers, eg. coffee, xmas	clarify what is possible, realistic for 3 sites	respect and understand each other's personalities	validate each other	Electronic mail	inter-site connectedness	resources need to be duplicated for staff at satellite
encourage visits to other sites	plan specifc events together i.e. open house	plan visits together	respect each others opinions and expertise	build success story into each agenda	bulletin boards	staff catalogue of strengths, interests, happenings	each site needs: office supplies, resources, equipment
rotate meetings from satellite to satellite	open house at every satellite location	market organization by geographic teams	acknowledge some staff feel undervalued	recognition to promote initiative	voice mail	develop a picture catalogue of all staff	share tasks and responsibilities with your team members
rotate social functions to each location	social activities, personal investment	personal accountability in team	empower and enable each other	acknowledge each other's accomplishments	newsletter on regular basis	who's who list of team members and clients	creative ideas should be encouraged from all team members
	calendar of social events for advance planning	develop tradition in team	develop understanding of each other's roles	recognize achievements and success	update website regularly		taking ownership of the team and its environment
	provide opportunities for social activities, centre and regional	have invited guests to team meetings	be appreciative of each other	share success stories			
	socialization - leisure acitivies with food in small teams		be sensitive and listen to each other				

FIGURE 7. Product of a consensus workshop

Focused conversation method

> *In many situations participation and involvement is an assumption, not a choice. The issue is how to structure the involvement. Without structure, involvement and participation remain tough routes to increased ownership and better decisions.*
> —*Linda Alton, ToP practitioner, Minneapolis, USA*

The ***focused conversation method*** provides a structured approach for discussing any topic safely and usefully by establishing a rational and experiential aim and then asking participants ever deeper questions, guided by the goals, at the objective, reflective, interpretive, and decisional levels. The focused conversation method is used by all ToP practitioners and is well documented in Brian Stanfield's *The Art of Focused Conversation: 100 Ways to Access Group Wisdom in the Workplace*. This method is integral to all ToP facilitation and is in widespread use throughout the world. Structured focused conversations are built into almost all the group interactions in ToP participatory strategic planning.

The master facilitator as an invisible consultant

Since ToP methods are transparent; the facilitator can focus the group on the content of the session and on the participants' relationships to each other. Participants are the experts on the topic and the facilitator remains an invisible consultant.

Whether it is a straightforward planning session or a potentially traumatic transformation, an extensive philosophical background prepares the practitioner with a thorough understanding of the human condition and the drama that is about to unfold. The life stances ground the practitioner solidly in values for relating to and empathizing with the everyday experiences of each participant. The social processes permit the practitioner to handle great complexity and not be overwhelmed, even when the content is beyond the practitioner's realm of expertise. The spiral process provides the facilitator a practical means to design the planning and methodology for engaging an entire group in all the relevant dialogue. As a thinking process, the spiral phases allow the facilitator to handle any size group with any time constraint and to engage participants using their own individual strengths. Finally, a variety of approaches, mental models, methods and tools, all of which are transparent and dynamic, focus individuals and the group toward commitment and empower them to act.

6
A complete framework of participation

This chapter contains detailed content on the overall participatory framework, and tools and best practices for each stage. A brief description of each tool or best practice will be given. To find detailed procedures for using each of the tools, see Chapter 9 starting on page 125.

Facilitation has been an important element in the work I have done throughout my career as both an educator and mental health practitioner. When I took the Group Facilitation Methods course, I felt like I had come home. I loved the fact that the methods were not only highly participatory, they honored and respected the participants. I then took the Participatory Strategic Planning course and used the methods in my work with my clients. I have worked with a wide range of clients in both the private and public sectors and facilitated them to achieve the results they declared they sought, from the creation of consensus on a challenging issue to the development of strategic and action plans. Seeing my institutional, business and community clients' amazement with the outcomes they have created by using the ToP processes, combined with their satisfaction with the results that lead them to become more productive, effective and inclusive, has been very gratifying.
—Nadine Bell, ToP practitioner, Austin, USA

Four stages of the participatory framework

The overall framework for participation that supports ToP strategic planning unfolds in four "stages":

I.   Preparing for strategic planning
II. Developing the planning context
III. Creating the strategies (using the spiral process)
IV. Implementing the plans

Within stage III of the four stages, the four "phases" of the spiral process take place. See Figure 1 on page 47.

Stage I: Preparing for strategic planning

Since the purpose of strategic planning is to consciously and intentionally prepare for change, planning events require careful preparation. When word gets out in an organization that major planning is going to take place, rumors may circulate like, "Why are we doing this now? Is something happening that we don't know about? Is there a budgetary problem, and are we going to lose our jobs?" While the simple answer might be, "We want to make thing better, so we have to plan for it," this answer will be unsatisfactory to many, causing even more speculation: "What's wrong with things the way they are? What do you mean by 'better'? Why are we really doing this? Can we actually pay for what we come up with, and is there commitment from the leadership, or is this just an exercise?"

The ToP practitioner needs to find out the type and scope of change the client has in mind for the strategic planning exercise. For instance:

a) Is the purpose of the planning related primarily to enhancing operations and prioritizing initiatives, so that everyone can "work from the same page or sing from the same song sheet?"
b) Is there an intention that some major new initiatives will be created or launched from this planning? If so, what level of commitment exists to direct resources to the new initiative?
c) Is the leadership team expecting that some structural changes will be needed to implement the strategic plan? Do they want to formalize some structural changes during the planning itself, especially changes to the organization chart?
d) Is the external environment putting large new demands and pressures on the organization, so that major systems change is needed? Is the organizational leadership prepared to undergo a systems change?
e) Is the purpose of this strategic plan to get the staff and leadership to create and operate out

of a joint set of new values, and embed behavioral changes throughout the organization? Is the leadership conscious of the size and scope of these shifts?

The listed changes are progressively more difficult, requiring progressively more discipline and intentionality in the various stages of the framework. It is critical to know the scope of the exercise before you start. It is possible that the client is interested only in a) even though the ToP practitioner is aware that c) or d) may eventually be required.

Stage II: Developing the planning context

After these questions have been answered, research or data gathering might be needed, so that real decisions can be made during the planning meetings. It may be necessary to gather information about the external environment, about the competition, or changes in demographics and surrounding social conditions. The history of the organization plays a part in the planning, especially if there is history from past planning or initiatives, or known weaknesses within the organization. Some ToP practitioners call this stage "determining the current situation," including the history and environment. The leadership team needs to assess whether it is time to revisit the current mission or mandate of the organization, or to leave those basics as they are. They need to ask if the planning process is intended to reinforce or rely on the existing values within the organization. Are people actually clear what those values are? Do they see the implications? Are any assumptions about the upcoming planning going to contravene beliefs or principles of any of the stakeholders? Do those principles need to be revisited first?

Stage III: Creating the strategies

At stage III, the spiral process is applied. This is where the highly participatory and transformative potential of the ToP approach excels. A master ToP practitioner can turn this stage of the planning process into an eventful and memorable time that the participants will look back upon for many years. People listen to each other intently, make many decisions together, and take on major responsibility for the future of their organization. Stage III includes some planning for implementation, but not the implementation itself. The last part of stage III can take several forms, depending on the purpose and intention of the planning.

Stage IV: Implementing the plans

When the first three stages have been done well, the implementation during stage IV is likely to flow easily. When the plans have been thought through well, and implementing teams have been empowered with time, staff, and budgets, significant results are possible. New patterns of behavior, including respectful dialogue, have emerged over and over during the process. The clients might not need the facilitators during implementation. Or it might be useful for the practitioners to return after six months or so for some participatory fine-tuning or a mid-course correction of the plan. Facilitators might also be retained to do specific work with a particular team, or to help with the transformation of a particular part of the organization that has some entrenched patterns of behavior that run counter to the larger plan.

Working with a client planning team and leadership team

The questions or choices in stages I and II might be handled in a simple meeting or conversation between the facilitator and the leadership team. Or they might require extensive internal and external dialogue, with data gathering from a wide variety of sources before the planning can proceed. The organization's leadership team needs to pull in the right people at the right time, to answer questions about the planning process and the data gathering.

The preparatory tool for the planning process (see page 262 in the appendix) is one way of assessing who needs to take part. The leadership team should consider the appropriate involvement of the Board of Directors, management, staff, other key stakeholders, and the larger community in each stage of the planning process. The ToP practitioner can advise on this, or at least discuss options with the leadership team.

At the very beginning, the leadership team might decide that this is to be a major planning process with a lot of participation and involvement from several levels or groups. In this case, they can delegate a planning team with representatives from within the organization, and entrust them with ensuring that the planning process is fair and transparent and involves all the right people. The planning team might meet several times, create some rules of engagement, and consider the best dates and times for the participation of the various stakeholders. The ToP practitioner should be part of or even convene the planning team meetings, since those decisions are so crucial to the outcome of the participatory process.

Meanwhile, the leadership team continues meeting separately, because they have to reach agreement on the proposed process, and the general content or directions they want to emerge from the planning process. On occasion, the leadership team will want to set parameters ("Let's not go there!"), or make difficult choices if the preparation process reveals a number of mutually exclusive directions.

Determining how much participation is appropriate

Stage I components generally need to be decided only by the leadership team, but the practitioner needs to ask about them in order to give advice on the full extent of participation needed in stages II and III.

While stage I seems obvious, it can be done well or not well at all. Here are some examples from my own experience.

A) Many years ago I was asked by two members of the Board of Directors of an NGO (on behalf of the Board) to conduct a stage III planning process, only to find a few days before that the Executive Director and management had a serious distrust of all external consultants, based on previous experiences, and didn't want me there at all. At the first joint meeting of the Board and senior management, it was clear that stage III could not happen because we ended up spending two hours working through a revised mission statement for the organization (a stage II item). Unbeknownst to me, a rift in the Board was the reason why it took two Board members to engage me in the first place. My initial questions had not uncovered the right or the urgent need for a new mission and mandate. After they had their new mission they decided they would go ahead with the stage III planning only at a much later date, and without me.

B) A government crown corporation wanted to create a strategy (stage III). I worked with the leadership team to consider all the stage I elements. They decided they wanted lots of participation from management and staff in stage II and from other stakeholders in stage III. After their strategy was completed I was asked to come back to help with some of the stage IV implementation. It was a great project and took about eight months.

Stage II activities can be done in a participatory manner, but only if the leadership or planning teams do adequate preparation. Staff, management, and other stakeholders benefit from being involved in reviewing the organization's history of successes and setbacks, its mission and values, and in analyzing current trends. There are ToP methodologies and tools for all of these activities, but the leadership team has to decide how much time and emphasis to put here, and whether stage II work is really needed to enhance participation in stage III, the spiral process.

The practitioner is often given authority over stage III (creating the strategies). This portion of the overall framework applies the spiral process to the organization: visioning, contradictions, strategies, and action planning. In this case, the practitioner has to review stages I and II with the client, generally asking simple questions, to ensure that the organization has allowed sufficient time and has sufficient participants for stage III.

The chart in Figure 8 can be used to help design the overall work plan. The chart can also provide a talking point with which to work with a client or team at the project's inception.

Stages and Steps in a Complete Participatory Strategic Planning Process			
Stage I. Preparing for strategic planning	Stage II. Developing the planning context	Stage III. Creating the strategies (spiral process)	Stage IV. Implementing the plans
Assessing the reasons for strategic planning	Analyzing the external environment	Stating the vision for the future	Preparing the action plans
• internal • external	• stakeholders & constituents • competitors & collaborators • events • trends • opportunities & threats	• hopes and dreams • 3–5 years • practical	• specific, measurable accomplishments • catalytic actions • focused campaigns • coordinated timelines • budgeting
Clarifying the planning objectives	Analyzing the internal environment	Identifying the underlying obstacles	Forming the implementing structures
• expectations • results • scope • group	• history • accomplishments & setbacks • resources • strengths & weaknesses	• obstacles, barriers, and roadblocks • underlying contradictions	• ongoing committees • special task forces • coordination team
Establishing the planning roles and guidelines	Clarifying the mandate, purpose, and mission	Creating the strategic directions	Monitoring and tracking results
• how much participation • steering committee • leadership • consultant/facilitator	• basic mandate • purpose & mission • reason for being	• 1–2 years or more • practical • implement yourself	• tracking action • action reviews • breakthroughs and gaps
Designing the planning process	Objectifying the primary values and philosophy	Designing the implementation scheme	Learnings and evaluation
• focus question • methods • time	• guiding principles • basic ethics • operating patterns	• priorities • phasing • action projects	• recreated objectives • actions and campaigns • implementing structures

FIGURE 8. Basic participation framework

Stage I. Preparing the groundwork for participation in strategic planning

Assessing the reasons for strategic planning

Why does a client want to do strategic planning? It takes a lot of energy to create a strategic plan, and the facilitator needs to know the real reason to determine if that is what is actually needed. Most clients state many good internal reasons for doing participatory strategic planning:

- We've been operating from the same strategic plan for many years and have accomplished much of it, so it's time to create a new one again.
- The company has grown, we have a lot of new staff, and we have a lot more potential than before.
- The staff has shrunk and our whole group needs to focus its efforts.
- The organization has gotten some large long-term new contracts and we have to shift to handle them.
- The budget has to be reduced and it will remain that way for a long time.
- There is a new board, and the new board members want to create a plan together using the wisdom of the whole group.
- The organization has a new mandate from a higher authority, and we have to get everyone operating on the same page.
- We all work well together and we just need to think about our future direction.
- There is a new CEO or executive director, and we need a new way of operating together.

However, a client might say, "We need to create a strategic plan because our funder has a requirement that we do one every five years. I really don't think we need it, but we have to for funding reasons." One would have to question that client's commitment to implementing the results of the plan. The facilitator's reputation could suffer if the plan was created and the leadership then decided it was only for show—which does occur.

While the clients may have a very good reason for writing up a strategic plan, they might not see any reason why it should be a participatory one. The plan they want might be created easily by a couple of people on behalf of the company. In that case, participatory strategic planning would be unnecessary, and might even raise expectations unnecessarily.

Figure 9 shows some typical situations in which ToP participatory strategic planning excels.

Type of change	General types of outcomes	Major emphasis of practitioner
Enhancing or changing current operating structures	reprioritization, refocusing, reorienting of the staff or board	Stage III spiral process
Creating new initiatives	new projects, programs, initiatives	Stage III spiral process with some Stage II analysis
Formalizing organizational structural changes	restructuring, new departments or lines of business	Some of Stages I, II, and III
Transforming whole systems	downsizing, mergers, re-engineering	Stages I, II, III, and some stage IV
Value-based behavioral change	values and behaviors must change because of internal and external pressures	Stages I, II, III, and some stage IV

FIGURE 9. Types of change and outcomes

While participatory strategic planning often happens at the organizational level, it can also be focused more narrowly at the department or even unit level. It is also possible to do participatory strategic planning sequentially throughout the organization. In the case of a government IT department (see page 109), the management team of a small branch office created a strategic plan that focused their staff on an important project. The plan was cohesive enough that the director of another branch said, "I'd like to do a similar process with my staff." This happened two more times, until each of the four branches had done their own strategic planning, involving about 50 people altogether. The chief information officer then recognized it would make sense to merge all four strategic plans: "Now that we have these four, let's roll them together into one big plan." While this might not appear to be the optimal way to run participatory strategic planning, it worked out well in this case. When merged, the big plan, which involved about 65 management staff, ended up requiring less work than the four individual plans.

External reasons

Shifts in society, in populations, in the marketplace, or in technology can easily provoke the need for a long range plan. Here are a few examples:

a) In the case study on regional economic development (see page 103), several small towns were forcibly amalgamated into one city. The economies of the city and the surrounding rural areas were being driven by external market forces in the resource sector.

b) A government department faced the possibility of being affected by an election within six months. Rather than having to deal with the whims of a new Minister, the Deputy Minister decided to engage all assistant deputy ministers and the directors in creating a thought-through proactive strategy for the future to show to the new minister regardless of which party actually won the election.

c) After September 11, 2001 many companies considered that their external environment had shifted sufficiently for them to rework the strategic plans for their entire companies.

d) Faced with rapidly changing demographics of its region, a social service agency found that all its existing plans were based on old demographics.

There are myriad external reasons why participatory strategic planning can be useful. The more complex the external reasons are, the more valuable a highly participatory strategic plan can be.

One reason often mentioned for doing participatory strategic planning is to "get buy-in from staff on a predetermined outcome." The president of a food processing company and two vice presidents were very enthusiastic about widespread participation throughout the plant. The president was delighted and said, "This is really great! Once we get their buy-in on managing the plant floor more efficiently, we can turn our attention to our real priority, which is selling the company." It was easy for me to turn down this exercise in token participation.

Risks are involved in participatory strategic planning. One risk is that the participants may come up with something contrary to what the acting leaders had in mind. The gains, however, generally outweigh the risks. When an entire team knows what they need to do and feels empowered to do it, and has a good plan underneath them, they are highly motivated to handle many of the external factors that society or the competition might throw their way. This sort of proactive commitment by staff cannot be mandated or legislated by a leader—it takes participation.

Clarifying the planning objectives

Getting clear on objectives and scope helps determine how much participation is key to the planning exercise, and from whom.

In the case study on regional economic development (see page 103), the city was faced with a diminishing resource-based economy that employed a significant percentage of the population. The strategic plan was designed to project out 25 years into the future. For this type of planning, as many people as possible should be involved. And indeed, about 540 people participated—a significant percentage of the population. Visioning, contradictions, and strategies were handled in thirty neighbourhood meetings, while the action planning was held in a large day-long conference, to which everyone was invited.

In another instance, a ratepayers association representing all the cottagers on a lake held a strategic planning session to figure out the focus and priorities for its volunteer board. The board members basically wanted to make cottage life more pleasant and protect their environment. Five years later the same group did another strategic plan, but the situation had changed. The ratepayers were facing higher taxes from the nearby municipality, so the scope of the strategic plan required involving all the ratepayers to influence how the tax money would be spent. Five years later another strategic plan was done, but this time the board wanted to hire an executive director and give clear instructions on what should be done. With each strategic planning exercise during that ten-year period, the focus of planning changed.

The scope of strategic planning may encompass helping a group clarify how they intend to work together. In the case study of a national board of a profession (see page 101), the executive spent a whole year discussing how they should be organized structurally. Finally they decided that form should follow function, and decided to create a strategic plan that would determine main future strategies and, consequently, how to structure the organization. In another instance, a city government already had a sound strategic plan. But some newly-elected regional politicians wanted to show the public that they were being sensitive and proactive to their needs, and asked for a new strategic plan to be created with participation from external stakeholders. When the additional planning process was complete, it contained only one new strategy.

How does a facilitator know when **operational planning** is preferable to **strategic planning**? Operational planning generally deals with things that are known and quantifiable, while strategic planning deals with the unknown—what needs to be created or re-created anew and is longer term.

Initiatives like large fundraising campaigns or building new buildings generally don't need strategic planning. Campaigns need some goals, perhaps a SWOT analysis (strengths, weaknesses, opportunities, threats), a few task forces, and some project planning. If a client already knows what they want or how to go about it, the facilitator will do well to ask them why they think a strategic plan is needed. The client might say, "We need some good strategies for how to get all this done." In this case, one might choose to do action planning, which is just the final phase of a strategic plan. If the client adds, "We need to get this done, but there is not a lot of clarity on what 'this' actually is. It has a variety of meanings, and we don't really know how to start," then perhaps strategic planning is needed after all.

Establishing the planning roles and guidelines

How does a practitioner know who actually needs to be involved in the various parts of the participatory strategic planning process? The best way to answer that question is to lay out the participatory framework, and then ask the leadership team or planning committee. The **comprehensive stakeholder involvement chart** in the appendix on page 262 helps with this determination. The facilitator can give advice on who and how many should be involved in various stages of the planning, but it is only advice, and the leadership team has to decide who will be made available for various parts of the process.

The leadership team might create a planning committee to help decide the roles and guidelines. The leadership team might also suggest which topics are "on the table" and which are not. They may have to indicate preferences that guide everything else. "We want to establish a research department, but we have to use current staffing." The facilitator may ask to engage other people in a dialogue, or to get more opinions, but the leadership team will make the choice. Another role of the leadership team is to indicate what sort of resources will be available for implementation. If there will be no new financial support, or no additional staff support, participants need to know this, so that they create implementation plans that they themselves can carry out.

A steering committee can be as few as three people or as many as ten, if it is a large organization with a number of departments. Steering committee members need to be representative, discreet, and trusted by their constituents. The purpose of a steering committee is to help decide the composition and timing of group events, to determine who must be involved in certain activities and to make sure that the planning does not interfere with all the other work of the organization. The steering committee also recognizes ideas that need to be referred to the leadership for vetting or be reviewed by a larger group. The committee knows where all the stakeholders are whenever it is necessary to get their input and involvement. A steering committee is an important ally for the practitioner, because it can steer the facilitator away from potential controversies that may arise, and warn of loaded language the facilitator should avoid, or of sensitivities that the facilitator could never know about. I once used the term "health promotion" as a simple generic description of some potential outcomes until the steering committee warned me that this term had a specific scientific meaning that would trigger participants to limit their thinking in a specific way.

Guidelines determine who participates in which stages and phases. These guidelines depend on factors such as who can be available when, how much time various stakeholder groups can spend on the process, and the underlying reason behind the strategic planning in the first place. One overriding value of a ToP practitioner is to involve in the planning those who will be responsible for implementing the final plans. How will each become involved in the planning and at what point?

The **ToP framework-building tool** (see page 206) can be used with a planning committee to find the whole range of stakeholders and how to involve them. Experts might be needed when technical information must be gathered. Forums might be needed to involve large numbers of people. A large consultation might need logistical support. Staff might need to be trained to facilitate smaller focus groups. This effort, of course, creates in-house capacity for future stakeholder dialogue, and could make future planning more affordable.

Designing a participatory process

Participatory processes might take place in a variety of types of session: forums, workshops, focus groups, plenary sessions, conferences, conversations, interviews, telephone interviews, email or fax input, online surveys, or online meetings.

Among the many participatory tools and methods are brainstorms, consensus workshops, focused conversations, historical and environmental scans, wave analysis, data scans, literature reviews, project plans, frameworks, timelines, presentations, and cooperative writing.

The main job in designing a participatory process is to figure out how to use the various participatory methods and tools during the various types of sessions to create dialogue and outcomes chronologically, according to the participatory framework in general, and specifically for the phases of the spiral process. Designing this process requires checking in regularly with the leadership team.

The facilitator can recommend and lay out options for types of sessions, tools, and how much participation is needed at what point. In general, the more participation, the better the plan, but there are almost an unlimited number of scenarios for designing a participatory process. Here are four simple scenarios.

Straightforward board-level planning
a) Staff members gather some information and input for the board.
b) The board goes through a cycle of stating the mission, vision, contradictions, and strategies.
c) Meetings with staff enhance contradictions and strategies, and send them back to the board.
d) Staff members do action planning, and send their final results to the board for approval.

Board and senior leadership team, together with staff input
a) A senior leadership team creates some background materials.
b) The board and senior leadership create a vision together.
c) A staff committee analyzes the underlying obstacles.
d) The vision and obstacles are sent to a larger staff group for reflection and input on strategies.
e) A representative group including staff and leadership create strategies and send them to the board for approval.

f) The entire staff are involved in action planning for implementation.

Staff planning
a) The entire staff are involved in a visioning day, ending with brainstorming of issues.
b) A representative group of staff work with the leadership team to determine underlying obstacles and formulate strategies.
c) Certain strategies are then sent out to relevant teams of staff to build action plans.

Stakeholder input
a) The leadership team does a historical scan and trends analysis to create a presentation for stakeholders.
b) External stakeholders participate in forums. They see the presentation and then provide input on the vision, contradictions, and strategies.
c) Staff go through a similar cycle using data from external stakeholders, plus their own perspectives.
d) The leadership team vets vision and strategies.
e) Stakeholders create action plans.

A participatory strategic planning process can sometimes be done in two days if all the right stakeholders are in the room. Other situations might require a month of data gathering, a month of staff discussions, another month or more of external stakeholders' input, and another month of the internal staff discussions, after which the approval process might take several weeks. Figure 10 shows a process timeline, an example of how the process played out in a city parks and recreation department with both a project team (PT), and a leadership team (LT), see page 86.

Space

ToP participatory strategic planning can be a very visual experience. Major space considerations include wall space, breakout space, and plenary space. Lots of unimpeded wall space is needed. Index cards, flipcharts, and results should be left up on the wall so the group can see them while they move on to the next workshop, with its own set of wall charts, index cards, and other visuals. A two-day planning retreat for 20 people can easily use 50 feet of well-lit, unbroken wall space, which can sustain charts with masking tape or adhesive putty.

Breakout discussion space, with moveable tables and chairs, is even more necessary. Space is needed for many small discussion groups of three to six people, optimally with their own small table and wall space. At a minimum, these groups should have enough privacy to hear each other well.

PROCESS TIMELINE City-wide community vision and strategic planning

PT = planning team
LT = Leadership team
VCS = Vision, contradictions, strategy

| Step | 1 2 3 | 4 - 6 | 7 - 8 | 9 - 10 | 11 | 12 | 13 | 14 - 15 | 16 | 17 | 18 - 19 | | | |

Step: Staff intro Feb 5

Meetings:
- PT Jan 21
- LT Jan 24
- Councillor invitations
- Community resource bank helps invitation process
- Presentation developed
- Community Forum March 4 VCS
- Community Forum March 5 VCS
- Sector Forum March 6 VCS
- Staff Review Mar 10
- Individual councillor input March 10
- Task force (×6)
- Program evaluation
- Cost and pricing
- Staff Consultation Mar 19 VCS
- PT Mar 20
- LT Mar 21
- Council Briefing Mar 18
- Project Team Leaders Mar 24
- Survey Launch Mar 28
- Proj. force (×6)
- Program evaluation
- Cost and pricing
- PT Apr 7 / LT Apr 9
- Survey Results Apr 18
- PT Apr 20 / LT Apr 21
- Staff Consultation Apr 29 AP
- PT May 8 / LT May 9
- PT May 15 / LT May 16
- Public Meeting May 15
- Council Report
- Council Report

Reports:
- Community Presentation (5)
- Community Vision Report
- Forum Review Report
- Draft Strategies Report
- Community Report printed (20)
- Action Plan and prioritize report
- Draft Report May 22 (23)
- Implementation Report May 29 (26)

FIGURE 10. Sample process timeline

Plenary space also has to be arranged, so that all the participants can see and hear both each other and the facilitator, and see all the material on the front active wall. Being too far from the front wall can kill the interactive dynamics. It is far preferable to be cozy and close in the plenary space, and be able to see and hear everything, than to be expansive and comfortable, yet too spread out for people to see and hear each other and the front wall perfectly.

The ToP practitioner generally has to reset hotel plenary space, because hotels almost always default to the expansive settings. Computers, LCD projectors, and screens are generally at the bottom of the space requirements, since they are often unnecessary to the planning process. They can be helpful for keeping notes and key points in front of large groups. They can be moved aside after presentations, unless you design them into the process. For more on meeting space, see page 205.

Stage II. Developing the planning context for the whole team

Participants need to be given a common context on why they have been asked to participate. If not, each person will make up their own often limited or unhelpful context. The context should provide a big picture. It should touch on the immediate and long-term aims, the external and internal factors, the historical and current situation, plus a common understanding of the organization's mission, philosophy, and values.

Analyzing the external environment

There are five ToP methods for external analysis in a participatory manner.

Stakeholder analysis

When the final plan is implemented, people outside the organization will likely be affected. Involving as many potential stakeholders as possible increases the value of your plan, and can also lead to greater assistance in implementation from collaborators, clients, and other stakeholders.

In the case study on page 105 the hospital and area health centre considered other health system stakeholders, members of the community, as well as suppliers and unions. All of these perspectives were included when they selected the actual participants in the planning sessions. In the case study on page 103, the regional economic development steering committee considered many large and small players, including members of the private sector, and then involved a very large sector of the general public in planning sessions, and in implementing the final decisions.

The practitioner can engage the steering committee in identifying external stakeholders and competitors. External stakeholders have valuable perspectives on the environment and may also be affected by the results of the planning. Knowing the competition can bring to light products, services, or pricing that are important to consider, and might also give new insight into sources of internal organizational blockages. Staff might learn some creative strategic breakthroughs from the competition.

Use of the ToP *framework-building tool* is a best practice for participative stakeholder analysis and helps determine core, involved, supportive, and peripheral stakeholders in each sector. See page 206.

Trend analysis

Changes within society might drive transformation in an organization and in the strategic planning process. *Trend analysis* involves looking at changes in society over time to determine those forces and drivers that will affect the future in a positive or a negative way. In the case study on regional economic development on page 103, it was quite clear that the forestry sector could not fuel the economy of the amalgamated city forever. Rising resource prices and general environmental concerns were making the local industry unsustainable. In the case study of an industry association on page 111, border restrictions caused by September 11th made it more difficult to get products across the border. In the case study of a professional association on page 101, pandemics and other illness outbreaks were dramatically affecting the profession. A thorough analysis of trends in society can give added insight for the participants' vision, the contradictions they articulate, and the strategies they develop. Major trends in society can drive a whole system transformation within an organization, requiring a transformational stance, continual affirmation and the courageous style mentioned in Chapter 5.

Some people are naturally on the lookout for trends in society, while others focus only on their immediate situation. Examining trends is not a simple matter of one group listing them, and hoping that the other group will see them. A trend often has to be illustrated with examples to be seen. When a trend is made visible, most people begin to recognize the implications, and acknowledge the need to create strategies in response. Some people like to use numerical quantifications and projections to analyze trends, making other people's eyes glaze over. Individuals who love the numbers may say, "The numbers show that people are buying $60,000 luxury suvs, so we should be making them. If we don't, we will lose 20% market share in two years."

Projecting numerical data to analyze trends can be helpful, but it can just as easily steer you away from what is important. One can easily abrogate the responsibility for decision-making by relying on information or data that supports what you want to do anyway. The biggest problem with projecting data to analyze trends is that every trend has a countervailing force. Sometimes that countervailing force can be just as visible as the trend itself, causing confusion in the data. For example, there seems to have been an inescapable trend toward global trade over the past 30 years. At the same time, there seems to be a countervailing force toward trade protectionism. Numbers will prove both.

The confusion over numbers to prove trends is real. Numbers can prove the necessity of increasing ethanol content in fuel, because petroleum is running out. Numbers can prove the disastrous effects of diverting ethanol into fuel by citing ethanol food shortages. One can show the expansion of the West Nile mosquito as it enters each province in the country. You can also prove the necessity of exposure to the virus, so that natural antibodies will develop to deal with it naturally. Trends always raise the question of values: which side do you want to be on? This is a valuable clue in participatory strategic planning.

A good time to consider trends and countervailing trends is just before long-range visioning. Since many people spend little time thinking about the future, engaging those people in a dialogue about future trends and the values they personally hold important helps make their latent vision of the future more explicit. Examining trends is a great exercise for considering alternative futures, before people choose the vision they most desire. There are three best practices for doing a participatory trend analysis: a **wave analysis**, an **historical scan**, or a **ToP trend analysis**.

Wave analysis

Wave analysis uses the image of a powerful ocean wave as an analogy for the lifespan of a trend. One spots events and clues on the distant horizon that look as if they might become a trend. Some of those items begin to gain energy and complexity as a surge. Some become full-blown trends at the crest of the wave, which are visible and forceful as more and more people put creative energy into it to make it peak. Then the trend crashes or subsides and is in the trough of the wave, depleted, and with some confusion over its value (see Figure 27 on page 209).

One can analyze the ten-year history of the dot.com companies in this light. When the Internet first started, a few companies on the distant horizon started providing services and getting rich; some could see a trend beginning. Throughout the 1990s, thousands of companies surged into schemes for making use of Internet capacity in get-rich-quick schemes. By the late '90s, the dot.com companies crested as thousands of new MBAs pursued dreams of getting rich though IPOs. Then on March 10, 2000, the dot.coms crashed, leaving hundreds of thousands of people dazed and confused. The dot.coms still exist, but the get-rich-quick-through-dot.coms trend is in the trough.

Historical scan

Strategic planning asks people to consider the future they want to see, and figure out how to move in a desired direction. But it can be counterproductive to ask a roomful of cynical people to create a vision of the future, or to create a vision while they are in the midst of very difficult times. Therefore, a facilitator sometimes needs a method to get participants to think about the future in a positive light. The *historical scan* is one of the most powerful and intuitive tools that a practitioner can use to re-create a group's story about its past, project it into the future, and determine its trends or how the group will relate to the trends.

Consider two competitive organizations that have just been required to merge due to a takeover or government legislation. Each organization has its own unique history, a series of events that have brought it to the present moment, and which need to be recognized by the other. Each organization has its own story of successes and struggles that have shaped it, which are probably not even known by its new partner. If a common story is not created between the two of them, the past patterns of competition will continue to be the norm, causing difficulties in the merger.

An historical scan plots the history of events from both organizations on one timeline. Newcomers who know little about the history of one or the other organizations gain a broader appreciation. Oldtimers bring closure to long-past events, so people can move ahead with less baggage. The participants are able to see what has already been done or tried, and they gain new respect for each other. It becomes obvious what has not been tried.

Whatever the history you are scanning, each past event brought up during an historical scan might have a different meaning for each participant. The past date on which many employees were fired might be traumatic for some, and a source of new beginnings for others. The historical scan creates a safe place for participants to talk about their different perspectives and learn from each other. After all the data is plotted, the discussion shifts to discerning major turning points in the history of the organization, and then finally to naming the various eras, epochs, or time periods.

In the case of some First Nations, an historical scan can reflect back on events a hundred years or more. But young organizations can also gain from completing an historical scan, by recalling the events in society or in their field of endeavor that have given rise to their organization.

By looking at events that have occurred over time, participants begin to see internal or external trends that project forward to the future. The further back one reflects in an historical scan, the further forward one will generally be able to project. When the scan looks back over a history of ten years, one may be able to project a few years forward. But when a hundred years of history is under review, there will be little difficulty projecting decades ahead, since that span of time can feel consistent for participants drawing upon a long heritage.

An historical scan for analyzing trends has nine basic questions:

1. What events have occurred internally in the organization?
2. What events in society have had an impact on the organization?
3. When did they happen?
4. What were high and low points during the whole time period?
5. What were turning points?
6. What name should be give to the periods between turning points?
7. What are future events that are scheduled to happen or are likely to occur?
8. What trends we can see through the chronology of events?
9. How will these impact the organization in the future?

An historical scan can create unique insight about the internal history of the organization. Brainstorming specific events and happenings from every branch and department ensures that no one is left out. The historical scan also records the history of accomplishments and setbacks since the last strategic plan. The naming of the eras between turning points reflects the current understanding about the past (see Figure 28 on page 210).

ToP trend analysis

A *ToP trend analysis* is a form of consensus workshop method, where the basic focus question is "What are all the trends we are seeing that are having an effect on our organization?" Practitioners often use the social process triangles to aid in the brainstorming. After the trends have been clustered, each overall trend is named, and its positive and negative aspects are discussed.

Examining the positive and negative aspects of each trend gives a way for participants to discuss the values associated with trends, and to project a vision that works for or against a particular trend. For instance, if participants see a trend toward more violence in their neighborhood, they may call that a negative trend, and project a positive vision to counter it. If they see a trend towards increased diversity in the neighborhood, they might choose to emphasize the positive aspects of that to inform their visioning.

Analyzing the Internal environment

Analyzing the internal environment creates awareness of problems, inequities, and structures that need to change. It also reveals capacities, potentials, and resources that are waiting to be put to good use. In the case study of a professional association (page 101), the board members were acutely aware that they had an outdated structure, but only decided to revamp it after creating a new vision and new strategies. In the case study of an international NGO (page 107), the directors saw the likelihood of large infusions of cash over the next several years and needed to improve their staff's capacity to handle steady, sustainable growth.

Reflecting on past strategic plans

Comparing the last strategic plan's goals and objectives with the actual results generates insight about the current internal environment. Goals that have been reached should be applauded and celebrated. Goals not reached may become part of a new strategic plan, or dropped because they are no longer necessary.

Assessing the results of a past strategic plan does more than simply clarify "what was done and what was not done." It also enables reflection on what was learned during implementation of that plan. These learnings can give very practical insight as the group moves from obstacles to strategies in its new strategic plan. What failed to happen is fertile ground for examining underlying obstacles.

Five key questions the facilitator can ask in reflecting on a past plan are:
1. What actually happened that was supposed to happen?
2. What did not happen, even though it was supposed to happen?
3. What else happened that was not intended?
4. What did we learn about how to do things?
5. What did we learn about how not to do things?

A previous strategic plan may have fully implemented several of its strategies. If those strategies are still important, they might evolve to a new level in a new vision of the future. One organization had a strategy of launching new research initiatives. After five years, they had so much success in launching these initiatives that everyone wanted to increase research in the new vision. In their new strategic plan, the old strategy became part of the new vision for a "full capacity research department."

SWOT analysis

SWOT analysis (strengths, weaknesses, opportunities, threats) is a well-known technique to analyze internal and external environments quickly. The SWOT analysis gives participants a strategic filter through which to study and analyze those environments. The more finely tuned the questions and the more categories used, the bigger the brainstorm will be and the more thoughtful people will become. In the SWOT analysis, positive and negative conditions are listed on one axis, and present and future time are listed on the other axis, giving four sections. However, the basic brainstorm is of two sorts, advantages and vulnerabilities, or whatever terms fit with the organization. For instance, a group could list "benefits and dangers" instead of "opportunities and threats." The positives and negatives are all variations of Kurt Lewin's force field analysis. A SWOT analysis can be done in a brainstorming session that lasts half an hour to an hour—although some organizations spend days capturing information from many sources to put into a comprehensive document…with questionable value.

John Epps tells his graduate business classes that although SWOT is not really a tool for environmental scans, it is often used as such. He asks them, "Strengths relative to what? Weaknesses relative to what? SWOT is a good tool to use prior to action planning, because then you have a strategy as an answer to that question." Some facilitators start every strategic plan with a SWOT analysis. This has its own benefits and dangers. Thinking about strengths and opportunities in the very broadest sense can help with visionary thinking, and thinking about weaknesses and threats can provide some data about the current reality. But getting too detailed too quickly about strengths and opportunities can circumvent several thought processes. It can turn visionary thinking superficial, and strategic thinking reactive. For example, a community might have a long-term practical vision of personal responsibility for health care, including nutrition, physical activities, and health promotion. However, if the SWOT analysis reveals a short window of opportunity for funding a new wing to the hospital, one can imagine all the forces lining up behind that quick fix. If a facilitator is not aware of how a SWOT analysis can circumvent visionary and strategic thinking, short-term strategies can end up becoming long-range visions. And this short circuit can ultimately be divisive, because the long-range visioning did not truly occur. One neighborhood wanted to do long-range participatory strategic planning, but after an initial SWOT analysis, the leadership opportunistically jumped on the bandwagon of funding a community center for which there was an available grant. Three years later, they found out the hard way that they had never dealt with their fundamental contradiction of internal divisions—and they had neither the community center nor the vision nor a plan. For clients who equate strategic planning with a SWOT analysis, the facilitator must spend time getting further clarity on the client's real motivation for doing a strategic plan.

Still, a SWOT analysis does spark both visionary and contradictional thinking, and a skilled practitioner can put this to good use. A very focused and useful SWOT analysis can be accomplished by first engaging the participants in determining major trends, and then doing the SWOT analysis on several of the selected trend topics. Here are two examples of SWOT analyses, one ill-conceived, the other well-conceived.

One health organization put several staff to work for several weeks, brainstorming and finding data on as many strengths, weaknesses, opportunities, and threats as they could on every conceivable subject of potential interest. The resulting 60-page document was full of charts, graphs, and demographic data, and looked very professional. When the board members got together to participate in the spiral process, they looked briefly at the document, and were unsure of how to use or interpret the glut of information. They commented on a few major points concerning demographics, but that was it.

A different health organization prepared for their strategic planning by identifying a dozen trends in society, such as, "an increasing use of best practices in standards and accountability," "a move towards multigenerational workplaces," and "the cultural diversification of the region." They assigned people to write short research papers and do a SWOT analysis of the dozen trends. In essence, they determined the department's strengths, weaknesses, opportunities, and threats in relation to larger trends, such as increasing cultural diversification or use of best practices. This research was compressed and precise and all of it was useful to the board, especially in the long-range practical visioning. The whole process helped to increase the flexibility within the organization and the competency of the staff.

A smaller SWOT analysis is a very necessary step during action planning, just prior to determining measurable accomplishments or strategic objectives. At this point, the analysis becomes part of tactical thinking, and helps dig out information to focus on relevant short term goals.

If a SWOT analysis is being done immediately before a strategies session, or immediately before determining measurable accomplishments, it is helpful to do the SWOT in the order of strengths, weaknesses, threats, and only then opportunities—which will lead directly into a form of positive strategic or tactical thinking.

Clarifying purpose, mission, mandate, and philosophy

Stating the purpose of an organization clarifies its reason for being. It answers the question, "*Why* are we in existence?"

Stating the organization's mission clarifies its role or task. It answers the question, "*What* do we do to fulfill our purpose?"

Stating the philosophy of an organization articulates the values it holds in carrying out its mission and purpose. This answers the question, "*How* do we do things here?"

Mission and philosophy are key elements of group culture. Enlightened leaders recognize that their staff's understanding of their collective mission generally connects to their own personal sense of purpose, and that connection yields enhanced motivation, commitment, and fulfillment. Some organizations have never written a mission statement, but operate on assumptions. However, the rapid and radical changes in the environment, the marketplace, and the workforce increasingly forces organizations to write, rehearse, re-examine, and sometimes revise their mission and philosophy.

The mission of an organization can remain the same for decades, and might never change. But it can also be subject to complex and rapid change, requiring nuanced shifts over time. Language is crucial. To say "Our mission is to create a healthy environment in our city" can be vastly different than "Our mission is to promote a healthy environment in our city." It could require many hours of deep discussion to decide which way to go because of the implications.

If the leadership team sees no reason to change or restate the mission, then it is only necessary to remind stakeholders or participants what the mission statement is, and to reiterate that the strategic plan will be driven by it.

Sometimes, however, strategic planning is done with the specific intention to revise the mission statement. The practitioner needs to determine if the desire is to change the mission or to update the mission statement. It is common enough that the mission has not changed at all, but the wording of the existing mission statement is causing some problems, and needs to be reworked for legal reasons or reasons of public perception. The change might be fairly straightforward. For instance the phrase "helping the handicapped" was decades out of date, and was changed to "helping people with physical disabilities." Later this was changed again, to "supporting people with physical challenges." When the leadership team talks about changing the mission, they might just need some simple wordsmithing, or they might need to change some very nuanced language that has important implications, or they might require a major shift in the mission itself.

The mission statement must be revised by the board since the board is the ultimate authority. The staff's involvement is only to inform the board of difficulties caused by the current mission statement, either because of the wording, or because the statement's inflexibility prevents them from carrying out the mission. The staff can point out inappropriate terminology. A shift in focus or in target audience can require that the mission statement be revised. Mandates, which are generally handed down by an external funding authority, are sometimes changed without the board's approval, and might require a revision of the mission statement.

Mission, mandate, and vision are often used interchangeably by clients. But they serve different functions, and a ToP practitioner needs to know the precise meaning of the client. Also, a mission can be broader than a mission statement, and a vision might be different from a vision statement. Generally speaking:

- A *mission* is relatively unchanging, and defines the role or task of the organization, stating succinctly "what we do to fulfill our purpose." For example: "Our mission is to research and develop cures for cancer and eradicate cancer in the population."
- A *vision* establishes what you want in place in the medium term. For example, "Our vision is to be a world leader in state-of-the-art cancer cures, with leading-edge research, strong partnerships, and reduced cancer rates in the population."
- A *mandate* often refers to a role predetermined by someone else, but is written in the organization's own language. For example: "Our mandate is to ensure that cancer research is made accessible to all health institutions." This is code for: "We are being funded primarily for public cancer research."

If unclarity about the mission is expressed by the leadership team, try to identify the root cause of the problem. Unclarity can generate long, unproductive discussions by a board, but can sometimes be cleared up quickly. The issue can range from simple dissatisfaction with the terminology, to differences of opinion about the purpose, up to serious disagreements over the meaning of the mission, the vision, or the mandate.

For the purposes of creating a plan, it is helpful to think of a mission statement as the unchanging purpose of the organization that exists regardless of staffing, funding, or any practical considerations. A mission statement should quickly allow others to say, "I understand that. That's important." A mission does not have to be practical; it only has to be important. "Our mission is to end hunger in the world." "Our mission is to create an umbrella of trees over the entire city." "Our mission is to promote the highest standards of products and services for the benefit of the consumer."

If some board members interchange vision, mission, mandate, and purpose, the resulting confusion does not necessarily pose a problem for strategic planning. As long as they do not change the main purpose of the organization (the mission), it is not too difficult to create a new practical vision to drive the strategic planning. On the other hand, if several board members agree that the organization's *raison d'être* has changed, both the mission and the vision have to be reworked.

In general, if the mission is clear, a long-range vision is easy to create, and a vision statement is easy to write. If the long range vision is clear, a mission statement can be enhanced easily. If the mission is not clear, the creation of a long range vision helps clarify the mission, the mission statement, and the vision statement.

However, if a mandate changes, both mission statement and long range vision might have to be reworked. For guidelines on how to facilitate in these situations, see "ToP mission and philosophy retreat," on page 213.

Objectifying philosophy and primary values

When creating a strategy for oneself, ethics and values operate in the background, more implicitly than explicitly. When my vision is "to own a house near my office for investment and as an art studio," my implicit philosophy and values determine whether the house has a one-car garage or no garage at all, or if the garden is for beauty or for planting vegetables for personal consumption, and if it is near a streetcar line or a highway. Philosophy and values also determine whether I hire my neighborhood realtor, or a specialist.

In a small organization where everyone knows each other, values and philosophy might be implicit, so that everyone just knows what they are. It may not be necessary to discuss values during the strategic planning. However, the bigger the organization and the more diverse the employees or stakeholders, the more important it is to explicitly state the values. The values affect the vision, how strategies are implemented, how programs are run, and how people are treated. Values come into play every time priorities are set or important choices are made in the strategic planning. A familiar example is 3M. Since the company's overriding value is innovation, new product development is an important strategy. This commitment has consistently inspired management to provide personal time for employees to develop new product ideas.

When stated values are held in common across the organization, clarity helps people decide among options when hard choices must be made. In a diverse organization with many different and even conflicting perspectives and behavior patterns, creating a common set of values together helps set expectations. If, in a hospital, the primary value is patient care, this value guides goal-setting if they adopt a strategy to increase efficiency throughout the hospital.

A ToP practitioners' understanding of *imaginal education theory* helps ensure that discussions of organization values are linked to organizational and individual behaviors. Imaginal education theory (see page 30), reveals practical linkages between group image, self-image, messages, and communication, as well as between values and behaviors. There are many examples of organizations that espouse particular values because they look good in their promotional material. When there is a gap, it is not because the organization does not believe that their stated values are important. More likely, they just don't know how to make them real and alive. This gap between stated and actual values causes a dilemma in participatory strategic planning, because the group's values are used to help determine or prioritize vision, strategies, and even action plans.

But when the time comes for implementation, the staff will not believe in the plans. Staff who are told that customer service is the number one priority, but find that resources and staff for customer service must be cut, do not believe that the action plans are serious or real.

ToP practitioners are biased toward implementation, so ensuring that the final implementation plans operate from "real" shared values involves linking those values to behavior, and matching the stated values to the real operational behaviors. ToP image, value, and behavior exercises help ensure that the values are stated properly, honestly, and realistically.

If the leadership team decides that a new set of values is needed, or that behaviors need to change within the organization to match the group's shared values, then the ToP practitioner can embed the exercises into the participatory strategic planning process. By the time the planning is done and implementation is ready to proceed, the staff and management will have stated their new values, experienced the new behaviors that are expected, and begun role modeling for how to "walk the talk." This is the type of transformation that ToP practitioners are trained for.

Part C

Four Transformational Phases
of the Spiral Process in Planning

7
Visible transformation
in ToP case studies

These case studies briefly illustrate the application of the spiral process in six very different settings. To see sample documentation for each of the case studies after the strategic planning process was complete, see Chapter 14.

Case study 1.
The board of a profession restructures for national prominence

The request by the organization

The national board of a health profession, made up of 12 people from several different provinces, wanted to hold a two and a half day retreat to come up with a cohesive plan that would be relevant in all regions of the country, to allow a potential membership of many thousands of people to "row in the same direction." They wanted to revisit the association's mission because of external problems and global pressures on their members, dilemmas that were never anticipated when the old mission statement was written. The board was aware that the organization's structure was not up to the task and that structural adjustments would be needed, despite their contract with an administration company that handled membership dues and some communication. The board members were all aware of their small financial reserves. None of these people had any particular solutions in mind, but they just knew that urgent decisions and actions were needed.

The situation and factors at play

Clearly, the organization needed to create an important plan broad enough to apply for at least the next four years. The association had a membership of only 1,600 people from a potential of 36,000 professionals across the country, and it was unincorporated, existing under the umbrella of a related regional organization. Recent major health threats including SARS, West Nile virus, and others had alarmed the international community, and the media was quick to publicize anything linked to those problems. The profession had members who were on the front line dealing with some of the issues and so the profession was, therefore, under constant scrutiny by the media. The news editors seized on unflattering facts and shortfalls of any group related to the crisis. The profession was receiving negative publicity, in spite of being on the front line, struggling to help people under difficult conditions.

In this case, the profession was under siege because of events in society. Their professional credibility was shaken, and some members were becoming depressed or burned out. The board of directors, all members for many years, wanted to renew their profession's morale and good standing. They wanted the association to grow and give quality service to all its members. The problems created by a global health crisis became a rallying point for the board. They decided to seize the moment and ensure their profession moved ahead despite all their recent challenges. They decided to re-strategize and to signal that common action was needed by all members, not just a few leaders.

The planning

Following telephone interviews with five of the board members, the ToP participatory strategic planning session lasted two and a half days. (See page 14.) The planning process included an historical scan; mission discussions; vision, contradictions, and strategy workshops; an organizational structure discussion; action planning for the coming two years; and team assignments. After the event, a first draft of the planning document was sent to the board members within two weeks.

Impact and results

The association was registered as a corporation with a new board and committee structure, which spread the workload and responsibility across the nationwide membership. The administration was shifted from the third party management firm to a full-time administrator. Before the strategic plan, the annual budget was about $10,000; five years later, the organization managed $500,000 in various project grants and initiatives. Its new structure enabled the association to handle about 20 major projects over the next five years, some of which are still having a positive impact in the field of health.

A series of well attended annual conferences increased the membership, the interaction among members, and the public profile of the organization. The profession extended its influence into several other partner bodies and professional groups through joint task forces, joint research, and subsequent collaboration. Executive directors and high-level experts from other professions regularly work with the organization. As a credible voice for the profession, they are sought for advice, partnerships, and joint funding proposals. Several seminal pieces of work have been undertaken with funding from government bodies, including national standards of practice.

Standards of practice for the profession, which already existed before the strategic plan, have now been applied extensively to shape curriculum, create toolkits, and write research papers and books to support the standards. A set of competencies with a process to certify professionals has been refined, implemented, and evaluated.

Almost all the strategies were accomplished within three years, so the board started another round of strategic planning earlier than expected. The practical components of the vision for the second plan were not very different from the first ones, but they envisioned a desire to affect society rather than just organize the profession. The strategies and action plans of the new strategic plan exhibit greater confidence than the earlier plan. The new plan reflects an expectation of success.

Learnings

When a new structure is being created, it is more useful to form the organizational structure after developing the strategies it will implement, rather than before. Some of the more important strategies might give rise to specific structural forms based on the plan being implemented, and not vice versa. An organization's mission changes with shifts in the environment and as the organization evolves.

See page 244 for sample documentation from this case study.

Case study 2.
Regional economic development refocuses from industry to tourism

The request by the organization

The Economic Development Commission of a new small city and its surrounding rural area wanted long-term regional planning that was fair and provided lots of opportunity for input from various stakeholders. The planning had to be highly participatory, with neutral facilitators engaging a large part of the general public to create a well-supported economic development plan. The Economic Development Commission wanted active teams of citizens by the end of the planning cycle. They did not want the plan to sit on a shelf, as plans so often do.

The situation and factors at play

Three small towns were mandated to amalgamate into the new city with a large rural catchment area to reduce administrative costs and rationalize the patchwork of local regulations that shaped business and day-to-day life across the region. The entire area depended heavily on a resource economy, but most people knew that this could not be sustained over the long term. City councilors and business leaders had formed an advisory group to create an economic development plan to provide a solid foundation for everyone in the region. This advisory group had had very little luck in creating a plan that everyone would back. After almost a year without getting very far in their planning, they decided on the ToP participatory approach.

The planning

This planning process involved demonstration sessions with the original advisory committee of politicians and business leaders. Three dozen open-focus groups and input sessions for the general public were held across the catchment area with good promotion by the local media. Since the sessions were open and public, no one knew how many people would show up for any particular session; therefore, the process had to be robust enough to work for however many people came, a handful or a hundred. Sessions were held in local community halls, golf clubs, and hotels. Two months after all the public sessions were complete, the advisory group met twice to consider the emerging vision, obstacles, and strategies. They invited all the participants from the three dozen public sessions to join them at a large plenary meeting in a local college gymnasium to review the emerging consensus plans, make recommendations, and launch implementation teams. The government leader opened the session, remarking that it was a "good example of democracy in action." Other people were invited to participate through email, fax, and surveys. In all about 540 people attended the various sessions.

Impact and results

By the end of the planning, eight new strategy teams were in place. The team to promote regional attractions was the largest. They revamped the schedule of celebrations among all the towns and villages to eliminate conflicting schedules. A new downtown business network replaced the three previous competing business associations, with a full-time marketing and events coordinator. The business district became the region's first historic district under the Historic Sites Protection Act. The team coordinated several new websites to offer a wider variety of tourism information. Within five years, tourist income had increased to $35 million per year. A one-source business team has since been created to encourage local investment. They help coordinate business associations, create local investment pools, seek out entrepreneurial efforts, and help micro-business startups.

Learnings

It is important to consider the timing of elections when deciding when to do large-scale public consultation strategic planning. Leading up to an election, politicians tend to stake out their favorite topics, using the public input sessions to promote their own priorities. This can create public conflict over high-profile choices, as in the common "tough on crime" posturing, which often has very little to do with good public policy. Immediately after an election, people expect political leaders to make decisions, not start a planning process. Therefore, a participatory planning process is best held midterm, when people are ready to listen to each other and electioneering has not yet started.

See page 247 for sample documentation from this case study.

Case study 3. A private hospital changes to a public health center

The request by the organization

A new hospital board and senior management wanted to assure the community that big changes in the hospital would not affect the care and compassionate service that had been emphasized in the past. The explicit purpose of the strategic plan was to enable a transition from being a hospital to becoming an area health center, with added emphasis on prevention, wellness, and public education. The stakeholders had extensive experience in running a hospital effectively, but wanted a strategic plan that would put them on the right course for their long-term future as an area health center. They were open to whatever would emerge from the plan.

The situation and factors at play

The town hospital was undergoing two major changes at once. The first was to shift from being a Roman Catholic organization to becoming a public institution. The religious order that had opened the hospital and served the population over many decades was stepping back, after having trained local professionals to take over the hospital administration and patient care. The second transition was from mainly helping sick and injured people to becoming a regional health center with a much larger mandate including wellness, education, and prevention.

For many decades, the town's population had trusted the religious order to provide competent, compassionate care. With the shift to becoming a public institution, a new set of values, especially fiscal responsibility, were added to the mix. This hospital attracted loyalty and commitment because of their deep ties with the community and the whole area.

The planning

The strategic planning process included 31 people: 12 board members, 11 managers, and 8 representatives of partner organizations. The board members represented a very good cross-section of the rural area, so there was no need to hold public sessions beyond the 31 people involved in the strategic planning process. The management team did some data gathering in advance and briefed the board members about current programs, services, and government mandates, so that the whole group could launch straight into the participatory process. The planning itself took three days over a weekend. It included an historical scan, a visioning session, contradictional analysis, a strategies workshop with phasing of strategies, and an action planning workshop. A draft of documented results was sent to the clients within three weeks. The staff took the results and did further implementation planning.

Impact and results

During the eight years following the planning, the hospital had three CEOs. The third CEO had been the new Chief Nursing Officer at the time of the planning, and was able to reflect on the results eight years later. According to him, about 70% of the long range practical vision had been realized.

A major tenet of the vision was a seamless care model for seniors, and this has largely been implemented with expanded community support services, apartments for assisted living, and many supports for people living in their own homes. Future senior service requirements are constantly monitored and projected. Expanded transit for seniors is improving accessibility of services. The Health Center offers acute care, long-term care, and community support, along with preventative and health promotion programs. A missing part of the puzzle is a retirement home, which would complete the seamless model by providing a medium-care alternative to the long-term care facility.

Another substantial part of the vision was increased and stable levels of qualified, satisfied staff. As a result of the plan, many approaches were tried to stabilize the part-time, professional health care staff. Eventually, the decision was taken to make all the part-time nursing positions into full-time positions, including both registered nurses and registered practical nurses. This change provided stability, but there are still some registered practical nurse shortages.

The Area Health Center partnered with a nearby college of applied arts and technology. Seven local residents decided to study for a health care profession by using videoconferences, so that they could stay in the area rather than moving out. The program also resulted in students from outlying communities coming to the Area Health Center for both theoretical education and laboratory experience.

It took a long time to realize the vision of satisfied staff. Four years after the strategic planning, a staff survey still showed a satisfaction level lower than 50%, largely a result of the constant turnover in CEOs. Many improvements were introduced in the following three years, and a similar survey showed staff satisfaction had increased to well over 80%.

The planning team also envisioned acquiring state-of-the-art equipment. After a sizeable investment, the diagnostic imaging suite was upgraded, and telediagnostic systems installed to permit rural patients to remain at home, rather than having to travel long distances for diagnostics.

Learnings

Hospitals have to shift the services they offer with shifts in technology and population. Hospitals are generally slow to make changes, because of the expensive infrastructure needed, staff training requirements, and the difficulty and expense of attracting staff.

Since the demand for health care generally expands, long-term strategic planning for a hospital must take into account community needs, government mandates, professional and union requirements, and new modes of service. A hospital's strategic planning needs involvement from the full range of stakeholders, including health professionals, unionized staff, administration and management, partner health delivery organizations, and the segments of the population who most use the hospital. In a hospital setting fully funded by government, strategies to ensure clarity and steadiness are more important than strategies for innovation. Measurable accomplishment tends to stress process rather than content. A crucial part of the process is to ensure that as many stakeholders as possible are on board at every stage of implementation.

See page 250 for sample documentation from this case study.

Case study 4. An international NGO expands size and scope dramatically

The request by the organization

A small non-government organization anticipated a period of global expansion and needed a long-range plan. The executive team intended to expand staff in the near future to several new countries. They needed specific long-range goals to focus on, but had few definite ideas in mind. The staff consisted largely of scientists, who said they had little familiarity with any form of long-range or organizational planning.

The situation and factors at play

This NGO started modestly in the late 1990s with a small staff within a related government department, some international grants, and a passion to increase public health around the world. The staff were primarily experts in their own fields of scientific endeavor. The government was ready to spin off this group of staff and to cut direct government ties. To act on their new mandate and become autonomous from the government, the entire staff embarked on a participatory strategic planning process that would launch the organization. They needed to articulate their new mission, register the NGO as a corporation, secure potential funding, create a public face, and plan for multilateral relationships with organizations in many other nations.

The planning

The participatory strategic planning occurred over three months, with a ToP practitioner leading the 14 staff and leaders over five separate daylong sessions, and the staff gathering additional data between sessions. The facilitated process included an historical scan; a societal trend analysis; a framework-building session to consider potential partners; vision, contradictions, and strategies workshops, with action planning to the strategic objective level. Over the next four years, the ToP practitioner worked with the executive and senior management, spending 50 days on curriculum building, international conferences, operational planning, and several think tanks, all of which were related to implementing the strategic plans.

Impact and results

One strategy was to promote advocacy and social marketing seminars. Within four years, international training programs had been held in Europe and the Middle East with trainees from 20 nations. The trainees were then able to promote and launch government-funded programs in each country, gathering and applying compelling scientific evidence from around the world.

Another objective was to conduct needs assessments for three continents. These assessments were completed and the partner organizations and governments that participated in the assessments became allies in the NGO's efforts.

The major objective of holding open partnership forums resulted in several forums, of which one of the largest was in Southeast Asia. Government ministers, officials, and industry owners from seven nations attended for five days, and the president of the host country visited the forum. This partnership forum resulted in the establishment of goals and objectives for each of the seven nations.

As a result of these efforts, hundreds of scientific papers have been written and shared widely to accelerate the health benefits in each nation. Media campaigns were launched in 30 nations, targeting people with authority to change public health policies. As this NGO has steadily grown and opened offices on three continents, positive health impacts have been documented for 250 million people in 65 countries.

Learnings

When working with civil society groups or with charitable organizations, participants and stakeholders are generally driven by high ethical standards, and are very interested in creative strategies. They are willing to work in teams across functions, even outside their normal areas of expertise, in order to create plans that maximize impact. Participants have little problem "telling it like it is," so the analysis of root problems and contradictions tends to be very revealing resulting in more grounded and effective strategies.

See page 254 for sample documentation from this case study.

Case study 5. Four government IT departments combine into one

The request by the organization

The director of a branch of a government department wanted his managers to create a strategic plan. The branch was mandated to roll out new information technology across the entire department, and potentially several other departments. The director wanted the managers to figure out how to accomplish this, and to lead their respective front line staff in all aspects of the rollout.

The situation and factors at play

In the late 1990s new technology and increased capacity of the Internet were encouraging government departments to envision new e-services, where people could access government information directly rather than having to visit branches and make requests. Until that time, most government departments purchased their own computers and bought their own programs, which were generally incompatible with each other. Some departments, however, had similar needs and were beginning to form clusters (or departments) with a matrix reporting structure.

For instance, social services have similar technology needs as education departments, and the needs of agriculture and environment departments are also similar. This particular branch was within a large department that had similar technological needs as three other large departments. The plan created by this branch would have repercussions on all four departments.

The planning event

The director and his seven managers allotted two full days to create a strategic plan for the branch. The managers had already done considerable research on the needs of the branch, their department, and the three other departments. Their planning event included a trend analysis for the past several years, a session to envision their best-case technological requirements, an analysis of the blockages they were experiencing in their work, a workshop to develop a set of strategic directions for all the staff, and a timeline of milestones for the next two years, along with a plan for key topics to be covered in monthly meetings over the next year. They also considered the complete set of stakeholders who would be affected by their plan.

Impact and results

The branch director and managers were able to report immediately to their Deputy Minister that they had a comprehensive plan of action and would create a set of deliverables that the other branches in the department could depend upon. The Deputy Minister shared the deliverables with the DMs of the three other departments. One by one, the information technology branches in each of the other three departments requested a similar strategic planning retreat. Within four months, all the information technology branches in that cluster of departments had their plans in place. The Chief Information Officer (Deputy Minister Level) of all four departments then requested a similar retreat for the 65 managers of all the departments at once, to ensure that the plans all had synergy between them.

Within three years, the new technology, information architecture, information management, and knowledge management were all in place, and the legacy data for the four departments had been consolidated. Help desks were up and running for government staff and external users. A voice-over-Internet protocol was being used to allow staff across the province to interact with each other to learn how to access the entire system and create or update new systems.

Learnings

The strategic plan created by the 65 managers had efficiencies beyond the four separate plans created by each department. While the larger plan included many of the milestones and planned accomplishments from the four departmental plans, the combined plan was able to remove some redundancies and duplications of effort across the smaller plans. Therefore, if everyone had created the larger plan together from the beginning, the four smaller plans would not have been needed. On the other hand, the creation of the four smaller plans first conditioned all staff members to the behavioral changes necessary for such a large project. In general, as in this experience, participatory strategic planning is very effective in matrix organizations, where communication is needed across the reporting systems as well as up and down the levels or the departments.

Sample documentation of the five strategic plans is too extensive for the appendix.

Case study 6. A competitive industry association turns collaborative

The request by the organization

The directors of this industry association decided that it was time to do major planning, but were stymied, partly because their member companies were in direct competition with each other. They needed a neutral way to conduct very frank discussions that were demonstrably transparent and open to all other members.

The situation and factors at play

Over 40 years previously, owners of companies in this industrial sector had created an association to give advice to government about legislation and regulation, to ensure that high quality persisted throughout the industry, and to serve as the industry's face to the public for marketing purposes. Federal legislation, product tariffs with the USA, and different provincial tax levels were creating inequities between members across the country. New plasticized materials and other manufacturing technologies were also transforming the industry, but training in the use of these materials was unequal. The association directors, as owners of companies that competed directly with each other, were naturally concerned to prevent any member of the association from taking advantage of the others to get contracts, free publicity, or exclude members who were not directors.

The planning event

The planning process was conducted with 14 directors of the industry association, who flew in from across the country to meet over a weekend at a hotel near a large airport. Owners or senior executives of their own companies, they had been directors of the industry association for between two to twenty years. The event included an historical scan, vision workshop, contradictions workshop, strategies workshop, and an action planning session which designated objectives, committee roles, and a timeline of activities.

Impact and results

The members of the association are all companies, and the membership increased 25% over a four year period. A partnership with another association has been strengthened continuing an annual joint convention and trade show. A volunteer executive secretary was brought on board to allow more consistent and stable operation of the organization. An award to help needy students pursue academic interests was established.

Learnings

In situations with built-in conflicts of interest between stakeholders or among participants, external facilitators can ensure neutrality. Facilitators or neutral consultants who lead participatory strategic planning in such situations must display an intention of fairness, and strive to ensure openness and transparency throughout the process. The facilitator needs to explain the process to everyone at once, and to ensure that any assignments made to individuals during the process are fairly distributed.

See page 255 for sample documentation from this case study.

8

Creating a practical vision together fuels the motivation to change

What keeps me going is the belief that a new type of politics is needed in the world, one that is more transparent and participatory, which respects our different integrities while building on our commonality as human beings sharing this planet together.
—Ahmed Badawi, ToP practitioner, Jerusalem, Israel

Groups of disabled peoples and their families and organizations want happiness and integration.
—Joaquina Rodriguez Ruz, ToP practitioner, Guatemala

The first strategic plan at Ozanam Industries enabled teamwork across the organization.
—Richard Maguire, ToP practitioner, Wentworthville, Australia

One requirement of strategic planning is a motivating vision of the future, preferably one that has been created by the participants and stakeholders. A long-range practical vision is essentially a snapshot of what the participants want to see in place after five years or more. This chapter explores visionary thinking, with special attention to the essential components of participatory visioning. It provides several exercises for orienting participants toward the future, with examples of practical visions from a number of organizations, and a step-by-step process for engaging participants in creating a motivating long-range practical vision.

Case study

Thirty-one people from the area health center in the case study on page 105 met for four hours to create a long-range practical vision to launch work on their participatory strategic plan. Twelve Board members, eleven managers, and eight people from partner organizations, including union and resident council members, met in a community centre on a December Saturday morning.

Each person took some time to write down personal answers to the question, "What do we want to see in place in our Area Health Center in five years?" They assembled into seven small groups to discuss their answers. Each group had at least one member from the board, from management, and from a partnering organization. Each little group generated eight answers to the focus question, and wrote each answer onto an index card with a thick magic marker so everyone would be able to read it.

Two index cards from each group, 14 in all, were taped randomly onto the large front wall. Participants began looking for patterns of similarity among the cards, and rearranged the cards into short columns. Another 14 cards were put up, and the emerging patterns of similarities were expanded until seven columns emerged. Participants were then asked for all other cards with dissimilar ideas. Another three clusters emerged, totaling ten columns of similar ideas. Then the participants brought all of their remaining cards up, and placed them into the columns they felt most appropriate. Each column of cards was read out one by one and discussed until the group could give a name to the pattern of ideas in the column.

During this naming process, it quickly became clear that everyone wanted to open a long-term care home under the auspices of the health center. They also decided that having a seamless care model for all seniors would be vital, supported by a philosophy of choice in client care. It was apparent that state-of-the-art equipment would be needed in the health center, especially long-distance diagnostics equipment. A competent, stable workforce would be needed in this rural area, and all the staff would have to be satisfied with their work situation in order to keep them in the area. One person wondered how all this visioning would get enacted, and asked if people should start listing things to do. The practitioner told the group that such action-oriented thinking was valuable, but that it was premature at this point and would be covered later in the process.

To complete the visioning exercise, teams of three people each took a column of cards and wrote a sentence describing the specifics of the five-year vision represented by those cards. The sentences were read out and discussed for clarity and for agreement on their long-range vision.

Links back to previous stages

A long-range practical vision can almost always be created in a participatory way, using the con-sensus workshop method. However, thinking about the future in a very general way (as when clarifying a mission or mandate) is different from thinking about very practical images and ideas about the future. Sometimes a short exercise is needed to spark people to articulate specific images of the future. The menu of visioning tools includes:

- Focused conversation
- Guided imagery reflection
- Mindmapping
- Wall of wonder or Historical scan
- Social process or dynamic process mapping
- Organizational journey mapping

Each of these tools is described briefly here or in more detail in Chapter 12.

Focused conversation

A series of open-ended questions can be asked at four levels in turn: objective, reflective, inter-pretive, and decisional. A sample *focused conversation* might ask these questions:

- What important projects and initiatives are currently being worked on in the organization?
- What future projects, programs, or initiatives are being anticipated over the next few years?
- Which of these are the most exciting or energizing?
- What else is missing in these images of the future?
- What are some long-range implications from all of these initiatives?
- What are some specifics that we need to think about or work on?
- What do you want to see in place in our organization in three to five years? (Note: this decisional level question can be the focus question of a practical vision workshop.)

For details on this type of conversation, see *The Art of Focused Conversation* by Brian Stanfield.

Guided imagery reflection

Guided imagery can help prepare for a practical vision workshop. It is best to plan the guided daydreaming carefully, using a comprehensiveness screen to encourage comprehensive brain-storming. Here are simple instructions for a type of guided daydream.

Ask participants to relax with both feet on the floor, close their eyes, and imagine themselves in a very comfortable lounge chair. Imagine waking up from a short snooze, looking at a calendar and seeing a date five years in the future. The facilitator can take the participants on an imaginary balloon ride or golf cart to see future places, scenes, or whatever they can see. The facilitator has to be very careful not to seed the participants' imagination too concretely, or else the participants will see what they think the facilitator wants rather than their own private visions. For instance, "Look around the new office and see all the new equipment that is there" is unacceptable for guided imagery because it guides people to imagine a specific vision. It would be less leading to suggest, "Look at a bulletin board and see photos of all the new and wonderful things that have happened in our office." Eventually, take people back to their comfortable lounge chair, and then get them to open their eyes and write down some of the things they saw on their imaginary trip into the future. You must prepare your guided daydream script with care, so that you point attention to many different aspects of the group's work, but to nothing in particular.

Wall of wonder or historical scan

Taking time to acknowledge and learn from past experience can liberate most groups to think about the future. At the end of an *historical scan*, after the participants have created their story about the organization's past, they can be asked about some things they anticipate happening within the next few years. On the right side of the historical scan timeline, you can list their ideas. Alternatively, participants can be asked to look across the whole scan to find trends that are likely to continue in the future. Anticipations and trends help link participants' thinking to the practical vision.

Social process or dynamic process mapping

The *social process* or *dynamic process triangles* can be used to develop a script that is aimed at generating a comprehensive vision. The triangles are placed on the wall, or individuals are given small copies, and then they are asked to jot down whatever they specifically see in the future of the organization as they range around the economic, political, and cultural dimensions of the first level, or the nine areas of the second level, or the 27 third-level triangles (see page 207).

A practical vision is a picture of the future

We begin by looking at the desired future, and the vision is a snapshot of that future. The orientation here is toward the positive—the situation we want to create and develop. A practical vision is a compelling, motivating description of the future we really want. We can see it and can almost taste the excitement. It is fun to get people together to think about the future, and it is motivating for everyone to hear from each other. If a group has never done visioning before, the participants are usually highly appreciative. However, many people equate strategic planning with only visioning, although visioning is only one part of a strategic planning process. Visioning is a stage that can feed into many other types of planning, including long-range, operational, program, project, or action planning.

Here are a few pointers about visioning:
- A vision is not necessarily a goal or a set of goals.
- A vision is not a mission.
- A vision is not a simple sentence.

People can become "visioned out" if they do it too frequently, especially if nothing happens as a result. One of the difficulties faced by ToP practitioners is explaining to clients how ToP participatory visioning differs from many other types of visioning, and that the visioning will be followed up by other steps that lead participants to become ready and empowered to act.

Key factors in creating a long range practical vision

More than a goal

A long-range practical vision is an overall description of what the participants really intend for the future. It is not a single goal grafted onto the future like "selling one million widgets," even though such a goal might be one solid feature of an overall vision. Many people have been enamored with the image of a leader who will take one element of an overall vision, and make it so succinct that it represents the vision of everyone. "To put a man on the moon by the end of this decade" is constantly used as an example of this. But the "man on the moon" vision was not a simple goal. It crystallized people's desire for rapid technological advancement, for emerging with a new spirit from post-war doldrums, and for a sense that democracy could win out over communism. The goal was not simple. It was very well researched and became something akin to poetry.

Visionary individuals in an organization can help state a vision, but only if they do it without trying to overshadow the vision of everyone else. It is best to engage everyone in creating a long-range, mutual, practical vision, which is comprehensive and which everyone can feel part of. Visionary thinkers have an important role to play, but can stifle others if their comments are allowed to eclipse the other people.

Balance between comprehensive and detailed

"You can't see the forest for the trees" goes the well-known saw, meaning one can get caught up in details and no longer see the big picture. However, developing a practical vision is a way to see both the forest and the trees. People in organizations often get so involved in the nitty-gritty details of their work that they forget why they are doing it. Creating or returning to their practical vision helps them "re-see" the whole picture, and do their nitty gritty in the context of the whole. Some organizations seem to have no vision at all except to keep doing what they have always done. Some people have the vision of doing what the boss says. Companies are finding that when their employees don't help with planning, they deprive themselves of a rich source of information. When an organization elicits wider participation in developing its practical vision, everyone gets a chance to "bracket" the trees for a while in order to see the woods, and to get fired up again over the possibilities of a future they want to help build.

When creating a vision in a participatory strategic planning process, the vision stage needs to be inclusive, so that everyone can see elements of their own vision in it. It needs to be motivating, so that in the midst of implementation people will remember why they're doing what they're doing. The vision needs to be practical enough to be more than a simple list of empty slogans.

When visioning is done well, it communicates what everybody naturally wants in the future. It may not be surprising or electrifying, but most people who have been part of the visioning will say, "Yes, of course, that is what we really want to move toward." The vision articulates what everybody would naturally move toward if there were no impediments or blockages in the way.

> *People were aware that they became more tolerant, listened to each other, integrated with the group, arrived at consensus rapidly, engaged in profound dialogue on specific themes, trusted each other's thoughts, and appreciated the different backgrounds, educations and capacities within the group.*
> *—Joaquina Rodriquez Ruz, ToP practitioner, Guatemala City, Guatemala*

Consider a company in which there are three prevailing attitudes about the organization. Some people work there only because it provides them with a steady income. They really don't care what the organization is about, as long as it keeps them employed. Other people like the camaraderie at the workplace and view it as a place to create social relationships and to develop friends. Some other people see the products or services of the organization as vital for the future of the community or the world, and that is what is important to them. The first group might have a vision about making good use of their skills, or getting opportunities to move up in the organization, make more money, and have more stability. The second group might have visions of a harmonious workplace where people appreciate each other, the workforce is kept intact, there is a positive spirit within the organization, and perhaps people join in social activities. The third group might have visions of an expanding organization with new lines of goods or services, that excels in customer service and generally has a positive impact on society. These three different visions of the company's future are not mutually exclusive, nor does any one person have only one of them. Any of these visions can motivate people to get up in the morning, bring them to work, and get them to do their best.

Now add into the mix a CEO, whose primary vision for the company is to be highly profitable by selling a million widgets in the next three years, or who wants to merge operations with another company, perhaps driven by the shareholders' or owners' requirements. All four of these visions might clash because they point to different intentions, but not necessarily. The three different versions of the staff vision can motivate the employees and keep them doing their best (assuming there is an organization to work for). And the CEO's vision might be based upon the survival of the organization, or other drivers might be at work such as share prices, bonuses, or the competition. The CEO might share her vision with others or might keep it private. The CEO might add elements of the staff's visions to her own to make her own visioning more robust. On the other hand, she might try to "sell" her own vision to the staff or even just announce it. She might decide that the staff visions are irrelevant as a company vision and treat them as strategies to keep the employees motivated while she pursues her "bigger" vision.

However, when one takes all of these vision elements together, they point toward a stable growing company, harmonious workforce, new product lines, opportunity for pay raises, a million widgets sold, a larger merged company. The best vision combines them all.

Common scope and horizon

In participatory strategic planning it is necessary to suggest a common scope or horizon for the visioning. Three to five years is relevant for many strategic plans, while six months might be used for a project plan. But what is a relevant scope for the plan?

In the health sector, Bob's vision might be to have the capacity to handle many of the town's health needs locally, without requiring people to travel to a nearby city. This vision might have a ten- or twenty-year horizon. Caitlin may envision a new wing in a hospital that can handle the ever-increasing needs of seniors. Derek might want to have a CAT scanner. A fourth person might see more health professionals, especially scanner technicians, living in the community and working at the hospital. For Bob and Caitlin, Derek's vision might simply be a strategy or even just a tactic. For Caitlin, who wants a new hospital, having a CAT scanner might be simply a small piece of her bigger vision. Derek, who wants the CAT scanner, might consider hiring the professional technicians as a tactic to make it all operational. These examples raise an important point about visioning with a group. How big are you going to go, and how long-range are you going to envision? In other words, what is the scope of the visioning? When a group of people discusses visioning for their organization, one can often note that a vision for one person is a strategy for another. People might begin to use vision and strategy interchangeably, which will add confusion. In this case Bob, Caitlin, and Derek will argue over what constitutes the vision, even though in the end they are all committed to the same thing.

Determining the scope or horizon of the vision will reduce the argument. In this case, Bob has the biggest scope in his vision (see Figure 11). Caitlin and Derek have a small scope, but both seem more practical. Practicality can be a highly motivating force in a vision.

Person	Vision	Strategy	Tactic
Bob	Healthcare for all	build local hospital	hold local funding campaign
Caitlin	State-of-art local hospital	decrease cancer rates	apply political pressure for CAT scanner
Derek	Accessible CAT scans for cancer patients	build public support	recruit technician

FIGURE 11. Visions within visions

Substance rather than style

Some consider visioning to be equivalent to coining a catchy, one-line vision statement, which has less to do with substance and more to do with style. In the 1990s, many consultants recommended vision statements that referred to "centers of excellence," "employers of choice," "top quality service," and "best in our field." We all know these to be simplistic templates of vision statements. Although powerful statements, they might not have any real significance for the people within the organization, especially if they did not create them. The statements are visionary in that they point to some idealized future state, but they do not state what that future state actually is. These are good branding slogans for third party consumption, rather than descriptions of the real vision.

Many organizations say "Employees are our most important asset," "Customers are our first priority," "Our future is in our people," or "Quality and service define us." While these are powerful statements and might have once been true, since the crash of 2008 they are easily recognized as manipulative and meaningless. They are great slogans for the media, or to put on a wall to remind people of important values, but they do not make a good vision, nor are they visionary, since they lack substance. One even gets a vague sense of discomfort. Such slogans have been used on occasion to lull people into a false sense of security, while the real vision and its strategies are playing out behind the scenes.

Being versus doing

This is what "lights" me up in the world: healing conflicts so that people can get back to being creative … being light. Life is the balance of light and dark. By teaching people how to engage their conflicts and build vision we are showing them how to sit with themselves and others, the good and the bad, and create the change they want to see in the world, both individually and as a whole. Recently I realized that one of the greatest privileges I have in my life is sitting at peoples' feet as they process their lives, their pain. It is a blessing more than anything to be able to do that. Recently with a colleague who was going through depression and grief, I listened. I acknowledged and shared my own story. He later told me this was a major turning point for him.
—Meghan Clarke, ToP practitioner, Cincinatti, USA

Vision is about being, while strategy is about doing. When this difference is not clearly articulated, vision and strategy are easily confused, especially when one person's vision is actually a strategy for another. The vision of a community garden for one person can be a strategy toward a healthy community for another. This confusion can be resolved by remembering that a vision refers to what will be in the future or a preferred state in the future. It is a category of "being." A strategy refers to how this will come about, or the approaches to be taken. It is a category of "doing."

Here is another example of how vision and strategy can get confused. Senior government workers do some research and agree among themselves on a long-range vision for their department. They spell out something that is motivating and compelling, using language that the public will recognize and see as necessary, such as "adequate inexpensive social housing." They communicate the long-range vision to elected representatives. The elected reps refer to it as a strategy, because politicians want to be associated with action (doing), not necessarily with vision. The workers realize the value of being associated with doing. The legitimate long-range vision ("adequate inexpensive social housing") is suddenly called a strategy of "building low-cost social housing," or "funding low cost social housing," because that appears more action-oriented. The politician then translates this terminology back for the public, either in bigger visionary terms: "better housing for all," or in strategic terms: "accessing housing options," whichever will get the better mileage.

When a person creates a strategic plan individually, there is an internal logic about vision, contradiction, and strategy that the person can understand, even if no one else understands that logic.

The plan is thought-through to the extent that the person can act on it. There is no big need to separate out the being from the doing. When two people create a strategic plan together, it is still fairly easy for them to have a consistent thought process that differentiates between vision and strategy. But in participatory planning with a large group, it is vital that everyone understand the terminology and the differences between being and doing so that they can come up with a common plan. If the being is not considered separately from the doing, people's responses in a meeting will in fact be answers to different questions.

Examples of long-range practical vision

The directors of an industry association (on page 111) agreed that they wanted their association to be recognized by everyone in that industry, that all members should be well-informed about the association's activities, that there needed to be a new generation of leaders to bolster the organization, and that they wanted healthy finances in the organization. While none of these were earth-shattering, they did state the real vision that the directors had for the association. That effort generated some new energy so that they wanted their annual trade shows to become much higher-profile affairs than in the past. Their full vision is available in Chapter 14 (see page 257).

A professional association (case study on page 101) required a much more practical dimension to their visioning. They decided that the profession itself needed to become an influential voice in the bigger field to which they were related. They wanted publicly identifiable leaders of their profession at all levels in the field. And to ensure that they were recognized as a real force, they envisioned that 50% of all practitioners in their field would be certified by a credible certification program. They also decided a new structure would be needed along with an Executive Director. These folks were thinking big and envisioning boldly, while being very practical. Their full vision is also available in Chapter 14.

It was clear during those both visioning sessions that the final vision captured what the participants really wanted, intended, and believed. It was also fairly certain that they did not yet know what they would have to do to get there, or what approaches they might take. There was no doubt that many difficulties would arise, but there was also no doubt that their vision was very important to them.

Visionary thinking: a thought process of planning

Master ToP practitioner and trainer John Epps of Malaysia has suggested several forms of visionary thinking: projected, effulgent, and latent. Distinguishing these levels can help a practitioner determine two aspects of a participatory vision, its practicality and its longevity.

Projected visionary thinking

Projected visionary thinking thrusts forward to reveal what will be visible. It is like a picture of the future from an LCD projector onto the wall, so that everyone can see it. Such visions are motivating and helpful because they are clear and easy to relate to: "We'll have a new research department housed in its own building, with full-time staff connected by Internet to every other research facility around the world. It will be wonderful!" Or, as Herbert Hoover put it in 1928, "a chicken in every pot and a car in every garage." Of course such projected images can get manipulative: "The new factory will provide jobs for everyone!" "If you are good, you might get an iPhone for your birthday." Projected visions are powerful, but unfortunately, just as with a projector, this type of visionary thinking can simply change the slide and create a new picture effortlessly: "There will not be a new factory. Instead it will be a mall." It is difficult to gauge actual commitment when one encounters projected visionary thinking.

Effulgent visionary thinking

Effulgent visionary thinking bubbles up effervescently from the deep resolve of an individual. When one bumps into a person with effulgent vision you see excitement, total commitment, and you can easily get caught up. It is a wonderful experience. "Save the rainforest!" "Save whales … or cats!" "Eradicate alcoholism!" "Beat cancer!" These are all extremely compelling visions, and you want to remain in the presence of such commitment and dedication. But an unfortunate side effect is that such compelling visions can tear a team apart. As long as members of the team are committed to the exact same thing as the person with the effulgent vision, everything goes fine. But if the team takes a one degree turn, they can lose their visionary colleague: "I meant the Amazon rainforests, not the African ones." "Sorry to have to part ways, but my passion is for breast cancer, not prostate cancer." And the same uncompromising commitment that makes this kind of visionary so energizing to be with, can also make him unable to shift his strategy and inflexible in implementation.

Latent visionary thinking

The hopes and dreams that make up the practical vision are usually latent. They are hidden in the depths of the subconscious, underneath all the daily workplace complaints. A participant might say, "Vision, I have zilch. But complaints, just listen to me." Underneath those woes is vision in disguise, waiting for a chance to get into the open. You generally find clues to the latent vision by simply asking people what they hope and dream for; what they need, or anticipate. More indirectly, you can discern it in stories, symbols, celebrations, or in architecture.

Latent visionary thinking is what most of us engage in most of the time. This unconscious vision propels our day-to-day behavior. It might be learned or picked up from the culture: "My summers as a child were spent swimming and fishing. I am now looking for property on the lake and have spent years saving up for a cottage." "In my new office I am expecting a window and a parking space. Managers and above have always gotten this." "Church every Sunday, and 2% to the collection plate." A latent vision expresses an important dimension of what people want in their lives and in their work. It may not be explicitly stated, but if you look carefully you will see that people's behavior is generally consistent with it. People operate from their latent visions.

> There is a good, simple test for the existence of a latent vision: ask people if the group feels cynical. If the answer is an exaggerated "Yes!!," you can smile and relax knowing that participants have a frustrated sense of how things could or should be. Hopes and dreams are there for the asking.
> —John Miller, ToP practitioner, Toronto, Canada

Imagination

Sometimes visions jump out and appear suddenly in "Eureka!" fashion. Sometimes they seem to crawl up through the floor or out of the walls in a slow, painstaking manner. The facilitator's job is to help participants make their own consciousness overt, and express their latent operating vision so they can see new possibilities, fresh alternatives that answer to specific needs. A good vision is practical, full of specific things you can see. A good vision makes your heart groan with hope at the very thought of it: "Employee profit sharing"—oh, yes!; "Introduction of teams— My O My!; "Permanent water supply—Glory, alleluia!" To get to this point, facilitators use techniques to go beyond linear thinking or knee-jerk visions of the future.

The facilitator needs to encourage freedom of imagination in the group, so it can express its real hopes and dreams. A vision covers both real needs and felt needs. It must go beyond the tame and fairly predictable to include items that provoke a few people to say "Wow!" Visionary thinking needs some elements of wildness. This wildness is in tension with the objectivity of the consultant, and the objective dimension of the vision. On occasion, hopes and dreams are expressed on behalf of the next generations—the group's children, grandchildren, and beyond. Sometimes an organization cannot know or understand its operating vision until it encounters something "outside" or "other." To create the practical vision requires both the objectivity of the other, and the subjectivity of the participants. The consultant or planning facilitator can play this "other" or objective role.

Visioning sessions are often the first occasions where large scale participation is invited, and in general, the more people involved, the better. Even so, participants can arrive at a visioning session without having given any thought to the subject, perhaps not even knowing why they are being invited. Some may be thinking, "Why doesn't the boss just tell us what he wants and how he intends to get there? That's all I need to know." This assumption eliminates all the latent visioning in stakeholders that is actually the source of most motivation or cooperation that exists within the organization. Getting them to share their latent vision can easily be as powerful as any projected or effulgent vision.

A three-hour classic ToP vision workshop

While there are many ways to create a participatory, long-range practical vision, here is an example of the procedures of a classic ToP Vision Workshop. This approach works well for a group of about 18 people who are all stakeholders in the vision. It could take up to three hours, and should be held in a room with a large, well-lit, vacant front wall, on which cards or charts can be taped. The tables are arranged in an open U, so that everyone can easily see the front wall, with some extra tables for break-out discussion groups at the back.

The aim of this session is to help the group clarify its hopes and dreams for the future. The product is a common, long range, practical vision. By the end of the session, the participants will feel and be unified and motivated. For the session below, a starting assumption is that the members know who they are, what they do, why they do it, and where they come from. If the people did not know one another they would need to spend some time for that purpose, not included here.

The following statements can help give the participants permission to join in on the visioning, and to clarify any questions being asked:
- Our long-range practical vision is based on the latent vision: the hidden, unconscious images of the future that are already in our heads, informing our actions whether we know it or not.
- This workshop brings the many individual latent visions to the surface, bringing the group's vision into shared awareness.
- Everyone has a piece of the puzzle. No one has the whole picture until the group creates it together.
- Each piece of the vision is necessary and important, therefore participants do not need to agree on every element of our initial thinking, but we do need to be clear.
- The whole picture we create together will be formed from the relationships among the many separate elements.
- The vision we create is not merely an assembly of separate ideas. It's like putting together a jigsaw puzzle without the cover picture, so the whole picture can emerge only when you see how all the pieces fit together.

The result of this visioning is *not* intended to be:
- Fatalistic—a projection of what is out there waiting to get us
- Subjective—a personal vision imposed upon the group
- Whimsical—wishful thinking about what "ought" to be a goal
- Mechanical—a roadmap of goals
- Easy—or uninspiring
- Scenarios—of alternative or preferred futures

The result of this visioning will be:
- Shared—a single, group product
- Practical—written in the concrete, descriptive language of nouns and adjectives in the present tense
- Intentional—describing where you will be when you get there
- Familiar—clearer and deeper, but not different from what each individual had in mind before
- Inspiring—calling participants to stretch a bit and take some responsibility for the future

As a facilitator during the workshop, you will be looking for the "Aha!" that is a shock of recognition for the hopes that lie behind people's daily activities and decisions.

Give a context to the participants

1) *Outline the process*: In this workshop we will develop a long-range practical vision for the organization. We will consider blockages and systemic constraints in a later workshop, and after that, we'll look at strategies for how to move ahead. Therefore, at this point we do not have to think about difficulties or about strategies—only what we want in our desired or preferred future. This workshop will take about two to three hours. We will brainstorm ideas, put them on the wall, and look for patterns. Then we will develop our vision from that.

2) *Outline the product:* By the time we are finished, we will have six to twelve short statements that express our shared, long-range practical vision.

3) *Highlight the focus question:* Write it on flipchart paper high on the wall, and keep it front and visible for the entire workshop. Ask questions like "What do we want to see in place in this organization in three to five years?" or "What do we want to see in society in three to five years as a result of this organization?"

Brainstorm ideas

1) *Brainstorm individually.* Each person list or sketch as many elements of your vision as you can see happening within five years from now. This is what you would like to see in place, not just what you think might be there. Try to get a list of at least eight ideas or as long a list as possible.

2) *Select your best ideas.* Choose your three most important yet clearest ideas, and draw a star on them. This is not to eliminate the others, but to speed up the next conversation.

3) *Brainstorm in a small discussion group.* Get into six small discussion groups of three people each. Take turns reading out your starred ideas to each other. From the total list, choose the eight clearest ideas. Start with ideas that more than one person had, and write them down. Try to get a range of ideas that honors the diversity of your discussion group. You do not have to agree with each other about each idea. The point is to help each other to be clear about what you mean. You can read out all your other ideas if you need to. Write each of your ideas on a card in three to five words, in big letters with a magic marker. You can add details on the back of the card, if you like. This will take about twenty minutes. When we are done, we should have about fifty cards altogether.

Cluster the ideas

1) *Discuss in the whole group.* Move back to the plenary space, but sit together with your group. Every person needs to be able to see the front wall clearly. Each group select three cards, and sends them up to the front. The three cards should include:
   a) the one you feel most passionate about
   b) the one that requires the least explanation
   c) the one that is least likely to come from any other small group
We will eventually get all the cards up front.
TIP: After the groups pass up about 18 total cards, read them out loud as you post them on the front wall, with tape, adhesive putty, or on a *Sticky Wall*, a nylon sheet sprayed with adhesive. Spread the cards out randomly. After all cards are posted, find out if any of them need clarification.

2) *Form four or five initial pairs of cards.* Let's look for any pairs of cards that have "a similar intent" and point them out.
TIP: If someone points out a pair, move those cards together, put a neutral symbol above them, and check the group's reaction to see if they agree. Ask the plenary to look for three more pairs of cards. On each pair, put a different symbol. When you are pairing these cards, avoid allowing anyone to add a third or fourth card to any pair, unless it is an obvious duplicate card. That will come next.

3) *Cluster beyond pairs.* Now we have four or five pairs of cards. Do you see any additional pairs, or do any of the remaining cards fit into existing pairs? Why do they fit together? TIP: Perhaps 14 of the original 18 cards on the wall might be clustered in columns by this time, each with a symbol on the top.

4) *Collect more cards.* Can each group pass up two more cards—the two that are most different from anything that is already on the wall? I'll read each one out loud as I post it on the wall. TIP: Spread them out randomly in empty spaces. Ask "Are there any questions of clarification about any cards?" At this point there should be 28 cards altogether on the wall.

5) *Continue clustering.* Let's cluster the cards in columns by similar intent, one at a time. We'll go in the order of whoever can see a new relationship among cards. TIP: If disagreement erupts over where a card should go, ask "What will you see when this whole column is accomplished, if we put this card here? What would we see in place if we put the card in this other proposed column? Where is the card most helpful? Most evocative?" Keep your focus on clarity. If disagreement continues, ask whoever wrote the card to rearticulate its intent, and where they think it should go. Or ask "Where is this card most needed to inform a larger element of our vision?" By this time, there will probably be about seven clusters or columns of cards, ranging from two to five cards per column. There may be several cards that do not fit with anything else.

6) *Relate extra cards.* Of the three cards left with each discussion group, try to relate them to the existing columns on the wall, and put the appropriate symbol on them. Do not try to force-fit cards into a column. Then ask them to send up the cards that do not have a symbol on them, or the ones that do not yet fit anywhere. TIP: Read these aloud as you put them on the wall. It would be normal to add another five to ten cards at this point, giving perhaps as many as 38 cards up front, in total.

7) *Create new clusters.* Do the new cards create any new clusters? Can someone suggest where they might go into existing clusters? TIP: There could be significant discussion around this point. Allow the group to explore options. Another three clusters might emerge. It is also possible that two existing clusters might collapse at this point to make one, resulting in eight or nine clusters. But do not ask about collapsing clusters unless the participants are analytical thinkers, or you have 12 or more columns on the wall.

8) *Bring up the remaining cards.* Put all your remaining cards on the wall in the appropriate categories. TIP: After they have put them up, this is an opportune time for everyone to take a short bio-

break, if necessary. When they come back from the break, rather than reading out all the new cards, you could count out loud how many new ones are in each cluster. You can see which cards are new because they have a small symbol on them (see Figure 12).

Name the clusters

By this time, there are about 50 cards on the wall, in about nine columns that range from three to twelve cards each. There will be a clear pattern, but the pattern is held only by the symbol cards. We will now name the columns and see what the pattern actually is.

1) *Select the longest column and discuss it for clarity and insight.*
TIP: This step involves asking a few questions to provoke group reflection:
a) Objective level—Read the cards in that one column out loud so everyone can hear.
b) Reflective level—Ask participants to call out their initial impressions: "What are the key words or phrases on these cards?"
c) Interpretive level—Invite people to discuss many answers and listen to one another carefully: "What is this column all about? What makes it different or special from all the other columns? What is the insight about our vision? What are clues to the vision that these cards are pointing to?"

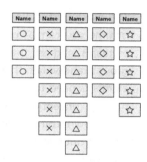

FIGURE 12. Columns grouped in a vision workshop

2) *Name the cluster.* These cards were all generated from the focus question "What do we want to see in place in our organization in 3 to 5 years?" What could we name the column, using a noun and at least one juicy adjective that describes what we want to see, such as "Dynamic waterfront park." We can always clean up or refine the language later. We are now only after clarity, not finality.
TIP: When you get a suggestion the group approves of, write the name on a card with a border around it, and put it at the top of the column. If the name does not come easily, here are some questions that can help:
• What have you heard us saying we want to see in place in three to five years?
• What is the recognizable condition you would hope to have in place in the next three to five years?
• What will we see when this is accomplished?
• How will we know when this vision element is in place?
• What will you see?

- How would other people know that this vision has been realized? What would they see?
- What is the noun (or the thing) that describes what is in place, such as a park?
- What are the qualities or features or characteristics of that thing that make it visionary, such as a dynamic waterfront park?
- Offer an off-topic example of a vision title. The best form for a name is *"juicy adjective + adjective + noun."* Another example could be "State-of-the-art research department."

3) *Continue naming the other clusters.* Let's go through the same steps with the second longest column.

TIP: Then do the third longest column, etc. The process gets easier with each column.

The more clusters you name together, the better the result. If you think you are running out of time you can, after naming four clusters all together, assign the leftover unnamed clusters to teams, and ask them to recommend a name to the whole group. Assign the clusters to the groups randomly rather than allowing them to select the cluster they want, because the vision elements need to honor the wisdom of the whole group. You need to remind everyone of the naming convention: *adjective + adjective + noun.* Each group might need to take their assigned cards down from the wall and find a spot to have their discussion, or they might be close enough to the front wall to see the cards. Each group needs a card with a border on it on which to write their recommended title. As each discussion group comes up with a name, they put the title card up on the wall, along with all the cards in the column.

Check the resolve of the group

1) *Acknowledge the results.* This was our focus question, and these are the titles we have decided on for each of the columns. We said by 2020 we want to see … .

TIP: Use a little drama when you read. At this point, they might give themselves a hand for getting so far, which is no easy feat.

2) *Ground the results.* Which title very clearly describes an important element of the vision? Which of the titles are you most passionate about? Which title could use some more work? Which are you most committed to? When this all comes into being, how will we be different?

TIP: Get several answers for each question.

3) *Create a chart to hold the consensus.* If we rearranged these columns to capture what you just heard us saying, which column would we put in the center, and how do the others relate to it? Let's arrange the columns to form a balanced whole. You might also name groups of similar columns.

TIP: See the example in Figure 13, on the next page. After the session you'll pull together some documentation like this.

Long-range practical vision: What do we want to see in place in five years?

Competent Renewable Stable Workforce	Business Management	State of the Art Equipment	Ongoing Staff Education	Satisfied, Stable Staffing	Engaged Community partnerships	Philosophy of client care	Sustained Essential Programs	Tertiary Prevention Programs	Seamless Care Model for Seniors
Recruitment planning Recruit and retain all professionals Emphasis on attracting local youth to health professionals Early retirement incentives Doctor recruiting program e.g. incentives Family doctor availability for new patients Early retirements incentives i.e. job sharing Adequate staffing Retention and recruitment policies Replacement for retiring CEO	Pleasant welcoming plant Manageable partnerships with other hospitals Self-reliant facility Maintain pride and confidence, self reliant secure facility Maintain reserves Sound stable economy within the community Maintain capital assets – cleanliness Balanced budget continued Strong financial health, capital reserves, balanced and surplus budgets, financial measurements, reporting systems	State of the art equipment (all areas for each department computers and applications) Telemedicine, more in-patient acute care program New diagnostic technology and access to it Video conference, telemedicine, telediagnostic Great computerization	Define skills required, skills available, and gap Competent well trained staff Staff monitoring Education all staff ongoing Changing roles i.e. nurses, doctors, multi-skilled workers Nurse practitioner Staff education program Well educated staff, healthy, enthusiastic, vital	Purpose and wellbeing for staff, rewards and recognition Staff recognition for good performance Expand employee health programs People may need counseling, financial, emotional, physical More staff functions, team spirit between groups of service providers, staff	Community involvement, youth and senior programs Greater use of volunteers Community loan cupboard Community interaction for residents Improve accessibility Cooperate with other facilities Home maintenance program for seniors Seniors outreach program Home support program More in-home services for elderly Expanded children's services Substance abuse, mental health Alternate medicine Alternative medicine and prevention	Emphasis on client care Link with referral centers Monitor demand and be proactive Increase LTC programs Health promotion clinic, NP, kinesiologist, recreation programs should be developed Adult volunteer program, community partnership Meet higher expectations of baby boomers' different needs Source types of health care for future or people can come in later Changing care model, medical to social	Palliative care on site and in the community Appropriate use of emergency Transit use, extend hours and use, no unfair competition with taxis Outpatient clinics Additional support clinics Procedure room, use of OR room Focus on wellness Enhance existing programs and eliminate others Expansion of palliative care program, more volunteers, increase awareness of teams' services Dementia gentle care program	Outpatient programming TV wellness channel Wellness clinic Becoming a center for education, training facility for variety of programs More outreach programs, nutrition, fitness, community teaching More caregivers for elderly More supportive housing Keep up morale of staff Continue diabetic program More volunteers	Increase rehab and psychogeriatric support teams LTC access system-locally, resident preferences More acute beds More nursing home beds Supportive housing beds Continuum of care: supportive housing, long-term, acute Easier access to supportive housing Supported independent living On-site supportive housing Seamless approach on site – supportive housing complex Supportive housing attached to the facility, full continuum

FIGURE 13. Sample vision documentation, showing all the data from the groups

4) *Discuss next steps.* Where did you notice a "That's all very nice, but …" reaction in the back of your mind? Did you have any other reactions? Those concerns are natural, and so our next step will be to look at those questions. The next workshop on identifying obstacles will clarify our issues. After that we'll continue with strategies and action plans.

A sample of the documentation of results

The facilitator normally types up the results of the workshop. This takes less than an hour. The table can be handed out for the contradiction session. If there is no time to type, move the columns to another wall to keep them visible to participants.

Sample vision chart

It is very common before the contradiction session to create a vision chart to help participants remember the vision in a more compact form. It usually takes about 15 minutes to create and can be done by two people who are known to be "big picture" thinkers along with one manager or director. They take the title cards from the workshop and look for an organizing principle between the cards, clustering the cards into a higher level consensus. If possible, they arrange the chart in some visually balanced way, as in Figure 14.

Vision element sentence

If time is available at the end of the vision workshop, or if there is a several day wait before the next session, you can ask small teams of two or three people to write up one paragraph for each column. The paragraph says "In five years we will see…. This is important because…. This will

Becoming a District Health Center		
In business	**In client care**	**In staffing**
State-of-the-art equipment Balanced business management	Seamless care model for seniors Community partnerships Tertiary prevention Essential programs Philosophy of choice in client care	Competent, stable, renewable workforce Staff education Satisfied staff

FIGURE 14. Sample vision chart, summarizing the group's decisions

look like…." The purpose of the sentences is not to be creative or to change anything, but to record the existing consensus of the group.

For each vision element, such as "Seamless care model for seniors," the small team can spell out the vision in a sentence. Here's an example:

In five years we want to see local continuous access to health care and support for individuals to be able to age in this community. This is important because:

- *It represents an expanding portion of our population.*
- *It will enhance the quality of life through augmenting support systems through familiarity of environment.*
- *It will maintain the economic viability of an area with a static senior population."*

This would look like:

- *Additional support housing units on-site to allow for continuous access to services, and reflecting the unique life style and spirit to which we are accustomed.*
- *Agreed-to programs to extend independent community living.*

In addition to creating a **vision chart** and writing ***vision sentences***, some groups will find it exciting to write a song, a story, or create a symbol at the end of a visioning session. Detailed ways to do this can be found in the section called "Stage IV tools to empower participants to implement" on page 226.

9
Articulating the contradiction is key to transformation

Between the idea and the action falls the shadow."
—T.S. Eliot

People become unafraid to present previously unspoken truths.
—Mollie Lakin-Haye, ToP practitioner, Atlanta, USA

People have hope even during conflict. The Technology of Participation has encouraged them to bring hope to their lives. Many participants have been able to transform their society through applying ToP methods.
—Tatwa Timsina, ToP practitioner, Kathmandu, Nepal

From hostile and confrontational to collaborative, and from hopeless and cynical to positive and willing to try, many efforts have been picked up and implemented because of their sincere belief.
—Dorcas Rose, ToP practitioner, Troy, USA

Understanding contradiction is the key to developing effective strategy. In their personal lives, people grasp and examine contradictions all the time, and then create strategies to deal with them. In our background thinking, we compare the differences between where we want to be and our actual reality of the moment. Then we determine what makes us complacent within the current reality, and a contradiction emerges. We must be truthful with ourselves to discern an underlying contradiction: "I would like to be 160 pounds and feel energized. But I am now 205 pounds, and have been that way for ten years. I eat rich food and my exercise consists of walking to work. My sedentary lifestyle is my contradiction."

Brian Stanfield puts it like this:

> The contradiction is the realm of that gap that any sensible person knows about—the gap between one's intention for a situation and what actually comes to be. In Western philosophy, Hegel came closest to describing what a contradiction is. His philosophy was based upon thesis and antithesis, out of which emerges synthesis. Out of the tension of a thrust and a counter-thrust comes the "not yet." The contradiction is the shadow that intervenes between what we want to do, and getting it done. The contradiction is whatever says "no" to the Practical Vision—contradicting and negating it.

ToP practitioners sometimes refer to **contradiction** as locating the underlying obstacles. But contradiction is a somewhat weightier term than *obstacle*. Another word is *block*—in the sense of a logjam in the river or a boulder in the road. Not only are those logs or boulders not going anywhere, but anything else coming down the way will also be blocked. Unless the block is cleared, nothing can happen.

This chapter examines the theory and practice of articulating contradictions during participatory strategic planning. It also discusses the reasons and ways that individuals or groups avoid looking at contradictions … and how to get beyond that reluctance. It suggests that developing transformational strategy depends on finding and confronting contradictions. Even though it is possible to develop strategies without naming contradictions, those strategies are usually less effective and non-transformational than strategies developed to resolve contradictions. A thorough understanding and practice of contradictional analysis is unique to ToP participatory strategic planning, and gives depth to the work of ToP practitioners.

Case study

In the case study of economic development (on page 109), the leadership group of the newly amalgamated city, including politicians, bureaucrats, and business people, were discussing a typed, rough document of verbatim results from 30 focus groups. The report repeatedly mentioned that participants really wanted regional unity since the recent amalgamation, along with increased tourism.

The discussion among the 15 leaders moved to some of the problems mentioned during the focus groups. Many issues and obstacles were listed, and the leaders wanted to figure out how to position these problems in the public report.

One businessman pointed to a large list of "lack of leadership" comments.

A bureaucrat said that this seemed similar to the list termed "leadership issues."

A couple of other councilors wondered aloud why people would make those comments. They asked "What is the coding on those comments?"—meaning which political wards did the comments come from.

"Many of them are in focus groups 4, 7, and 23."

"I don't think those particular ward references are relevant," another ward councilor responded. "They are from many places."

An older, long-time councilor said that these probably meant "communication issues between leaders" rather than actual leadership issues.

Another businessperson read a comment that said "Petty disputes. Local politics gets in the way of getting things done."

The official in charge of tourism said that this sort of comment should not be put in the report. A councilor said it should be. The group went back and forth on this point for a while, wondering who the comment was about. The tourism official repeated, "We certainly can't publish that in a report. If we publish 'petty local politics' in the report, it would make us look bad."

The first businessman, who had been flipping quickly though the lists, said, "Look, the same point shows up 53 times in all of these public comments from across the region. If we don't acknowledge that we've heard this, none of those people will believe the report."

Another councilor said, "If it shows up that many times, there might be another hundred or more who didn't say it because it wasn't the most important thing on their list. If we don't mention this point, many people will consider this report to be a whitewash."

The older councilor said, "I know we don't like it, and it's not pleasant to say so, but we will have to point out that petty local politics is a major block in this community. And it applies to everyone, not just a few." There was some nodding around the room, and he continued, "You know, if we want regional unity to really work, we are going to have to get some new young blood on our city committees, and maybe even the council as well. That could make a difference. And we'll need to come up with some other things as well."

Links back to previous stages

Sometimes previous stages of the overall planning framework bring up comments that can eventually point to contradictions. And a practitioner can review notes from these earlier stages in order to ask participants about those comments during the contradictions workshop. Here are stages worth examining:

- Weaknesses and threats were identified while analyzing the internal or external environment.
- Low points or turning points were found during the historical scan of the organization.
- If the mission is changing during this cycle of strategic planning, some contradictions were apparent in comparing the old and new missions.
- The leadership team indicates that some stakeholders do not need to be engaged in the larger strategic planning process. When asked why, they were unable or unwilling to say. This could be an area to examine during contradiction analysis.
- When probing primary values or philosophy, the values demonstrated through behavior in the organization differ from its stated values.

A contradiction analysis can be done immediately after visioning: the best time is the very next session. If several days or weeks elapse between vision and contradiction workshops, or if many new participants arrive for the contradiction analysis, start by reading through the vision again. Confirm or ground the vision by asking individuals to give examples of the future vision.

Contradictions and systemic blocks you participate in

A contradiction is a social reality that causes group paralysis. This paralyzing factor might be passively accepted as "the way things are," or it could be an object of hopeless complaints. Most people don't know what to do about it, because they don't know how to talk about it. A contradiction is like a family secret that people avoid mentioning. Slavery was a social reality that paralyzed the emergence of a fully equitable society.

Although a contradiction can be the source of great pain, it is not simply negative. In fact, it can become the doorway to the future. When people recognize it and come to terms with it, it can leverage an organization or a whole society into the future. Tiny, marginal farms were the painful reality that led to the creation of the cooperative farming movement.

A contradiction is a complex phenomenon—a vortex of underlying irritants, deterrents, and blocks. It is a coagulation of factors that reveal the focal point of social paralysis. A "vicious colonial salt tax" was the doorway to Gandhi's Indian revolution. It is always a struggle to capture a contradiction in a memorable short phrase.

Generally, people do not talk about contradictions around the water fountain. In fact, one definition of a contradiction is that it's the unmentioned item in every conversation, "the elephant in the room." It's what everyone shies away from, yet it permeates the whole community. In this sense, a contradiction is a timely social truth which, if allowed into the light, will shake the rafters and create a new situation. In some communities, child abuse was unmentionable for decades.

Locating a contradiction is the most painful part of planning, but it is the key to any creative change. It is important to take enough time to discuss and name each contradiction carefully, since the rest of the planning process builds on this insight as the foundation of a plan for the future.

However, a contradiction is not just a practical problem. A problem might be: "We're losing fax messages because we've run out of paper, and no one has ordered a fresh supply because we haven't paid our stationery bill." Problems are dealt with by solving them: "Well, let's pay the bill, and get the copier paper." Contradictions run a lot deeper than that.

Contradictions are not psychological, but sociological. They are related to structures, policies, and social patterns that say "no" to contradict the vision. Encountering unlikeable qualities in people can be unpleasant, but they are not contradictions. The fact that certain people don't get along is not a contradiction—that will always be the case. But systematic racial discrimination in the workplace is a true contradiction. In looking for contradictions, we are not concerned with personal quirks or symptoms, but with social structures and policies that cut a group of people off from their desired future.

Similarly, contradictions should never be stated as moralisms. "Students are lazy" is not a contradiction. You have to dig deeper to find out why they might appear to be lazy. Maybe they're coming to school hungry and need to be fed.

Because contradictions are real entities, never state them in the negative. A contradiction does not begin with the phrase "a lack of." A lack of money is not a contradiction, while wasteful spending priorities might be.

Key factors in articulating a contradiction

I have seen people and organizations move on and develop as a result of my work, I have seen extraordinary "aha" moments and a light in people's eyes which tells me they are in a new place. Equally, I have seen my efforts defeated in cases where internal and external forces conspire against the sort of being, thinking, and doing on which ToP is based. Taking time to identify the real contradictions means I hear more "ahas" and see more of those lights.
—Jonathan Dudding, ToP practitioner, London, UK

Doorway to strategy

Millions of people wake up each morning with one thing on their mind ... to get their kids off to school. Those little children, however, can create lots of difficulties for their parents. They don't want to get washed or to eat their breakfast in time. They want to play video games instead of brushing their teeth. They pick little fights with each other. When a parent's vision is to get the kids off to school, but the children's boisterous nature blocks this from happening, high-level strategy comes into play. One strategy is to make a game out of who can get dressed first. Praising the children and saying wonderful things might work. Other strategies are to get one child to help the other, or to create a diversion to pull them away from their video screen, or to use threats of punishment. You could employ a strategy of preparing breakfast and packing lunches the night before. You might have to consider all these strategies all at once. But the success of the strategies depends on understanding the nature of the children and what they are actually doing.

Strategy is not restricted to the boardrooms of banks or closed-door executive meetings. We all use strategies every day, but they are *not* done simply by implementing a vision. You cannot just will your kids to get washed, dressed, fed, and off to school. You cannot tell them your vision and hope that everything turns out. Strategy requires that you thoroughly understand both your vision and the current reality that is stopping the vision from becoming a reality. Current reality could be "Jackie, are you teasing Jeffrey again? Or is he teasing you?" Are the children's clean clothes easily accessible in their drawer, or still in the dryer in the basement? Has that video game they want to play before breakfast become too addictive for them to put down? Are the kids old enough yet to test me and my "consequences" speech?

Current reality

Knowing what strategy to use, or even how to develop strategy, requires separating what is real from what is guesswork. It's not always easy to know what blocks our vision from becoming reality.

In fact, we tend to be complicit in the blocks themselves, and then we try to ignore our own complicity. "Didn't I buy the video game precisely to keep the kids from constantly complaining that they were bored? Didn't I leave the clothes in the dryer precisely because I didn't want to wake the kids up by putting their clothes in their drawer late at night? Aren't I really more happy when I don't have to act on my 'consequences' speech because, after all, they are my little darlings?"

All too often, the current reality that stops you from moving toward your vision is partially your own creation. As the cartoon character Pogo puts it, "I have seen the enemy and it is us!" Or as Brian Stanfield once told a colleague about her emotional attachments, "You can't complain about not being able to get out. It is your own warm puppies that keep you at home, distracted and poor."

We can fool ourselves by hiding current reality behind excuses. When the truth is too painful, it takes an outside intervention to reveal it. In participatory strategic planning, a whole group of people are able to multiply the excuses and make it very difficult to discern the real facts. Luckily, a group of people can also do their own intervention because they have multiple perspectives on the truth.

The unspoken truth

When facilitators try to uncover contradictions during a participatory planning session, they have to listen just as carefully to what is not being said, as to what *is* being said. Every participant has explicit reasons for why they've been unable to move ahead. Most participants also know of blockages they don't want to talk about, because it might make them vulnerable, put them in a bad light, or hurt someone else.

In one instance slow accounting procedures were blocking people from making timely decisions. But to say this implied incompetence in the accounting department, and since everyone liked the head accountant no one wanted to mention it. In another situation two senior managers worked in the same communication office, each with five subordinates. When the old director left, one of these senior managers became a director and the other did not. This caused internal problems based on split loyalties, but no one would actually talk about it. Most employees in the participatory sessions would only talk about "gaps in communication" or "coordination problems." One brave soul called it "a leadership issue." Eventually they agreed that the promotion protocol had caused a low-level rivalry between two different groups in the office that was beginning to poison the atmosphere of an otherwise very good team. This was a big admission. The new director and existing senior manager had no idea how much effect this was having on the whole team, and they agreed to get together and work things out.

The facilitator has to ensure that the realities about contradictions are verbalized, so that they can be heard, clarified, understood, or challenged. People may not want to publicly name the elephant in the room. But when a participant mistakenly thinks that a contradiction is obvious and goes straight to strategies from the vision, everyone in the room might assume a different contradiction, and therefore the strategies come helter skelter from different directions. The strategies may even work at cross-purposes. There will be arguments over strategy, and many will not believe that the selected strategy will actually solve the problem. Conversely, one person might want to blame someone in the room, in order to disguise or divert attention from a contradiction in which the first person is personally implicated.

> An industrial plant belonging to a large US company had a very strong union leader who called a strike just when the current plant manager (PM) was being transferred into this plant from the company's flagship plant in another state. Even after a year the PM was still in shock from the strike, permitting the union leader to assume unhelpful power by filing one grievance after another for various small infractions. A newly assigned unit manager to a small unit in the plant couldn't understand why the PM didn't take a stronger stand. Participatory strategic planning with all the managers brought things out into the open, especially when the PM drew a picture of one contradiction that he named "the bunnies getting out of the cage" (managers taking thoughtless risks). The picture was drawn well, and I still remember how the unit manager rose straight up in his chair when he realized that he and the other managers were considered to be the bunnies. As a result he himself began carefully pushing back at the union leader and was able (despite the PM's fears) to bring more of a reasoned balance (through participation) to the working style of the plant. After several years this younger leader rose to be works manager of the company's flagship plant, the highest operational position in the division.
> —Richard West, ToP practitioner, Taipei, Taiwan

Not about the money

People often blame not having enough money as the root problem, but it hardly ever is. Groups talk about wanting new buildings, capital projects, or programs that can expand from one year to the next. In the planning session they may complain about not having enough money. When you start to dig a little to clarify the real blockage, you often find that they actually do have some money, but few of them knew about it. They might admit that money actually does exist, but that it would take some reprioritizing to make it accessible. Especially with groups that use government funding, they might have money at the end of the year that regulations require them to use up or else give back. That annual funding envelope requiring all money to be spent by March 31 might be the actual block. Many blockages are more real than "lack of funding."

Hidden expenditures that cannot be quantified or vague accounting categories might be the actual block. A competing priority could be the real block. For one group, an external funding authority was the block. They didn't actually know if the external authority would agree to fund new proposals… they just made assumptions about it. Whenever "no money" or "lack of funding" is mentioned as a contradiction, it must be clarified and generally challenged.

> *A small computer company with ten people on staff and eleven on the board received some funding support from a Swedish agency. Even though the company was well organized, the external funding began to create internal problems, basically financial disagreements.*
> —*Tatwa Timsina, ToP practitioner, Kathmandu, Nepal*

Must feel safe

An important function of a facilitator is to create safety while discussing potential contradictions. Perhaps no one else in the room can create that safe, neutral space where people can explore the nature of the real contradiction, and get to the real truth of the matter. In one sense, the less the facilitator knows about the nature of the contradiction, the more objectivity can be brought to bear by asking simple straightforward questions that cut through the fog.

Creating safety can require a special room setup, seating arrangements, a neutral location, or having food available. Setting the right context can free people to say what they really think without being interrupted or fearing repercussion. Safety might require asking people to avoid language that triggers or sets others off. The practitioner may need a softer, slower body language and a calmer voice in order to put people at ease. Sometimes it helps to give people time to write down what they think, and let them check their written notes in pairs before saying things to the whole group, and perhaps not having to talk to their own supervisors. Creating a safe environment requires showing compassion and acknowledging when someone says something risky. It also means acknowledging that a participant's unease is personal and real, and should not be dismissed. It might mean allowing people to draw pictures of the contradiction rather than trying to verbalize it.

Affirmation is key

Practitioners will not be able to get a group to talk about contradictions if they display any sort of judgment toward the group members or their situation. While it is rare that legal or moral problems come up in contradictional analysis, participants often talk about things that make the facilitator uneasy, squeamish, or judgmental. The practitioner must stay neutral and affirm each person's contribution, modeling how all the participants are to treat each other. Here is an example:

Pradip complains, *"There are people in this office who never listen to what I have to say."* Brenda retorts, *"Our management meetings are at the end of the month. That's when we discuss ideas."*

This type of exchange, if not properly handled, can lead back and forth to recrimination and can easily deteriorate into he-said, she-said. The practitioner has to step right in the midst of this: "Now let's all of us listen carefully to what Pradip is saying. Regardless of what is happening at the management meetings, Pradip has the impression that he is not being listened to. Is that correct, Pradip? From your perspective, Pradip, how often does this occur and what impact has it had on you?"

Then the practitioner turns to Brenda: "OK, now let's listen carefully to Brenda's comments. Brenda, you mentioned monthly meetings. Is this the time when suggestions made by Pradip and others are looked at in detail? What actually happens to these types of suggestions?" Then, "From the managers' perspectives how important is it that these types of ideas are actually carefully considered?" "It is difficult to know what another person is actually experiencing. But everyone does have their own personal experience from which they draw their conclusions. It is helpful to affirm another person's experience, so that we can see what is really happening within the whole group."

Examples of contradictions

Example 1. Accident-free status subverts a culture of safety

A mining company had a vision of being profitable while having a great safety record. The share-holders, management, and the employees all found this vision reasonable and motivating. Prizes were awarded to departments with the most accident-free days. A large highway sign listed how many accident-free days they had. One could see that there was great pride in being accident-free. They also had a well-stocked nursing station with great equipment.

"So why do you need that nursing station if you are accident-free?"

"It is legally required of a plant our size. And of course people get sick and we want to look after them. We are very proud of our accident record, which does not take into account sick days. The station is very well stocked with equipment and bandages."

"So why would you need such a stock of equipment and bandages, especially since people stay home from work when they are sick?"

"Somebody might occasionally stub their toe. But we have a good hard hats and boots pro-tocol, which is what really counts. We have hats and splints and everything. We even have a doctor who comes to the plant regularly."

"So why would you need splints and hard hats for stubbed toes?"

"We need all that in case an accident does happen. But we don't report stubbed toes. A ham-mer or wrench might occasionally fall off a table and hit a foot, but we wouldn't report that or we might lose our 450-day accident-free status. Nobody really wants to report those little accidents that don't matter or else we would lose our status."

"Why do you not report a wrench falling off a table onto a foot? What sort of accidents would you report?"

"We have discussions on what constitutes a reportable accident. But not reporting an accident has never led to a grievance yet, and we are pretty sure the other mines do it as well."

"So why would someone report a grievance over something like a small accident?"

"No one would really want to report a grievance because it would affect that departments' accident status. But someone looking for an excuse for a grievance could use a small accident. And as I said, each department is very proud of its accident record."

Suddenly an elephant has appeared in the middle of the room, as if a spotlight has just turned on. A real contradiction has been exposed between the desired future reality and the current reality. Departmental pride in their accident-free status has put competitive pressure on every department not to report accidents. Employee resentment for any reason could use the non-reporting of an accident as a grievance. To avoid grievances management does not keeps records about the small accidents, but just deals with them outside the system. As long as accidents are not reported, the company keeps its accident-free record. This reporting anomaly has begun to show up in other areas of work, and is beginning to cause some internal rifts.

Example 2. The dual nature of evaluation discourages continuous improvement

An evaluation unit of a government corporation stated a long-range practical vision of spreading a culture of evaluation throughout the corporation. Their vision was that the organization would become more productive and people would all learn from each other's experiences. Evaluation would help everyone improve.

When the unit members talked about what was blocking an evaluation culture from emerging, they mentioned how difficult it was to motivate people to do evaluation. They blamed a few influential individuals in other departments for subverting evaluation methods and processes. They considered various leadership issues and communication issues within the corporation. They mentioned that evaluation reports were communicated vertically to the upper levels of management to help them create good policy, but their reports were often not acted upon. Someone mentioned that occasionally people were not entirely truthful in their evaluations. This sparked an illuminating discussion on why people would not be truthful, and how prevalent this was.

Management tended to come down hard on someone if production was not at full capacity or if mistakes were made. People began to realize that what was blocking them from moving ahead with a culture of evaluation was the dual nature of the evaluation itself, and the double role that evaluation played within the organization. While some considered evaluation a way to improve, others considered it to be a tool for accountability. The evaluation unit saw that it was not the lack of motivation or leadership that kept them from moving ahead, but that dual nature. This contradictory nature of evaluation was the root problem. The leadership within the corporation would have to be re-educated about the purpose that evaluation should play in improving the corporation, and stop punishing people who made mistakes. As soon as the team named a real contradiction, their attention went to developing strategy.

Example 3. Our consumer orientation promotes unhealthy lifestyles

Contradictions can occur at the level of society as well as of the internal organization. The board of a public health department had just finished discussing their vision of a healthy society where people eat well, exercise, and are generally happy. The department had good programs and services in place for inspecting restaurants and helping people deal with mental, oral, and other health problems, all run by qualified health practitioners who really knew their stuff.

The board members talked of their desire that everyone have good nutrition, and how exercise is so important for a variety of reasons:

"If we could just get everyone to exercise and eat good food, we would be a healthy society."

"Why don't people eat healthily?"

"The supermarket aisles are full of junk food that is cheap and easy. The chain stores and advertisers really push it. The junk food is a loss leader that gets people into their stores."

"Why don't people exercise?"

"People are just so busy. There was even an attempt to hold exercises during lunch hours in the office, but people were just too busy to come."

"Why wouldn't they come, if they know it will make them healthier?"

"It just takes too much effort to do it. Some buy exercise videos to help motivate them to do their exercise."

Suddenly one board member looked very thoughtful. "You know when you walk down one aisle at the bulk food store and all you see is junk food? Well when you turn the corner at the end of the aisle you see a whole rack of exercise videos. Those stores don't really care whether we eat healthy food or not. They only see us as walking wallets. If we are going to make a difference in public health, we are going to have to be very savvy in advertising and marketing our message, just like the supermarkets and ad companies."

The board member was pointing out a societal contradiction that even though many companies give lip service to a healthy lifestyle, especially the food giants, they promote both healthy and unhealthy lifestyles, whatever makes a profit. We are all seen simply as consumers. More importantly, we generally see ourselves only as consumers, and consumers of contradictory items. What was even more interesting was that as soon as that board member became aware of a contradiction, she immediately flipped into thinking about strategies.

Contradictional thinking: a thought process of planning

Levels of discernment is a tool to help people move from surface issues and smokescreens, down to the real contradictions beneath the surface. Using the levels of discernment with the consensus workshop method allows a group to find and name contradictions safely. The tool examines seven different layers of problem analysis, starting at a superficial level where discussion is simple and easy, and ending up at the root causes of problems where the underlying contradictions exist. The tool deepens discernment of root causes and discovery of what is real.

Level 1. Irritation

At the very top, the most superficial level, is irritation. People are simply irritated because they know they want to get someplace, they're not getting there, and they don't know why. Participants can experience a resentment or sense of dis-ease, or an unspecified anger over the fact that they can't move ahead. They might feel anxiety or even panic that nothing is going the way it should. This is the basic reflective level of thinking, which needs to come before real analysis of the situation.

On the positive side, discovering irritation about the realization of a vision is preferable to finding that participants have only unblinking obedience to a vision, with no feelings about it at all. Irritation at least implies interest and even perhaps passion. When a facilitator asks questions like "What irritates you about our inability to move ahead?" or "What irritates you personally about the fact that we aren't moving quickly enough toward this element of our vision?" the answers test the validity of the vision as well as surfacing potential contradictions. Acknowledging people's irritation and frustration validates their experiences and can help them proceed to deeper analysis. Discussing irritation about not moving ahead quickly enough is a fairly safe level of discussion. Watching heads nods in agreement tells a facilitator that this is a topic to bring up again when you start discussing contradictions.

Level 2. Blame

Irritation can quickly give way to blame. Everyone has their favorite person or group to blame for not being able to move toward the vision they so desperately want. But everyone knows that festering blame can create real difficulties within a group. People most often blame forces outside the group, such as the government, the media, the competition, the general public, or apathetic people. Facilitators can safely traverse this level and even have some fun doing it, by asking a question like "In relation to our vision, whom do we often blame the most for not being able to move ahead? Come on, now, you can say." Participants generally name half a dozen roles or people who they like to blame, and they might even laugh a little bit about each other's answers. As long as you are objective and do not treat this part too lightly, somebody might actually give a reasonable answer. Listen carefully for pointers toward a real contradiction. When someone is named, everyone gets quiet, or there might be nodding. Always be ready to reply, "Say more." While blame is almost never the central blockage, everyone can gather valuable insight by talking about it.

You can always go deeper with a closed question like "Are any of us in this room ever to blame? Come on now, we all have big shoulders and can take it." A few people laughingly protest, "Oh, not us. Never!" Someone might grin sheepishly and say, "Well, I probably get blamed a bit, but people are nice enough not to tell me to my face." It is very helpful if participants start acknowledging their own part in the blame. This builds trust and truthfulness in the group, and will allow real contradictions to be named much more easily later. The primary purpose for asking about blame is to get it out of the way, so that people can start thinking at a deeper level.

Level 3. Lack of, or gaps

The next level of discernment is "lack of" sometimes referred to as "gaps." Saying the problem is a "lack of" something is a slightly deeper level of analysis than simply blaming somebody else. A lack implies some understanding of the problem, but is also a complex mix of denial and ownership, as in "We lack the proper tools to do our job well" or "We lack the necessary training to move ahead."

But a "lack of" something is never really a contradiction. It is a negative way of stating a strategy that you want to propose. "We lack the proper tools, and I propose we get them." "We lack the necessary training so I propose we build that training into our budget." Whenever someone says "We are blocked by a lack of xxx," they are in fact suggesting a strategy or a course of action. A lack of communication is really suggesting a strategy of more communication. A "lack of motivation" is calling for a strategy to ramp up the motivation. It is certainly helpful to list and acknowledge all of the "lack of's" that people mention. But it is important to point out that these are suggestions for strategy, not root causes of the problem.

"Lack of" and gap analysis has a very useful role to play in operational and project planning. If you are clear on the gaps, you can figure out what you have to do to bridge them. But in strategic planning, "lack of" and gap analysis is used primarily to get to the deeper level of contradiction.

Some of those "lack of" answers can begin an analysis: "I think I heard there is a lack of leadership. Now, if I hear you right, there actually is some leadership. So how would you describe why the type of leadership that we currently have is actually blocking us? What is it about how the leadership currently operates that is the blockage? For example, is the leadership too far from the frontlines? Is the leadership too involved in administering legal affairs? Is the leadership of the informal type?"

Questions like these will spark some comments about what is actually going on, and move a "lack of" discussion closer toward the contradiction. A "lack of training" indicates that whatever training is available might be delivered poorly, irrelevant, or packaged in a boring way. A "lack of money" indicates that the money there is might be locked up in savings, or directed toward one priority rather than another, or reflect an obscure budget process. A good question to take the conversation deeper is "What is going on that causes or sustains this lack?" You might get a blockage like a "budget process" or "pattern of not saving monthly."

Level 4. Issues

While irritation, blame, and "lacks" are all relatively superficial levels of discernment, issues tend to pull people into deeper analysis. Issues are generally abstract concepts that point to an arena where a contradiction might exist. Participants might talk about a policy issue, a communication issue, or a training issue that is blocking them from moving toward the vision. These are but three of a myriad of such examples.

When participants mention "a policy issue" what do they really mean? Is there no policy, or is the existing policy too old or too obscure? The "policy issue" might well point to a real contradiction, such as two sets of clashing policies made at different times that work against one another and stall everyone. It could just as easily point to an irritant that someone just wanted to get off their chest.

What does "a communication issue" really mean? Is there too little? Too much? Is it unreliable, or does it come from the wrong source? There might be a deep-rooted contradiction, such as in an organization that wants to be a highly collaborative learning organization, but requires all external communication to go through a tightly controlled communication department. On the other hand, participants might just want to hear directly from the CEO on occasion because the organization is going through some difficult times, and they want reassurance.

Issues can show you areas in which to look for a contradiction, but they are often abstract and vague. All issues, however, must be acknowledged and written down, and you might discover interesting relationships to explore between issues. To push an issue a little deeper, ask questions such as "What is it about this issue that actually blocks us?" or "What do you most often do to avoid dealing with this issue?"

Level 5. Blocks or obstacles

When you get to blocks or obstacles, you are reaching fertile ground for finding a contradiction. An obstacle or block is real and tangible. It is not intellectually abstract like issues, gaps, or a lack of something, nor is it merely an irritating feeling. It is like a large boulder fallen in the middle of a narrow, winding mountain road that blocks you from getting where you want.

For a Mac computer user, a System 9 operating system blocks the use of Creative Suite 4. It doesn't matter that System 9 worked well for many years and allowed self-publishing with Creative Suite 2, it became a block when more design capacity was needed.

A tendering policy worked really well when there was only one department in the organization and only a few large contracts per year. However, now that there are dozens of small mini-contracts in several departments, the tendering policy has become a major bottleneck, especially when it is clear who really needs to do the work and it has to get done fast.

All of a company's routines are based on a nine-to-five, five-day-a–week work schedule, which has allowed the firm to grow and prosper for several decades. The company now has to move to shiftwork because of a competitor, but highly valued routines are a block.

Blockages can be clear to some people but not to others. What is an obvious block from one person's point of view might look to another like a carefully crafted structure that has held back chaos for a long time. Blocks, blockages, and obstacles, three terms for one thing, must be teased out of the participants. A facilitator has to acknowledge the blocking nature that appears important to some, while affirming the past contribution of the block that is important to others. Blocks are not bad, nor should they be judged. They are what they were designed to be, even if they are now in the way.

The facilitator honors both sides by asking such questions as "Since you have mentioned that that work routine is a block, tell us what part of the vision it actually blocks and how?" and "What was that work routine originally designed to help with? How did it actually work? Should we perhaps refer to it as a legacy work routine, or as a nine-to-five work schedule? Let's not judge it by using language like old or inefficient."

Level 6. Underlying blocks or obstacles

An underlying block or obstacle is similar to the tree root growing into the basement drainpipe of an apartment building I once lived in. It slowed down the flushing of every toilet and sink in the building. Everyone believed there was a clog somewhere in their own pipes. Everyone used Draino in their own apartment, but to no avail. After people shared their embarrassing stories and it was confirmed that it must be a tree root, they all breathed a sigh of relief; now something useful could be done.

Finding underlying blocks and obstacles requires thorough analysis. Some participants become deeply involved and expressive. Some watch quietly, but remain involved inwardly. A few say nothing because they have been trained to talk only about "positive" things. They join back in the conversation after the contradictions have been named.

Here are examples of underlying obstacles.

- Two branches of a department contributed staff to a joint task force with one big vision. One group had always been managed with clear plans, a paper trail, and an accountability framework. The other group was managed in a freewheeling intuitive way, but was always successful. Each found the other difficult to work with because of their differing management modes, and they regularly tried to persuade each other to change. They determined their underlying block to be "competitive operating and management patterns." While each operating pattern worked for its particular group, it ended up creating a competition between them that undermined them both. They would have to resolve this obstacle before they could be successful as a team.

- The board of a not-for-profit organization had reasonable funding for the important work that they did, but passionate board members constantly took on projects that were too big, then failed and burned out, negatively affecting the potential of the other members' projects. This board called their underlying obstacle a "volunteer project mentality." The volunteer project mentality worked well when the organization had no funding and ran totally on personal passion. But when money became available for all the projects and some professionals were hired to do background research, the projects became interlinked. Any project that did not finish on time blocked all the others. As long as the passionate board members continued from this volunteer project mentality, they would continue to fail.

- A franchise company determined through hard experience what it took for a franchisee to win over the long term, and created many supports and financial mechanisms to help the franchisees. But in a changed economic climate, no new franchisees were coming forward to grow the business. The company determined that burdensome long-term investment was the major underlying block to company growth. The financial cushions that had protected all the franchisees were now discouraging them, because of the cost of maintaining them. A new decision would have to be taken about the support structures, or less expensive support mechanisms would have to be created.

In Taiwan, participatory strategic planning was held offsite with the 25 local senior members of an international advertising company. The contradictions session was the highlight, especially for one contradiction cluster which seemed impossible to name. Finally the CEO said, "I think the real contradiction here is that "individuals learn, but the company does not learn." It was a moment of breakthrough, an aha! moment which opened up new understanding for the cultural change needed.
—Richard West, ToP practitioner, Taipei, Taiwan

Level 7. Contradictions

A couple of good underlying obstacles are generally sufficient to generate strategy. However, sometimes the facilitator and group are fortunate and discern an actual contradiction. This does not always happen, nor does it need to. But when a contradiction is found and articulated, it can occasion an avalanche of strategy and motivation that begins to transform the organization immediately.

A contradiction is beyond an underlying obstacle, because it points to current behaviors, beliefs and patterns of the participants that actually contradict the behavior envisioned in the long-range practical vision. When participants acknowledge this, the contradiction becomes visible, and immediate transformation can begin to unfold. In the first case study in this chapter (on page 103), as soon as the local politicians recognized that their own petty politicking was blocking regional unity, they immediately began to strategize a different way of operating.

The immediacy of the transformation can be illustrated by a neighborhood in which people did not feel safe from violence or crime, and generally stayed indoors isolated from one another, so none of the neighbors knew each other very well. A group got together tentatively to create a strategic plan for the community. Their main vision was to work together to create a safe neighborhood. As they considered the obstacles, they recognized that it was primarily the isolation from each other that fed the fear and blocked them from working together. It was an immediate "Aha," and in recognizing this fact there was an immediate transformation. They went out and got others to join them, further breaking the cycle of isolation. This illustrates the cyclical nature of transformation that occurs when a real contradiction is discerned.

A facilitator coaxes participants to as deep a level of discernment as they will go, recognizing that some people do not necessarily want to see too clearly. If the participants can get at least as far as underlying obstacles, they will be able to come up with effective strategic directions. If they can name even one contradiction, a doorway to the future opens up, and they will feel as if they have made a real breakthrough.

Getting out a full set of contradictions can overwhelm even the stoutest soul. In some situations social scientists even give us statistical reasons why nothing can be done. The situation seems to say to the vision, "No, no, impossible!" It takes courage for the group to pick itself up to look at where real possibility might lie.

To illustrate very simply how people actually participate in the contradiction, let's imagine a fellow with a bingo problem who wants to attract ladies (see Figure 15).

Level of analysis	The guy with the problem
There is a natural tendency to analyze problems in a simplistic and easy way. This tends to prevent a person from taking real responsibility for the situation.	*"I want to look good for the girls but I can't afford a fine jacket,"* he complained every night to the buddies that he lost bingo games with.
A superficial analysis might try to divorce oneself from the problem, affix blame on someone else, or abstractly theorize or rationalize.	*"Wow. Tonight I got my lucky seat at the bingo."* *"That bingo caller mumbled that last time. Only the close people could hear."* *"I've gotten four letters, three times in a row. I'm so close I can't stop now."*
However, when pushed to its depth, and at its most discerning, contradictional thinking provides a doorway to the future.	*"My daily bingo gamble to strike it rich is really stifling my social life, wasting both time and money."*

FIGURE 15. A personal contradiction

Example of company contradiction: Personalized customer service

In this example, the stated practical vision of the company is to have personalized customer service. Here are some examples of levels of discernment that are related to that vision.

1. **Irritants** .... *"The time it takes me to respond to a customer request through our internal system is really awful."*

2. **Blame** .... *"Maybe it's the receptionist's fault, for not getting the call through to you quickly."*

3. **Lack of** .... *"Isn't the problem that there are not enough receptionists and online customer service reps?"*

4. **Issues** .... *"It's not just reception. We have a bigger communication issue that relates to our overall computer usage."*

5. **Blocks/obstacles** .... *"I get totally blocked until I get the client's company number and transaction number. My computer takes several minutes just to do that simple search."*

6. **Underlying obstacle** ... *"We have a ten-year-old, slow computer system, which cannot do the work we want it to do."*

7. **Contradiction** .... *"Even though our vision is personalized customer service, we depend 100% on a computer system that make us terribly impersonal."*

Doorway .... *"Slow communication technology is de-personalizing vital customer contact."*

Naming convention for contradictions

When helping participants name a contradiction, use a three-step process: name the *blockage* itself, *what* it is actually blocking, and *how* the blockage is occurring. This matches the deeper understanding of a contradiction: the current reality (what the block is), the desired future state (what is it blocking), and the tensional relationship between the two (how it is blocking). Naming in this way can assist a group considerably in understanding the contradiction. If naming is not done well, it can lead to generalization and abstraction.

Examples of contradictions from the case studies in Chapter 14:
- A protective attitude by older members restricts new members and their involvement.
- Outside interests divide and conquer local leadership.
- Our organization's single-year funding envelope erodes the ability to plan long term.
- Our "at capacity" volunteer structure hinders the emergence of a professionalized system.

In the midst of a contradictions workshop, while the facilitator was at the naming stage, a participant ("P1") suggested an actual block:

> P1: *I really think a big block we face is our own protective attitude amongst ourselves and some older members.*

Several participants indicated affirmation of this by nodding. The facilitator ("F"), asked,

> F: *What does this block appear to be blocking? Take a look at the vision and see if there is something specific that this block is actually stopping.*
> P1: *The vision talks about having many new members. Our current attitudes make it difficult to get new members.*
> P2: *Actually, it really creates difficulties in any type of involvement that we want from new members.*
> F: *So we have a block called "our protective attitude," and what it appears to be blocking is "new members" and "involvement of members." Is that right? Let me write that down on a flipchart. Now how does "our protective attitude" affect or block "new members and their involvement"?*
> P2: *Our attitudes actually drive some of them away. It certainly restricts them from suggesting new things, when we are so protective.*
> F: *What I think I hear you saying is that "our own protective attitude amongst older members restricts new members and their involvement." Is this true? Can anyone confirm that? Have any of you actually participated in that?*
> P3: *Well, yes.*

And several examples followed.

Sample set of contradictions

Several service organizations formed a coalition and felt they were on the leading edge of diversity and inclusivity in their board composition, staff, members, services, and policies. They wanted to ensure that all types of diversity were embedded into the structure and practice of all other service organizations in the urban area. As they discussed the difficulties they faced, they found several systemic root problems that they would have to work to overcome, including some within their own service organizations.

- Naïve, shortsighted executive headspace treats diversity as "icing" rather than as fundamental, and resists diversity because of its short-term cost.
- Token, reactive, diversity activities divert attention from substantial change.
- Single-year grant funding erodes the ability to do good long-range planning.
- Translation into other languages is a simplistic reflex strategy for diversity, and clouds the need for deeper diversity.
- A "piecemeal individual response" mentality.

A three-hour classic ToP contradictions workshop

The ToP practitioner can enable conversation in a contradictions workshop by having a number of short contextual statements ready to deal with any difficulties. Here are some examples:

- We are active participants in the world we create; therefore we are part of the problem as well as the solution.
- There is no one to blame for a contradiction. It is historical residue—the result of past actions to solve problems of a previous time, now blocking the changes called for in our time.
- A contradiction is not a negative thing or an absence of something. It is a real relationship that exists between events, actions, or things.
- A contradiction is like a dandelion root—neither good nor bad in itself, but sustaining the visible manifestations of a block to the vision of a smooth grassy lawn.
- A contradiction is not an I-it relationship. It is an I-thou relationship when you discover how your pets need all your time, and you require a new relationship.
- The contradictions workshop is about ownership of the patterns of attitudes, behaviors, actions, and structures that inhibit or block effectiveness.
- It is not comfortable to take ownership of contradictions. Struggle is normal and necessary for breakthrough.
- We are seeing right through problems and obstacles to find the keys and release points that allow the future to unfold in our lives.

- Later, in the clustering part of the process, you will be asked to work at discerning the patterns of relationships that make up a contradiction.
- We are helping each other here to push through the data to deeper levels. Probe the data for the insights that it reveals.

You know you've got at a contradiction when it becomes clear to people how they participate in keeping it alive. It is unlikely that the group will name "the contradiction" beneath every cluster of data. They don't need to. The key is that they do it at least once or twice. If that happens, the unblocking can begin. Contradictions are the turning point in the strategic planning process. They catalyze the question, "If this is what is blocking us, what can we do about it?" As a facilitator, listen for answers to this question during the naming process. When people start mentioning actions to take instead of naming the contradiction, it is a clue that some have grasped the contradiction and have gone a step further. The contradiction is whatever that suggested action is dealing with.

After a contradictions workshop, do not take a lengthy or overnight break without at least beginning the brainstorm of strategies to deal with them. It is a normal reaction to try to escape ownership and fall back into helplessness. It is best to do contradictions and strategies back-to-back if you can.

While there are many ways to get people to discuss contradictions, you can easily modify a standard *ToP consensus workshop* to provide the safety and depth necessary to discern and name underlying obstacles and contradictions. The name "underlying obstacles workshop" is used interchangeably with "contradictions workshop" because both are trying to reveal the systemic root blockages, so that breakthrough strategy can then be developed. This kind of workshop has dual objectives:

   Rational aim: *to identify the obstacles to our vision*

   Experiential aim: *to create confidence that we can deal with the real issues facing us*

Use the following practical step-by-step guide to the contradiction workshop process. Of course each situation will require modifications, but this guide can serve as a checklist in preparing for the session.

Give a context to the participants

1) *Outline process and timeline.* Here's where we are in the strategic planning spiral, and in the process of vision, obstacles, strategic directions, and action planning. For this workshop we will focus on obstacles, deterrents, problems, and issues. This will take about two and a half to three hours. TIP: Use the spiral image on the wall.

2) *Explain product and outcome.* What we will come up with at the end of this workshop are those systemic root problems that are stopping us from moving ahead. In this workshop we do not have to worry about what to do, or about any sort of solution. That will come later. We will be looking here for the roots of the dandelion, which generally stay hidden. Everyone has experiences that it will be important to examine. Please do not judge other people's comments, because they will be talking about what they have experienced, which is very real for them but might differ from your experience. Since we will be talking about difficult situations, please refrain from using any language that you know will "trigger" someone else, or make them feel unsafe or feel as if they are being judged.

3) *Highlight focus question* "What is blocking us from realizing our vision?"
TIP: Write the question at the center of the board or paper so everyone can see it.

Brainstorm ideas

Image or story: Rock in the middle of the road. We are looking for concrete blocks. Here is an example of what we mean.

The village of Woburn Lawn is about 5,000 feet up in the Blue Mountains in Jamaica. Cedar Valley, which is the nearest post office and public transit stop, is about two and a half miles away—over a steep ridge 1,000 feet high. The village decided to cut a steep, narrow road into the soft volcanic soil, just wide enough for one four-wheel-drive vehicle to get over the ridge. This road reduced the time it took to walk to the bus stop by at least an hour. On the mountain-side, almost at the top, was a huge rock outcropping. In May of 1986, the tail-end of a tropical depression settled over the island, and 40 inches of rain fell within four days. Of course, the soft soil washed away. The rock outcropping, about ten feet wide and six feet tall, washed out of the mountainside and fell into the middle of the road, completely blocking it. The villagers had to survey that situation—describe the rock and the surrounding factors that contributed to the blockage—before they could decide on a working plan. Later we will get to our own strategies session and make a practical plan for what to do. But first we need to identify the objective, hard, concrete realities that are blocking our vision—our road to the future.

TIP: Put up a flipchart sheet with the *levels of discernment* and discuss for two minutes.

1) *Do an individual brainstorm*. Each person list (or sketch) five or six blocks that keep us from moving on our vision. Try to cover all aspects of the vision, anything that can be blocked in a way that stops other parts of the vision from being realized as well. If you like, you can base your answers on an actual experience you had. Or you can describe a pattern you have seen over time. Any insights you have will be useful.

2) *Select your best idea*. Each person choose your biggest blocks, the most important ones on your list and draw a star beside them.

3) *Brainstorm as a small discussion group*. Get into pairs of two people (no more than three), choosing someone that you can have a good conversation with. Safety in your discussion is important. Read through your blocks, starting with the ones that have been starred. After you have read and discussed them all, choose six that are really big problems, that cause real difficulties. Try to include blocks that affect several parts of the vision. Read your priority items out to each other to make sure that they are clear and understood. You may have to rewrite some to make sure they communicate when written. Select six to eight issues and print them on cards in big bold letters, one idea per card, and four to seven words per card. Please do not use just one word. You do not have to agree with each other on your selection of blocks. It is only important that they be very clear.

TIP: If needed, you can assign teams to focus on each vision element to make sure they are all covered, in addition to other blocks they want to add.

Cluster the ideas

Image or story: I'm drawing the parts of a dandelion, starting with what is above ground.

A dandelion is neither good or bad, but when it is in the middle of your vision of a smooth lawn, and if that's the kind of garden you like, it is an obstacle. What happens if you cut it off at ground level? It grows back and may even scatter seeds. What happens if you get the roots just under the surface? It comes back again, but just takes a little longer. You have to identify the deep tap root, and when you do, you can design the tools to eradicate it. In the same way, your cards are like leaves, visible manifestations. We will cluster them to see the deep root issues that are sustaining them, that are under the ground. When we name those, then we can brainstorm the strategies.

1) *Each group choose two cards at random*. Gather back as one group in the plenary space, but sit with your small discussion group. Make sure you can see the front wall. Turn your cards over so you cannot see them, and then select two at random. This will give us 12 to 16 cards from the whole

group. Send your two cards up front. We will get all the rest a little later. I will read them out loud as I stick them on the wall. Do you have any questions of clarity about any of these cards?

2) *Look for any pairs of similar cards.* Which of any of these cards can form a pair because they have a similar root cause? I am only looking for pairs at this point. I will simply move one of the cards closer to the other, and put a symbol on them.

3) *Cluster beyond pairs.* After we have three or four pairs of cards we can add other cards to the pairs, as long as they have a similar root cause. If any card seems to fit into two different pairs, I'll move the pairs a little closer together and put the new card halfway between them both. We are not creating columns here, but rather clusters of cards that will start to look like "continents" on a world map. This is called a **polar gestalt**, where similar cards are clustered together, and clusters arranged roughly by degree of relationship around a central point (as in Figure 16).

TIP: Keep cards well spread out since the extra space will be important later. Eventually, the clusters of cards will look like Figure 16.

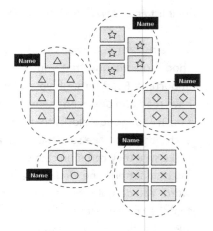

FIGURE 16. Polar gestalt for the contradictions workshop

4) *Collect more cards.* Can each group supply another set of two random cards.

TIP: Read them out loud as you stick them all around the wall in any open empty spaces. Ask if there are any questions of clarity. This will give us about 30 cards up front in all.

5) *Continue clustering.* Are any new pairs or clusters emerging here? Do any new cards fit in existing clusters?

TIP: Constantly ask what appears to be the root cause of any cluster when a new card is added, especially when it does not appear obvious. Cards that people suggest have two differing root causes can be placed in between existing clusters. It is not vital to force-fit cards into particular clusters. The nature of these cards is that they might fit several places at once. For groups of cards that seem to cluster together, assign a neutral symbol, such as a square, circle, or star.

6) *Relate extra cards.* Of the cards you have left, try to relate cards to the existing clusters on the wall and put the appropriate symbol on each. Avoid force-fitting cards into a column. If they don't seem to fit anywhere, leave them without any symbol. When you're done, send up the cards that do *not* have a symbol on them—the ones that do *not* yet fit anywhere.

TIP: Read these cards out loud as you put them on the wall. It would be normal to add another five or ten cards at this point, resulting in perhaps as many as 40 cards up front, in total.

7) *Create new clusters.* Do the new cards create any new clusters? Can someone suggest where this card might go into an existing cluster?
TIP: There could be significant discussion around this point. Allow the group to explore options. They are looking for clusters that seem to point to a similar root cause, even though that root cause has not yet been named, except in a rough holding title.

8) *Have remaining cards brought up front.* Bring up all your remaining cards, and stick them on the wall in their appropriate cluster.
TIP: This would be an appropriate time for a bio-break. During the break, you can move cards around within their clusters to make sure that each cluster stands out from the others, and give some spatial definition to the clusters. You can draw lines around the clusters if they are on a whiteboard or on paper, or use some tape to fashion lines around the clusters.

The result will be a polar gestalt of cards, which is helpful in discerning the root causes or underlying obstacles from a brainstorm of issues. Root causes are usually hidden or obscure, and may require an understanding of the relationships between clusters of data. The cards are clustered around a central point, with similar clusters close to each other. After the boundaries of the clusters become apparent, the naming process can begin.

Name the clusters

Participants may need to be reminded to name the clusters as real underlying blocks that are often hidden from view. This short story can make that point.

Image or story: Dragon. We are looking for what is keeping the fire-breathing dragon within the clusters.

Once upon a time there were two villages connected by a single road. One village produced food for itself and its neighbor; the other provided both with hunting equipment. One day a huge dragon settled across the road, blocking travel between the two villages. Villagers attacked it with spears, which splintered against the beast's thick

hide. They tried to lasso it, but the dragon's flames burned the ropes to ashes. Week after week they labored, sacrificing many lives and finally giving up in despair. Their food was depleted and the supply of hunting equipment exhausted in the battle against the dragon. But one day a youth climbed a tree to observe the dragon and discovered a remarkable thing; a farmer from a distant village was dumping garbage right under the dragon's snout. An envoy was soon dispatched to ask the farmer to move his dump to a remote field. The dragon relocated to this new feeding area, and the two villages were once again able to travel the road and serve each other.

1) *Select the biggest cluster and discuss it for clarity and insight.*

TIP: To discuss what root issue lies behind each cluster of cards requires a kind of structured reflection. The conversation has a series of levels, leading toward a collective insight. The questions can reflect the previously discussed **levels of discernment**, and you might refer to the list on the wall. But more basically, the conversation follows a deepening pattern of objective, reflective, interpretive, and decisional questions.

a) *Objective level*—Read the cards in that one column out loud so everyone can hear.

b) *Reflective level*—Ask people to say which words from the cards seem to stand out as important.

c) *Interpretive level*—Raise several questions to lead the discussion deeper toward a contradiction:

  1. What does this cluster seem to be about?
  2. Could a couple of people talk about personal experiences that illustrate this block?
  3. What appears to be the underlying blockage here—the real thing that causes the difficulties?
  4. How do we participate in this block? What do any of us do that actually helps keep it in being?

d) *Decisional level*—Let's name the actual underlying obstacle or contradiction.

TIP: Listen carefully and be prepared to challenge and cajole participants to make sure that the obstacle is named as a real block, not as an intellectual abstraction, or something to blame, or a "lack of something."

- What in our long-range practical vision does this actually block?
- How does it block the vision?
- Let's name it according to this naming convention: Summarize the insight in a phrase, in this format: "block, how it blocks, what it blocks."(You might write the naming convention on a flipchart so all can see it. Example of naming syntax: "Hierarchical leadership stifles individual creativity.")
- Who can confirm that we really have an underlying obstacle here?
- Is it real? Do we participate in it (if only in keeping it alive)?

- Can we do anything about it?

Write the agreed name for the underlying obstacle on a card, draw a highlighting border around it, and post it above the cluster concerned.

2) *Select another cluster.*
TIP: Go through the same process above. This time it will be quicker.

3) *Select another cluster.*
TIP: This time it will be much quicker.

4) *Name the rest of the clusters.*
TIP: If time permits, you can go through them all, one by one. If not, you can farm them out to small discussion groups and get them to name them and then read the titles to the group.

Other interpretive level questions can help in naming a contradiction:
- How do you experience this block? When has it happened to you?
- How does this stop us from realizing our vision? Why?
- How do we participate in it?
- What is the root cause that is preventing us from moving ahead?
- How is this blocking us?
- What is the part or process or dynamic of society where this block shows up?
- What is going on in society that sustains these blocks?
- What is the current reality that is a contradiction to our vision?
- What is the block? What does it block? How does that block operate?

Check the resolve of the group

Next the conversation turns to interpreting the whole set of issue clusters, and reaching a conclusion.

1) *Hold a focused conversation.*
TIP: The same basic levels of conversation apply in reflecting on the whole board.
a) Objective—Read the title cards out loud.
b) Reflective—Which do you experience as heaviest, and which is lightest?
c) Interpretive—How do any two or three of these work together to really tie us up into knots?
e) Decisional—Choose one. If we deal with it, which elements of the vision will it release? What are some approaches we could take, or things that we could begin to do, to deal with this underlying obstacle? Let's get half a dozen ideas out before we break. When we come back

together, we will consider what we can do to deal with these blocks and move toward our vision.

2) *Create a chart.* Arrange clusters into columns for documentation, from longest at the left to shortest at right, as a clue to priority, as in Figure 17. Tape the columns up on the wall. Rewrite the title cards to be big and easy to see, on 8.5 x 11 inch paper. The result should look something like Figure 17.

A sample of the documentation of results

3) *Write sample contradiction sentences.* For each column of obstacles, assign a group to express that contradiction as a written statement. Use the column name as the title, and write a one-sentence explanation that summarizes the data. As an example, you might post the following title and sample sentence for all to see:

"Protective attitude amongst members restricts recruitment and involvement."
Members of the chapter might be competitors, suppliers, and clients with one another, which leads to caution in recruiting new members and in involvement with the industry association.

Additional tools and variations

This workshop provides ample scope for the whole range of creativity. Depending on the nature of the group, different ways of expressing issues or different kinds of questions might be appropriate.

Drawing pictures

Issues, blocks, and underlying obstacles are difficult to speak about. Drawing, however, can be used to express some of the insight and open the door to conversation. After visioning, and before an underlying obstacles workshop, you could ask participants to "Draw a picture of what you see going on in this organization" or "How would you draw a picture of some of the issues that we are facing as an organization? Make the picture as detailed and colorful as you like." People need time for this, and they might need some privacy to keep others from seeing what they have drawn. These pictures should never be signed.

Once the pictures are collected anonymously and put on the wall, hold a focused conversation. Under no circumstances would you comment on quality, ask someone to explain their drawing, or even ask who drew what picture.

What is blocking us from realizing our vision?				
Unfocused, undeveloped message, causing waning interest	**Protective attitude amongst members restricts recruitment and involvement**	**Inadequate staffing levels**	**Conventional face-to-face meetings not drawing us together**	**Short-term, past-oriented cash accounting**
members don't see value in membership; join for social aspect and relationship development	members not open to sharing information that may leave their customer base open to attack	lack of time to invest in lobbying members	conventional management style	not a good use of current resources
companies don't feel they need the affiliation	overly competitive market (information, not parking)	lack of administrative support	lack of succession plan for leadership	not good financial management and reporting
insufficient communication with membership emphasizing positive aspects	inability to enforce ethics, lack of regulation	unrealistic vision	national BoD does not focus on chapter development	old style finance system
lack of institutional memory	members not letting go	where are we now?	lack of leadership at chapter level	
members don't know/see what the board does and don't understand direction of organization				
lack of membership participation at chapter level				

FIGURE 17. Sample contradiction workshop documentation, showing key input from the group

Once the drawings are posted on a wall, you can ask the group questions such as these:
- Which drawing do you find interesting or intriguing?
- What details would you like to point out?
- Which drawing pulls you in? Why?
- What is it about any of the drawings that you can relate to?

- What does the choice of colors say?
- Tell a story about one of the drawings and what it says to you.

This methodology must be done slowly and with deliberation, with great respect to all participants, and without any kind of time rush. You can write your questions on a flipchart on the wall, but let participants know that your intention is to work your way down the list one by one. This is not a method to go around the room and require everyone to speak. But you should allow most people to speak once before opening up to second comments from those who spoke first. Participants should direct their comments to you, not to someone else. Wait patiently if there are long periods of silence between comments.

While this methodology does not give a left brain analysis of blocks and obstacles, it opens up people to have safer and deeper conversations about the underlying obstacles and contradictions that do exist. At the end of the conversation about the drawings, you can ask "What insight did you get about what we are facing as an organization, and in what arena we are going to need a breakthrough in order to move ahead?" You can go around the room and ask everyone to answer this question, since it is no longer about the drawings. Drawing issues does not replace a contradictions workshop, but it can provide a safe way to talk about a very difficult situation.

World Café

You can use the World Café process with an entire group before a contradictions workshop to allow people to safely engage in dialogue about underlying contradictions. Before the dialogue, have someone make a short presentation about the long-range vision of the organization, and explain the levels of discernment. Each round of dialogue could explore a couple of the levels of discernment more fully. The first round could be about irritants and gaps, but blame is likely to surface. The second round could include issues and blockages. The third round could be about underlying blockages and contradictions. The conversation at the end can begin to capture the essence of the underlying blocks and contradictions.

10
Strategic thinking
forges breakthrough strategy

Strategy gives a way to move forward toward a practical vision by focusing on and releasing the energy that is being blocked by underlying obstacles. Strategy shows the way toward transformation when it is focused on a blockage of energy or motivation which has been caused by a contradiction. This chapter examines the central source of strategic thinking, what drives the insight necessary to create effective strategy, and some of the essential components of participatory strategy development. It provides several illustrations of participatory strategy, and presents in some detail what a strategy consensus workshop looks like.

Case study

A group of First Nations representatives met to develop strategies for their regional health coalition. They had already analyzed the major blockages to their vision of a healthy community, which included constantly changing leadership, chronic addiction, and community resistance to change. The strategy session was held for an hour and a half with 50 people on a late Thursday afternoon. It was opened with a smudge ceremony and a prayer by elders.

Participants reviewed the vision chart and three contradictions, then took time to write down their own individual ideas about strategy. Sitting at eight tables in groups of six, they shared their ideas, and then wrote them with magic markers on large cards. In all they produced 51 ideas.

Each team picked their boldest, most creative ideas first. They taped these to the front wall, and read them out loud. Participants quickly found a synergy between some of the suggestions. They then contributed some of their other "important" approaches, and the clusters of ideas were expanded. By the time all of the ideas were posted on the wall, eight main approaches were discerned. While small groups created strategy names for the eight clusters, another group tried to see if the clusters had any sense of priority attached to them.

During the plenary they determined that the most important strategy was "increasing community ownership and control of health issues, programs, awareness, and communication." They said this strategy would create a larger pool of joint leadership, and would increase community familiarity with health issues, while reducing the resistance to change. Two more strategies of "supporting personal healing" and "focusing on traditional practices" would begin to deal with the contradiction of chronic addiction, which had roots in solitary interior suffering. "Networking community support systems" would begin to deal with all three contradictions at once. Four more strategies were determined, which would play a more secondary role. Participants saw and created a way to move forward and were ready to generate action plans.

Links back to previous stages

Strategy emerges directly from an unstinting analysis of the tension between the vision, or the future desired state, and the current reality. Therefore a reminder of the elements of the practical vision is essential before you create strategy, as is a review of the contradictions. Other stages that can be helpful to review at this point are:
- A look at the opportunities and threats from a previous SWOT analysis.
- The "from" and "to" phrases found in the transition points of an historical scan.
- The positive and negative values of a trend analysis.
- The indicators of readiness from an organizational journey mapping exercise.
- The weakest triangles in any imbalance analysis of the social process.
- Notes from the client on why they wanted to do the strategic plan in the first place.

Strategic thinking and strategies that transform

Before embarking on creation of strategies, it is helpful to discuss what strategy means in the context of the Technology of Participation (ToP) methods.
- Strategy is more process than goal, in that it sets the direction for moving "toward" something, while allowing a way to discover the real nature of the path along the way.
- Without a strategic framework of directions, action is willy-nilly rather than comprehensive.
- The strategic directions workshop uses high creativity. It employs both intuition (to see all the

possibilities), and rationality (to order them into aligned directions that are wise to do).

- Strategic directions are paths of discovery. The discovery starts with where you are, and moves along a line of revelation and pattern-seeking, providing the flexibility to deal with rapidly changing times. It also allows organizational learning, with regular reflection on what is working and what is not, to enable changes in direction. Setting long-term objectives and figuring out how to get to them is a far less flexible type of thinking that decreases organizational and personal learning.
- Not every strategy needs to be bold and new. In times of transition, some things you are already doing need to be protected, so they undergird the more venturesome strategies.

Key factors in formulating strategic directions

As a long-time staff member, I was exposed to the basic methods in Fifth City [a Chicago neighbourhood and ICA's first project] and helped refine and develop them during summer programs. I was honored to spend a year with my wife Judy, and Joe and Marilyn Crocker doing village development consultations and refining that version of ToP strategic planning. For the past 15 years, facilitating and training in ToP methods have been my primary work, for the past four years as an independent professional. I have worked with over 177 groups. I continue to be fascinated by the commitment of people to full participation, and to the light that comes in their eyes as they experience ToP methods giving form and shape to what they intend.
—Jim Wiegel, ToP practitioner, Phoenix, USA

Strategy emerges out of an intention to create a desired future state from an existing current reality. However, if strategy aims only at the future state you want to see, it is based on an abstraction. And if it aims only at the current reality, then it is based on current patterns that no longer work.

Deals with blocks

When a vision is well-formed and motivating, people naturally want to move toward it. But no matter how much extra energy or initiative is put toward that vision, the constraints will still block it and might even intensify. An organization is powered by its vision, but great leaders are always contradiction-oriented. They look for models and scenarios that can break the logjam of the contradictions by creating models for new directions. To get rid of the British in India, civil disobedience was Gandhi's strategy, not his vision for the future.

Directing strategy at blocks to the future automatically releases the energy of the vision. A small rock sitting on the string of a helium balloon holds it down. If you want to release the balloon, it is more efficient to slightly shift the rock than to fill the balloon and make it bigger.

During contradictional analysis, as soon as a group becomes aware of an obstacle, they see a hint of what can be done about it, of what can begin to move the whole situation into the future. Rather than hopes of what might occur, strategy focuses on the approaches that must be taken because of the situation. For instance, as soon as a group knows that wasteful spending procedures are stifling future expansion, ideas emerge for what must be done.

Strategy also asks people to go beyond their latest good ideas and commit to change. Their judgments and decisions have the potential to transform the situation. A strategy of "moving into fundraising" is too obvious a response to learning that 100% government funding will end in a year. On the other hand, a strategy of "Investigating long-range funding opportunities by every department" might have the potential for transformation built right in.

Most people do not contemplate the military very much in everyday life, but military images can help in understanding how strategy is directed at blocks. For a commander to take a hill, getting the troops to run straight up that hill can be very unwise, like trying to simply implement a vision. Strategy is created by understanding the nature of the hill, the enemy troops guarding it, and the real blockages to taking the hill. Strategy emerges from knowing the number and the nature of the enemy troops, how they are armed, and the type of terrain on the hill. Strategy emerges from realizing that the enemy troops are half-hearted, very frightened, and might run if enough noise is made. It emerges from recognizing that the enemy troops are armed only with sticks and stones, or discovering that there is a route that goes around them, or that some of the enemy troops resent their commander and are open to inducements.

For many organizations, researching such detailed information is why consultants are hired. It's why they often start strategic planning with an analysis of strengths, weaknesses, opportunities, and threats—even before they know what their vision is. Sun Tzu, in his treatise *The Art of War*, said "Immature strategy is the cause of grief." Sending more and more people to run up the hill could be an example of that grief.

Sets direction

A strategy is a directional pointer to a crucial arena of action. Once a strategic direction is determined, tactics can be designed to accomplish all the detailed steps the strategy requires. Direction is determined by strategy, and change actually happens by doing tactics. Sun Tzu says strategy is one against ten, and tactics are ten against one. Strategy is the necessary approach for achieving the impossible of one against ten. Sun Tzu adds, "Many calculations win the war." Tactics, on the other hand, are about succeeding in implementation, by putting everything into it, ten against one.

A key directional question is "What is new about the direction we must take?"

Creative insight

John Epps, a ToP practitioner in Kuala Lumpur, said, "Many writers link strategy to various types of analysis, for instance pricing, competitive analysis, differentiation. But that isn't strategy. Those are just categories, or maybe types of strategies, and they certainly don't tell you what to do. Many people are so caught up in analysis and procedure that they miss insight. Developing creative insight is what we try to do in the ToP process, providing occasions for creativity and insight to happen."

Creative insight might seem like a tall order, but it comes naturally to all of us. When we shine the light of the real onto the impossible, or vice versa, creativity emerges. When we see a pattern within that tension, we are having a moment of insight. The key in using creative insight to inform strategy is to ensure that participants stay in the tension between the future vision and current reality long enough, and look at it from enough different perspectives. To collapse the tension too early leads to mundane approaches that are not strategic.

A key creativity question is "What creative insight can we glean from this tension?"

Focus on breakthrough

Current reality has its own inertia. That inertia continues until new energy pushes in a different direction. Strategy seeks a pathway towards breakthrough. At the very least a new direction will be forged, while at best a transformation will occur. Strategy occurs at the point where participants are able to say, "Now I see what we will have to do to move ahead!" It is actually less a list of actions they have to do, and more an image of the approach they will have to take. For instance, when the staff of an NGO complained that their sole donor determined where all the money went and gave no control to the staff, a sudden breakthrough in strategy occurred: "I now realize that if we as staff want to control where some of the funds are spent, we will have to take responsibility for raising some of those funds."

A key focus question is "What is the real breakthrough we need here?"

Participation becomes a necessity

Strategy used to be the purview of people at the top, the decision makers, the CEOs, the board. And while a mystique is attached to this type of strategy, the myth has run its course in today's society. Once upon a time, the people at the top were the only ones with the opportunity to think about the desired state that helps drive strategy. Only those people received reports about the issues arising throughout the entire organization. They were the only ones who had the information with which to create strategy, so they were the only ones who could reasonably be expected to do so.

Those people at the top now realize that everything is too complex in today's society to go it alone. The awareness, sensitivity, and knowledge of those on the front line is too great to ignore. The front-line folks on the telephones hear what the customers are really saying and what they really want. The nursing staff and inspectors on the front-line of a public health department see the immediate effects of a plant closure on families in the area, without having to wait six months or a year to see the statistics on depression, or the increase in spousal abuse. Even more important, when strategies are finally determined, those same people on the front lines are the ones who will be called upon to implement them.

Because of society's complexity, the variables that help determine strategy are shifting all the time. If the people who must implement a strategy don't understand the strategic intent and how it's supposed to work, every changing variable will cause them to stall until the Generals upstairs come up with the new plan. Until the new plan tells them which bolt to put on the proper place in which car, the whole assembly line stops. If, on the other hand, the front line already knows about the thinking behind the strategies, they'll be able to have a quick team meeting, innovate, and keep moving. They will be empowered to ask "What can we do to help? Not someone else, but us."

When people put their heads together to determine the real nature of their situation, strategy can emerge that makes participatory strategic planning effective. The more minds and perspectives are brought to bear on a situation, the better the current reality will be understood, and the more effective the strategy will be.

Examples of strategy

An organization with a long history of management with a "volunteer project mentality" finally received several new long-term funding sources. In response, they spelled out several new strategies:

1. Create a centralized project management system to make sure that no project gets too far behind, thereby stalling other projects.
2. Provide administrative support for project leaders, especially for those requiring large amounts of data input and analysis.
3. Develop an invoicing protocol so that the volunteer project leaders can legitimately charge for their time, and use the money to hire their own administrative support.

An evaluation unit of a crown corporation recognized that their evaluations were being used for accountability more than for continuous improvement and learning, which was why employees avoided evaluation activities. The unit promptly shifted to different strategies:

1. Develop a rewards system for evaluation work, so that those who participate in an evaluation process could expect something positive, not just accountability.
2. Foster a corporate evaluation system, one that would educate the directors on the learning function of evaluation.
3. Train more staff in evaluation processes throughout the corporation.

In a newly amalgamated city, the leadership recognized that old rivalries between previous municipalities and between older leaders were a great impediment to moving forward. The strategies they devised included:

1. Encourage new young leaders to come forward, since there were many young people who could be interested in civic engagement and who did not have the old histories.
2. Create new systems of dialogue, to add processes beyond the mayor and council meetings, in which the old rivalries had played out as theatre.
3. Expose hidden agendas. This was a radical strategy, but necessary because of the large outside vested interests at play in the city.

Strategic thinking: a thought process of planning

While everyone already uses basic forms of strategic thinking in their everyday lives, they can take their capacity for strategy to a whole new level with the help of certain widely used images. John Epps has catalogued a few images that have been helpful in his facilitation in Asia.

Thinking several moves ahead

A strategic chess player tries to think several moves ahead of the opponent, considering possible responses of the competition at each step. This is a time-honored tenet of good management. Thinking about how the whole situation can shift as one moves is perhaps mechanistic, but it can be quite effective. The entire science-based management process of Elliott Jaques' *Requisite Organization* is based on gradations of the ability to think ahead, while taking hundreds of variables into account. In our case study of the professional association on page 101, the leadership of the association recognized that creating a certification process and promoting or requiring certification of its members would be a real game changer. It would make their profession unassailable by others who claimed to represent the membership, as well as those who questioned the credentials of their members.

The ability to think several moves ahead is exercised in ToP participatory planning, partly by asking participants to think about strategies and approaches for each of the underlying obstacles independently. If there are five underlying obstacles, ask each person to consider at least one approach or strategy for each obstacle. The variety of strategies that emerge will span the short and long term. If the facilitator simply asks in a general sense, "What can we do to deal with the obstacles?" the ideas generated will tend be shorter term. But if the facilitator asks, "What approaches would you take to deal with each of these obstacles?" the ideas will tend to be longer term. All ideas should be welcomed, so the group can consider a greater span of possible options.

The negative implications of not changing

Any tendency to neglect strategic thinking vanishes if we consider the negative implications of not changing. If the current reality is clearly not tenable, then the desired future cannot come into being without some changes. This is most easy to see in our home life, where as a parent or a spouse we contemplate a lifetime of unwanted behavior from other family members, and suddenly become innovative in developing a strategy. In the case study of the area health center on page 105, the staff considered the negative implications of keeping the staff complement as it was. They saw how untenable this would be, and came up with several strategies for bringing new, younger health professionals on board.

This is the easiest way for a facilitator to get participants thinking strategically. The facilitator can ask, "What approaches can we take to deal with these obstacles, and at the same time move toward our vision?" Another way of getting strategic thinking going is to ask participants three questions just before they personally brainstorm their ideas. (They need not answer them out loud.)

- Looking at the vision chart, which of these elements of the vision are you most committed to?
- Looking at our contradiction analysis, how will these underlying obstacles affect us if something is not done about them?
- What can you or we do to deal with those obstacles, and at the same time move forward toward our vision?

Bold move or conservative approach

Another image of strategy is held by the yin/yang symbol of the Tao. Bold, creative, aggressive yang strategy may come up with new ideas and new ways to do things, which might be a real breakthrough. But yang must be balanced with the soft, slow, conservative yin strategy, which is rooted in tranquility and moves slowly but surely. Having coffee breaks with individual staff members on a regular basis is a conservative strategy that can get all sorts of things done. The big emergency meeting that focuses everyone's attention and boldly announces an important point has its place, too.

The facilitator can elicit both types of thinking by asking for them explicitly. Drawing a yin/yang conservative/bold image on the wall, and telling participants that we need both, gives permission to people who generally practice one or the other in their thinking. You can say before brainstorming, "Come up with at least one bold strategy that everyone will say 'Wow! If only we did that!' And come up with at least one that will slowly and inevitably result in progress." To seed the brainstorming, you can ask a couple of people to read their boldest idea out loud, and thank them for sparking the creative juices of others: "Who has an idea that would really turn our underlying obstacle on its head? Who has an idea that would really upset the applecart, but that has merit anyway?" "Who has an idea that if everyone did the same small thing, it would make an immediate difference in how we operate? Who has an idea that is just so obvious that no one else will think of mentioning it?" Most people simply need permission, a little prompting, and a little safety, to get this type of strategic thinking going.

In the government IT department case study on page 109, one major strategy was a series of regular meetings between managers of the three different departments, plus permission for the staff of each department to talk directly with the staff of other departments. One of the conservative strategies they decided on was to practice active listening. When everyone began practicing active listening, it had a positive effect throughout the organization. It directly supported another strategy of engaging in two-way lateral and vertical communication.

Point of leverage

Archimedes' archetypal strategy was "Give me a lever long enough, and a fulcrum on which to place it, and I shall move the world." The way a facilitator gets this type of strategic thinking going is by asking, just before brainstorming, "Looking carefully at the vision and at the contradictions, where are some places we could put some energy that would begin to shift things?" Sometimes very particular actions can be done or approaches taken that will begin to shift the whole context and move the entire organization forward.

In the industry association case study on page 111, two of the key strategies were to invigorate committee structures and inform or educate members about the association. As the leadership team talked about these strategies, they realized that the annual trade show, which was always a high point for members, could be used as a lever to ramp up both of these strategies. Up to that point, the trade show had been handled by a couple of volunteers with some professional advice. Now the association decided to use several different committees to pull off various parts of the trade show, and use the trade show news materials to inform the membership of other important things they needed to know.

Redirecting energy

The martial arts are full of images of leveraged strategy, in which one deflects the energy of an opponent, as in *aikido* or *tai chi*. Indirection in strategy is counterintuitive, since many people want to move straight ahead toward implementing some component of the vision. But an even more powerful image is using the energy of an opponent against that very opponent. In the case study of the professional association, the leadership was able to use negative media attention to rally the membership and focus them on some key goals.

Another image of strategic thinking comes from the practice of sailing. You want to get to a particular island, but the wind is directly against you. Most of us would throw up our hands and figure it can't be done. Sailors, on the other hand, know that by holding the sail and the boat in a very precise direction, the wind will push the whole boat sideways but forward. By regularly changing the precise direction of the sail and boat, the boat will go back and forth, zigzagging to the island. This "tacking" strategy is well known to sailors, and uses the energy of the wind blowing against the sail, along with the properties of a boat in water, to propel the boat ahead.

A three-hour classic ToP strategic directions workshop

Like other stages of the ToP process, a strategic directions session has a twofold objective:
Rational Aim: Identify the innovative practical actions that will release the contradictions
Experiential Aim: Release excitement about new possibilities

Give a context to the participants

Start by getting all members of the group on the same page.

1) *Outline process and timeline.* Show the stage you are all at in the planning process and tell how much time there will be to do the workshop.

2) *Explain the product and outcome.*
   TIP: This is a time to be bold and creative. Give examples of approaches. Take one of the group's obstacles and quickly brainstorm some approaches for it together. A useful image to share is a rock in the middle of a road with several arrows going around, under, over, or through the rock.

3) *Highlight the focus question.* What can we do to deal with the obstacles and realize our vision? What approaches can be taken to deal with the obstacles and move toward the vision?

Brainstorm ideas

Then move to open the floodgates of each person's creativity.

1) *Individual brainstorm.* Each person list two or three actions for each obstacle.
TIP: These could be actions, or they could be approaches. It is best if they are concrete and specific, as this helps the clustering process later.

2) *Select your best ideas.* Each person chooses three key actions and stars them.

3) *Brainstorm in small discussion groups.* Let's work in groups of two or three people so that all obstacles are covered. In the small groups, take turns reading proposed actions out to each other. Then discuss and select eight that cover a wide range of actions and strategies. Select overlapping actions first. Strike a balance between wildly creative and conserving action. Write each action on a card in big letters, using three to five words. You can write details on the back of the card if you like. This will take about 20 minutes. When we are done we should have about 50 cards altogether.
TIP: All discussion groups could cover all obstacles, or each discussion group could focus on one obstacle in depth, with secondary focus on the other obstacles.

Cluster the ideas

This workshop uses a "Tic-tac-toe cluster." Tape a matrix of nine half-sheets of flipchart paper to the wall—three columns by three rows, as in Figure 18:

Each sheet should be at least 25.5 inches wide by 16.5 inches high, big enough to hold nine 8.5 by 5.5 inch index cards. Each of the sheets will eventually hold a cluster of index cards (a strategy). The sheets should be taped to the wall, securely enough to take the weight of the cards, but not with too much tape, since the sheets will have to be moved around later. After all the cards are clustered on these sheets (and named as approximately nine strategies), each strategy sheet can be rearranged, so that related strategies are grouped on the same horizontal row.

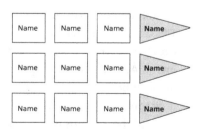

FIGURE 18. Tac-tac-toe gestalt
in a strategies workshop

The horizontal rows of strategies will then be named, as two, three, or four strategic directions.

1) *Share the boldest actions*. Each group select the three cards that are the boldest actions, and send them up to the front. We will eventually get all the cards up front.

TIP: Have the small groups reassemble in the plenary space, but sit beside each other. Every person needs to be able to see the front clearly. As you receive the 18 or so cards, read them out loud, and post them on the front wall, beside the set of sheets. Once they are all read out, ask if any of the cards are not clear and need clarification.

2) *Look for any pairs of similar cards. Look for pairs of similar cards.*

TIP: If someone points out a pair, move them together onto one sheet and put a neutral symbol on that sheet. Ask the whole group to look for three more pairs of cards. While you are pairing these cards, do not allow anyone to add a third or fourth card with any pair. After this step, three or four of the large sheets will have pairs of cards and a symbol.

3) *Cluster beyond pairs.*

TIP: When you have four pairs of cards, ask if there are additional pairs, or if any of the remaining ten or so cards fit into existing pairs. Get people to explain why they fit together, and how they might be clues to a larger strategy. Perhaps 12 of the original 18 cards on the wall might be clustered by this time onto sheets with a symbol on them.

4) *Collect more cards.*

TIP: Collect two more cards from each small discussion group—two they are most confident about. Read each one out loud as you post them on the sheets, spreading them randomly across the empty spaces on the sheets. Ask if there are any questions of clarification about any cards. At this point there should be 28 cards altogether on the wall.

5) *Continue clustering*. Continue clustering the cards, by similar actions or actions that can be done together to create momentum.

TIP: Go in the order of whoever can see a new relationship between cards. If disagreement occurs over where a card should go, This usually indicates that someone wants to try clustering by intent. Ask: Where would this card most illuminate a larger strategy? Is it a similar type of activity, or can it be done together with another of the actions? Where would it help build momentum? If disagreement continues, ask whomever wrote the card where they think it should go. By this time, of the 28 cards of the wall, there will probably be seven clusters on the sheets, each with two to five cards per cluster. There may be several cards that do not fit.

6) *Relate extra cards*. For the three to five cards left with each discussion group, try relating them

to the existing columns on the wall and putting the appropriate symbol on them. Do not try to force-fit cards into a cluster. Say: send up to me "the cards that do not have a symbol on them," or the ones that do not seem to fit anywhere yet.

TIP: Read these out loud as you put them on the wall. It would be normal to add another five to ten cards at this point, giving perhaps 38 cards up front, in total. Ask if there are any questions of clarity about the new cards.

7) *Create new clusters.*
TIP: See if the new cards create any new clusters, or if someone can suggest where a card might go into an existing cluster. There could be significant discussion around this. Allow the group to explore options. Another two clusters might emerge, giving a total of nine clusters. It is also possible that two existing clusters might collapse together to make one, giving seven or eight clusters in total.

8) *Bring remaining cards up front.* Participants bring up all the remaining cards and put them on the wall in their appropriate cluster.

TIP: Once the cards are posted, this is an opportune time for everyone to take a short bio-break, if necessary. When the group comes back from the break, rather than reading out all the new cards, you could count out loud how many new ones are in each cluster and tell the plenary group. You will be able to tell the new cards because they have a small symbol on them.

Name the clusters

By this time, there are around 48 cards on the wall, in about eight or nine clusters, with between three and ten cards per cluster. There will be a clear pattern, but the pattern is held only by the symbol cards. We will now name the clusters and see what the pattern actually is.

1) *Summarize one cluster.*
Select the largest cluster and discuss it for clarity and insight.
This step needs another guided conversation:
    a) *Objective level*—Read the cards in the largest cluster out loud so everyone can hear.
    b) *Reflective level*—Ask for some of the key words people heard from the cards.
    c) *Interpretive level*—What are some clues to the larger strategy that these cards illuminate?

These cards were all generated from the focus question, "What can we do to deal with the underlying obstacles and move toward the vision?"

Get the group to summarize the cluster with a verb that describes the action, and a phrase that tells the focus of the action, such as "Generating positive media reports" or "Building research capacity." Write the agreed name on a card with a border on it, and put it at the top of the cluster.

We can always clean up or refine the language later. At this point we are after clarity about the action and the focus.

TIP: Sometimes a strategy name does not emerge easily, and the facilitator must engage the group in more dialogue to get a good title. Here are some questions that can help to spark a good name for a strategy:

- How do these actions go together to produce catalytic new directions?
- What is this new direction that these cards say we must move in to resolve the contradictions and realize our vision? What new direction are we proposing?
- What is the action these cards are proposing? What is the verb that describes the action?
- What is the focus of these actions?
- What would you call this type of strategy?
- What is strategic about what we are proposing here?
- Haven't we already been doing this type of thing already? What is new and refreshing in this direction or activity?

2) *Continue naming the other clusters.*

TIP: Select the second longest column, and go through the same steps as with the first column. The process gets easier with each column.

The more clusters you name together, the better the result. If you think you are running out of time you could, after naming four clusters altogether, assign the leftover unnamed clusters to the discussion group teams of three people, and ask them to recommend a name to the whole group. You must assign the clusters out to the discussion groups randomly and fairly, and not allow participants to select the cluster they want. You will need to remind everyone of the naming convention. They should use either a gerundial phrase (such as "generating positive media reports") or an action verb + object (such as "generate positive media reports"). Each group needs to be close enough to the front wall to see its cards. Each group needs a card with a border on it, on which to write its recommended title. As soon as any discussion group has completed its task, its members put the title card up on the sheet.

Check the resolve of the group

Now comes the stage of putting the strategies into one big picture.

1) *Acknowledge the results.*

TIP: Read to the group the focus question and the seven to nine title cards out loud. At this point participants might give themselves a round of applause for getting this done.

2) *Ground the results.*

Let's get several answers for each of these questions:

- Which strategy is the most exciting? Scariest?
- Which will be easiest to do? Hardest?
- Which will have the most impact?
- Let's look back at our obstacles. Which obstacles are being dealt with by this set of strategies?
- Let's look back at our vision. Which vision elements are we moving toward?
- Which strategy or strategies are you committed to work on? Come and write your name on it.

3) *Create a chart to hold the consensus.*

Which of these strategies fit together to form a strategic direction?

TIP: Rearrange the sheets so that the linkages between strategies show as horizontal (not vertical) sets of strategies. Get the group to name the three or four sets of strategic directions.

Congratulate the group on its work. Allow a break, reminding them that the next workshop will be to create an Action Plan for each of these strategies, to put wheels under the whole effort.

A sample of the documentation of results

The result of the strategic directions workshop needs the visual look of forward momentum in it and could appear something like Figure 19.

Build capacity through training	Seek and involve partners in diverse sectors	Generate demand that leads to committed action	Enhance and expand new dialogue with partners	**Creating multi-level partnerships**
Monitor and evaluate programs and their structure		Disseminate results and success widely and routinely		**Broadcasting results of successful interventions**
Hold constraint assessments and gap analysis		Develop technologies and other initiatives	Expand long-term donor base with collaboration	**Focusing targets for maximum impact**
Identify and assign priorities with a concrete schedule		Clarify roles, responsibilities and accountability	Share information systematically	**Systematizing staff interaction**

FIGURE 19. Sample strategy chart and documentation

11
Action planning generates commitment to implementation

In Timor–Leste [East Timor], the production of an actual strategic plan is exciting and follow-up calls usually show that implementation of the plan is well under way.
—Carol Borovic, ToP practitioner, Darwin, Australia

In strategic planning, groups express hope about their ability to accomplish the implementation. The ToP approach excels in the implementation of participatory strategic plans. Therefore, trainees are choosing to become certified ToP facilitators and applying the methods in their work.
—Marilyn Oyler, ToP practitioner, Phoenix, USA.

Effective implementation of strategies requires detailed thinking about who, what, when, where, and how. Planning for implementation can sometimes be straightforward, taking a few measurable accomplishments (also known as outcomes, goals or strategic objectives), some actions, timelines with assignments, and some resource support. In many cases, ToP action planning provides sufficient planning to launch and sustain implementation. If strategies are very big, or are outside-of-the-box creative, they add considerable stress to the implementation system—especially those strategies that are intended to lead to a vital transformation. In such cases, additional methods can be used before action planning.

Every strategy requires its own implementation plan. The practitioner or team has to consider:
- Permissions, and who can give them
- Levels and types of support
- Leadership and teams responsible for the implementation
- Order in which implementation will proceed

In many cases, ToP action planning handles all those questions. ToP action planning is done for each strategy separately. It creates measurable accomplishments for each strategy, develops lists of tactics, and puts the implementing steps onto timelines.

This chapter explains the key elements of participatory implementation planning, the thinking process of tactical thinking, detailed procedures for ToP action planning, and special participatory tools to prepare for complex situations.

Fourteen employees of the international NGO (see page 107) convened to create an action plan for their strategies. They were still employees of the government but knew that they would soon be registered as a non-profit organization. They had already determined that eleven strategies within four overall strategic directions were necessary (see Figure 19).

To determine potential partners for the strategies, they began with an hour-long framework-building exercise that identified over 100 specific people within various organizations. Since they were a small group they did a SWOT analysis together, making flipchart lists of strengths, weaknesses, opportunities and threats for the whole organization along with much shorter lists for each of the four strategic directions. The director of the organization involved himself heavily in this brainstorming because he had such a long history in the field and wanted everyone to benefit from his knowledge.

Four teams of three people looked through the SWOT lists and the strategy brainstorms of their assigned strategic direction for about an hour. Each team formulated a set of measurable accomplishments that they called strategic objectives, one per strategy, and posted them on the front wall on a very large timeline. One team proposed pilot needs assessments in three countries on three different continents to be completed within two years to focus one of their assigned strategies. Another team proposed success story packages for highly targeted audiences reporting on great programs and models that already existed. A third team proposed an advocacy and social marketing seminar targeted to consultants and government departments on two continents to transfer compelling cases for specific interventions. The last team proposed partnership forums to encourage open dialogue during nine existing global events.

Eight strategic objectives were placed on the wall timeline. A conversation on the relative merits of each objective and the synergy between them elevated the understanding and commitment of the entire team. The director questioned team members on the realism and efficacy of each objective. About an hour into the plenary, several teams commented that not only could the goals be done over the three-year period, but they needed to be done if the organization was going to have the impact that it wanted. Since everyone nodded in agreement, three teams convened again to decide some key tasks for each strategy over the next six months. A fourth team, including the director, went aside to look at budgets and the plan for hiring new staff. Those timelines were collected later by a project leader.

Links back to previous stages

Some of the brainstorming during visioning, but especially the brainstorming during strategy development, contains plenty of raw data which can be brought forward and used as spark plugs during ToP action planning. In addition, if a SWOT analysis was done in Stage 2, that information can be considered during ToP action planning.

If the complexity of the organization's situation precludes the use of ToP action planning immediately after the strategies have been developed, the facilitator and client can consider the use of additional participatory tools, and then follow up with ToP action planning. The reasons for using any of these tools are found in "Stage 1: Preparing the groundwork for participation," under "Types of change and outcomes" (see Figure 9). Each of these tools is given more detailed treatment in "Stage 3 tools: Between strategy development and action planning" (page 217).

1. Prioritizing strategies

Prioritizing helps decide which strategies to create implementation plans for first. It can also help determine which strategy to launch first, or how much relative energy to put into each strategy. This prioritization is not about one strategy being more important or urgent than any other strategy. It is about deciding which strategies need immediate action plans created by the available participants, and which strategies can wait for planning and implementation. For instance, a set of five strategies could be prioritized to create three action plans immediately and two more at some later date.

2. Phasing the strategies

Phasing takes unfamiliar or very big strategies, and spreads them out over time with a set of process outcomes. It spreads out the pressure for action, and shows how implementation can proceed. Rather than just building an action plan with goals, a phased strategy divides big tasks into several phases of implementation, such as a research phase, a business plan phase, a launch phase. Each phase builds on the previous phase, and the final outcome is the implementation of the entire strategy. Action planning is done at the beginning of each phase.

3. Creating a tactical system

A set of big complex strategies can become manageable by generating tactics or action items that are common to several strategies at once. This approach is most useful when implementation of strategies will involve a large number of staff over a long period of time. Instead of creating goals and timelines for each strategy, another round of brainstorming is done on tactics or methods for implementing each strategy. Patterns of implementation are then identified among the strategies, and that creates the tactical system. For example, for two of the strategies for a city department, "Engage the public in large scale initiatives" and "Enhance communication across all units," the department's tactical system included:

- Hold a regular schedule of joint staff meetings.
- Generate public information and discussion on the website.
- Open leadership and facilitation training to all staff.
- Publicize all city projects in various media.

Action plans are then created for each part of the tactical system.

4. Developing structural solutions or restructuring

This approach creates a rationale for the reconfiguration of teams and task forces that will implement the strategies. It can link strategies and implementation to *organizational restructuring*, especially in cases when the purpose of the strategic planning is explicitly to restructure the organization. Sometimes a strategy calls for an action plan that focuses on launching the restructuring. But other times there is an expectation of accomplishing the reorganization during the strategic planning event rather than later. If this is the case, the strategies chosen can give important clues to the new structure. When the participants have the authority to create the new formalized structure, there might be no reason to wait. The new structure can be formalized before any action planning takes place, creating immediate motivation for the action planning and even determining the implementation teams.

Key factors in launching implementation from an action plan

Action will remove the doubt that theory cannot solve.
—Chinese epigram collected by Tehyi Hsieh

In building action or implementation plans, the ToP approach is designed to produce integrated thinking, and a qualitative change in how people work together. Several key factors converge in creating this change.

Clearly links back

All implementation eventually comes down to doing tactics, with timelines, assignments, and resources. Implementation can create a blizzard of detail. But the great power of ToP participatory strategic planning is that participants can easily link implementation back to the vision, which was the original motivation for the plan. They can also ensure that the implementation is done in a way that deals with underlying obstacles or contradictions. This approach also enables teams to quickly change a plan when external or internal factors require it, because they are clear about all the intentions behind the implementation plan, in contrast to implementation that loses its reference to the big picture.

Breaks inertia

ToP action planning takes the group out of the realm of routine implementation and cog-in-the-fog operations. After generating several measurable accomplishments for each strategy, the group considers or creates a synthesis of those measurable accomplishments which are the most catalytic. The team makes a conscious decision to win on those measurable accomplishments (or goals, outcomes, or strategic objectives) that will irrevocably alter the future, selecting those that could break through the inertia that has kept them mired in the past situation. These measurable accomplishments become symbols of the vision, as well as practical examples of breaking down the barriers which have been blocking the entire organization.

Builds momentum

Timelines are created to ensure synergy between the measurable accomplishments that build momentum toward final outcomes of the strategic plan. The facilitator finds out who needs to approve the plans and in what level of detail so that implementation can begin. It is common for board or senior management teams to approve initiatives and targeted measurable milestones for the first three years of a strategic plan.

Makes it real

Action planning requires knowing what is to be done, who will do it, when and how it will be done, plus what resources will be required. As ToP practitioner Jo Nelson puts it, "History doesn't change from the big things that you ought to do. History changes from the little things you actually do." The operative questions for any practitioner during action planning are "Can it be done? Will it be done?" No question is too detailed to ask during this phase of the planning. "*If* something will get done" is not the operative paradigm during action planning—only "*when* will it get done?" This means that measurable accomplishments, tactics, and implementing steps can be small, and can always be put on a timeline, with the name of an individual who is responsible to follow through. A small implementing step can break through inertia as surely as a big one, so small is good.

Creates campaigns

While implementation is always accomplished by doing tactics or implementing steps, it can almost always be organized into campaigns, maneuvers, programs, and projects. Project managers know the secret of having specific goals is having enough action items on a timeline, with someone responsible for each one, with the time, money and resources to do it, and someone assigned to coordinate the whole thing. ToP practitioners know a further secret, that motivation flows from imagery, slogans, and maneuvers to support the work.

"Jump ship! Join the Pirates" was the slogan for a team whose action plan was to hold celebrations toward creating a third new culture in the workplace, as distinct from their two previous cultures. The "Search and Rescue" team was assigned to recruit a new communications manager. "Spring Training" was the baseball imagery used to empower a staff orientation and training maneuver. Such imagery does not always have to be used, but never underestimate its power. The imagery needs to come from the participants themselves rather than being grafted on after the fact by an external source. ToP action planning builds this aspect of planning right in. If done carefully, it can turn the long drudgery of implementation into memories of fun and creativity that outlast the plan and its implementation.

Leads to self-assignment

When strategies have been created with participation from those involved, participants can often choose the strategy they want to work on in creating the action plan. There is a balance between who works on creating an action plan, and who is actually needed to implement the plan. Of course, teams may already exist for specific strategies, and this should be taken into account.

Who should create the action plan for each strategy? The best answer is that those who will do the implementation should create the plan. In fact, if those who are going to implement the plan cannot personally participate in any other part of a ToP participatory strategic planning process, at least they should be involved in the action planning to build commitment to the results.

Self-assignment, where participants pick the strategy they are really interested in and work with others who are similarly motivated, can lead to creativity and energy. Of course, there may be occasions when every participant wants or needs to give input into the action plan for every strategy. In this situation, the facilitator has to make it clear that the action planning group needs to recommend an implementation team for completing details of the plan. Upper management usually has to approve the teams as well.

Do your tactics

The real secret to transformation is "Do your tactics." Once you have a complete strategic plan, there is no reason to think anymore about vision, to worry about contradictions, or to plot over the strategy. If you do your tactics, the strategies will be implemented, the contradictions will be dealt with, and the future will unfold. Doing tactics is like gardening. The tactics are to mulch the soil, plant seeds a quarter of an inch under the soil, water the plants regularly, pull weeds weekly, scare off raccoons nightly. If you do those things, the garden will grow and take care of itself. This is the secret of implementing a strategic plan. Simply do your tactics. You may have the most compelling and wonderful vision. You may have done a superlative analysis of blockages. Your strategic approaches might be highly creative. But it is only when you do your tactics that any change actually happens.

Examples of action plans

For a strategy of "Maximizing public dialogue," one of the measurable accomplishments was a "series of community forums involving a total of 300 people by October 15th."

For a strategy of "Formalizing internal communications," a measurable accomplishment was "a quarterly six-page newsletter for all staff by June 30."

While one measurable accomplishment is often sufficient to focus the action of a strategy, some-times a series of measurable accomplishments done together can create great momentum. For instance, the strategy "Formalizing internal communications" could include several measurable accomplishments such as:
1. A clearly written e-mail reduction protocol by February
2. Monthly staff meetings for all 30 staff, launched in April
3. A quarterly newsletter to staff and partners by June 30
4. A full-time communications consultant on staff by September

If enough people are available to deliver on all these measurable accomplishments, the action plan could include all four. Accomplishment #3 (the quarterly newsletter) might also be used for the strategy of "Maximizing public dialogue."

Tactical thinking: a thought process of planning

To get people into a fruitful frame of mind in creating tactics, several images are helpful.

The Victory Circle

The **Victory Circle** is an image from racing, in which the winning horse, car, or runner does one more lap after the race, basking in the sheer exultation of success. A similar thinking process in participatory action planning is to put all participants into the "Victory Circle" before starting any implementation, to build up a state of confidence about goals in which all participants can "taste and smell" the victory before the victory. This creates the high motivation necessary to do the detailed tactical thinking that is necessary to ensure success.

To achieve this state of mind first make sure everyone understands the purpose of the planning, by linking the strategies back to the vision and contradictions out of which they were built, and recapping why the strategy is important. Second, look at all the advantages and vulnerabilities of the strategy, so everyone can see how it is possible to win. Third, craft a goal that is compelling in its simplicity and necessity—so clear that everyone can see how it will inspire the necessary creativity and attention to detail.

In Victory Circle thinking, it is not necessary to detail *how* the accomplishment will occur, but simply to ensure that everyone understands *why* it is crucial, *what* it will look like, and what difference it will make. One can see this type of thinking when a small think tank creates a conference theme so compelling that everyone becomes committed to the conference and wants to jump on board to make the event happen.

The key to generating this type of thinking is to link measurable outcomes to the lasting impact they will have, and to show how the measurable outcome is directly related to the vision.

Maneuvers

This French military term for "open hand" refers to the type of thinking that demonstrates how a small number of simple moves, done together, will win the battle. Using the conference example above, now that the winning theme is in place, all that is left is to:

1. Get the right exciting keynote speakers.

2. Set a date and location that everyone can get to.
3. Make a budget that makes it inexpensive for our targets to attend.
4. Send promo material out to all our targets as soon as possible.
5. Put a team to work on the logistics.

Maneuvers can seem simple or obvious, but creativity and clarity on these actions can allow a free-flowing organization of people and resources, so that everyone knows the details of their own maneuver, and victory is assured. Maneuvers have less to do with timing, and more to do with marshalling the required resources. The thinking required in making maneuvers entails getting everyone involved in making long lists of "to do's," that cover every possible aspect of accomplishing the goal, then clustering these into specific tasks that are related, and then creating a compelling image that holds the maneuvers together into a cohesive whole. A team is then assigned to implement each maneuver.

The key to this type of thinking is to be comprehensive and detailed in the types of actions that will be needed for success, and to name the patterns of action.

Deadlines

Deadlines add urgency to the thinking process, because they indicate when each part of the plan must be accomplished to enable the next phase. Having deadlines allows participants to know when they have to play their part, and, by extension, when they don't. Posting deadlines for each action on large Gantt charts or timelines gives everyone a way to know that their deadline is really real. Getting participants to figure those deadlines out for themselves has an even greater impact on their personal commitment, by making them comfortable with the implementation. The way people engage in action planning is very revealing. When you hear a participant say, "Just a minute, we have to complete this action on the timeline two weeks sooner, because several of us will be away on a course during that period"—you have just heard the sound of commitment.

The key to this type of thinking is in the sequencing of activities and actions, and in the synergy and synchronicity between actions and milestones.

A four-hour classic ToP action planning workshop

After our community mobilization using ToP methods, communities begin to see how their participation can lead to success and start activities such as collecting funds to implement a specific project. We prioritize community problems using ToP methods, and then the community can make decisions about how to address the problems and issues. We train communities

to create local institutions/organizations to support their work over time.
—Marina Safarova, ToP practitioner, Khujand, Tajikistan

Each strategy of the strategic plan requires its own action plan. The group should pick which strategy to start with, and the whole group should experience the process together. After that, it will be possible to break into subgroups to work on remaining strategies. This workshop demonstrates the three major steps in participatory action planning:

1. Forging catalytic measurable accomplishments
2. Generating comprehensive detailed actions
3. Timelining the implementation steps

Forging catalytic measurable accomplishments

To generate creative, do-able action plans for each strategy, it's helpful to start by reading through the brainstorm of ideas that led to the strategy at hand. A quick revisit of the original vision can remind the group of the focus of this strategic plan. In starting to think about catalytic action, the team can do its own SWOT analysis—naming their strengths and weaknesses, opportunities and threats, or benefits and dangers in relation to a given strategy. SWOT is a fine tool to use prior to action planning, because you have a strategy as an answer to the question: "Strengths relative to what?" For example, "Where are we strong relative to improving communication between levels in the organization?" Each team member may know of advantages or vulnerabilities that the other team members should be aware of. This quick analysis will move the team toward considering innovative actions that might be worth pursuing.

To ensure that each participant has a chance to put forward some goals to focus the strategy, a stage called "possible accomplishments" is necessary. Ensure that each team member has a chance to speak. There's a tendency for certain strong or loud team members to propose a goal, and then take time persuading other team members to support it. Assure them their ideas are recorded, and ask for others. The group should generate a minimum of three possible accomplishments, but there could be up to ten. Make sure there is creativity and diversity in the mix. Each proposed accomplishment will have some merit, which must be considered. Most likely, the final measurable accomplishment will be a blend of several of them.

After several possible accomplishments have been generated, each is gauged against several criteria for a good measurable accomplishment. What impact will the accomplishment have on people? How will it inspire people to win on this strategy and the long range vision of the whole plan? How catalytic is the measurable accomplishment? In other words, how much will it empower other parts of the whole plan?

Another set of criteria for evaluating proposals is "SMART goals": (specific, measurable, achievable, realistic, and timebound). SMART goals are useful as a criteria for proposals, but consider other relevant criteria, such as creativity or cultural fit. A ***measurable accomplishment*** must be stated as an accomplishment, rather than an activity. It must say, "conference plan finished," rather than "plan the conference." It must be measurable rather than vague, for example "$20,000 in hand" rather than "increased income." And it must also be timebound: "by September 1st." Challenging the team to be this specific empowers their commitment and realism.

In creating a measurable accomplishment, it is far more important to have a small goal that people are actually committed to, than a large goal that might be inspiring or visionary, but some group members believe can never happen. Test to make sure that every member of the small team actually believes it is possible. Ask what they feel able to do personally.

Here are some examples of specific, measurable accomplishments:
- By June 1st, we will have a re-credentialing process in place for 200 members, with core competencies and an administrative body.
- On July 15th, we will hold a major multicultural event with 400 participants.
- Within 12 months, 25% of the technical staff will have shifted from legacy data to new projects.

Generating comprehensive detailed actions

Next, each accomplishment will need a set of detailed actions to implement it. And creating a comprehensive plan of detailed actions involves three basic steps. First the group brainstorms a large number of actions or tactics, then clusters the actions into maneuvers or action campaigns, and finally creates motivating images or slogans that will capture the intent.

When measurable accomplishments are already quite clear, all this may seem unnecessary. There is a tendency to think, "We are all adults here. Everybody knows what they need to do. We don't need to do another brainstorm of actions." This assumption, however, can cause an entire plan to fall apart. Involving the whole team in brainstorming a complete list of "tactics to do" for measurable accomplishments avoids pitfalls like the following: "The sessions we planned for were all exciting. The invitation lists were well-targeted. The promo materials were superlative and on time. Unfortunately, we forgot about the week delay in getting checks from the finance department to the mailing house, which was a new mailing house that required the money in advance. That was most unfortunate."

That example and this next one illustrates the meaning of Sun Tzu's quotes, "Strategy is one against ten; tactics are ten against one," and "Many calculations win the battle." The more detail that goes into brainstorming tactics and things to do, the less likely the plan will fall through the cracks, and the greater the likelihood of success.

In 1977 I participated in a brainstorming session with Joe Slicker, one of the founders of ICA, and 25 other staff. The focus question was "What do we need to do to be successful in the New Village Effort of 250 village demonstration projects in India within three years?" The brainstorm of things to do was very long, and every piece of wall was covered with flipcharts. We were in uncharted territory in launching a village development movement, so exhaustive brainstorming was very important. After our initial brainstorm of three items from each person, he asked, "What else?" After 90 items were on the flipcharts, he turned and said, "Good list so far. Now that we have all the obvious psychic sludge out of the way, let's get down to business and figure out what really has to be done" We continued until there were 300 items. A good learning about brainstorming is that the first several ideas from each person are generally obvious ones. If the object of the brainstorming is creativity, it will be necessary to brainstorm a lot of ideas so that one idea sparks another.

If the list of actions to be generated is very long, they can be printed individually on index cards, posted on the wall, and clustered as in the consensus workshop method (see page 68). This clustering of actions by similar activity will create a set of basic maneuvers, or directional activities, to actually implement the measurable accomplishment. The maneuvers still have all the detailed actions behind them, which will be used.

As much fun as brainstorming actions can be, it will eventually get tiring for some people, but tactical thinkers revel in it. Visionary thinkers can get antsy because it's too detailed for them. Contradictional thinkers may be skeptical, but their realism adds value when they ask, "But what about *x*?" Strategic thinkers are happy with the process and usually look for patterns in the data.

Since these brainstormed actions or maneuvers are going to guide the team's work for months or years to come, it is wise to make them as memorable as possible. An element of fun will help keep people going when they are deep into the task of implementation. This is why the third step, of creating images and slogans for each of the maneuvers, is crucial. Images and slogans add a creative and imaginative element to the action planning. They help create team spirit, and make the effort memorable.

Timelining the implementation steps

A plan doesn't implement itself. Until a timeline is put up on the wall for everyone to see, and each action item on that timeline gets a person or team name assigned to it, the plan is very unlikely to be realized.

Even though this is obvious to most facilitators and to all project planners, it is a major discovery for many participants in participatory planning. The energy level in a room immediately increases when a large timeline is put on a wall. Suddenly everything becomes real. The tone changes to thoughtful commitment. No longer are good intentions sufficient. A timeline on the wall is the main symbol that the rubber is about to hit the road. Everybody now feels permission to ask whether there is real commitment to do any action item that goes up onto the timeline.

There are several steps to creating a good timeline. The first step is arranging all the actions, tactics, and implementation steps on the timeline in the most realistic way. The second step is making explicit assignments for all those actions. If names are not put on those activities, then it is only guesswork that someone actually intends to do them. The third step is estimating a budget, be it resources or money, to show how the plan can be supported.

Ask the participants to arrange the actions in sequence first. Then ask them to suggest actual dates for the actions in the sequence. When you begin to hear animated dialogue about the correct sequence, or about an actual date for an action item on a timeline, this generally indicates commitment to the outcome.

There is no one correct way to record actions on a timeline. It is helpful to signify the launch, and perhaps the duration, of the action. Gantt Charts and computer programs are available for this. But the key to the participatory nature of timelining is to keep it entirely visible during the process, to make it possible for anyone to easily make a change or modification, and to transfer control over to the participants while they are making commitments about their future work. The best way is to tape a very long paper on the wall for the timeline, and to hand out colored paper shapes on which to print various kinds of actions, and then move them around as needed during the discussion.

In a plenary meeting, when several action plans are being reported for several strategies, it is a declaration of commitment every time a team member steps up to the front of the room to report on the team's timeline of implementation.

An entire strategic plan will have a timeline with several strategies, measurable accomplishments, and implementation steps spread out horizontally. The timeline is an extremely valuable tool for use in the final plenary of a participatory planning session. The practitioner can lead a group conversation on the realism of the actions with questions like "What synergy can you see between the timing of some of these measurable accomplishments?" Participants often point out that if one measurable accomplishment is moved a couple of months earlier or later, the results will feed into the implementation of another accomplishment. This type of conversation benefits everyone when they see how one outcome affects another.

The same question can be asked of specific actions or milestones on a timeline: "How can the actions of one plan be used to help implement another plan?" Participants may point out that doing the survey for one measurable accomplishment could be combined with the survey for another. Or that one mailing could be done for several measurable accomplishments at once, if only the timing is shifted slightly.

Action planning requires assignments for implementation. To introduce this discussion, the context depends on how implementation is to be carried out. For example, "Just because you are in a small team working on an action plan for a particular strategy for the next hour does *not* mean that you are the only ones responsible for implementing that action plan for the next six months. It *is* your responsibility, however, to suggest or recommend who does need to be on the implementation team." In some cases, if action planning is already assigned to the relevant professional teams, it may be accurate to say, "By being on this action planning team, you will be responsible for the implementation of the measurable accomplishment, once you have made your recommendation to the whole team and it is deemed appropriate."

Other possible contexts for the assignments task are:
- In recommending assignments for your team's action plan, consider who will champion the team, who needs to give permissions, and who will be needed to help with the work of the team, especially if they are not present. Be careful when assigning someone who is not present. They may not have the time.
- At this point we are suggesting assignments. When an action planning team puts a name on a tactic or implementation step, this is only a recommendation to be given to managers or directors.
- When all the names are up on the wall, we will need a criteria for balancing the workload so that nobody is overloaded. We need rules such as "everyone is on at least one team" or "no more than two teams for any one person" or "every team needs a different champion."

After a team has made a complete timeline and added the implementation team assignments, they need to discuss the budget that will be required to do the work. This budget can be refined later, but a starting budget will help to determine the realism of the plan.

Action planning templates

In doing this workshop, the following charts or templates may be helpful as guides for each group to work through the process. Figures 20, 21 and 22 are templates for action planning that you might want to hand out as worksheets.

1. Strategy Write in the name of the strategy.		**6. Possible Accomplishments** Brainstorm possible accomplishments for this time period that build on the advantages and acknowledge the limits.

	Advantages	Limits
Present	**2. Strengths** In implementing this strategy at this time, we have the following strengths:	**3. Weaknesses** In implementing this strategy at this time, we have the following weaknesses:
Future	**5. Benefits** in the future of implementing this strategy are:	**4. Dangers** in the future of implementing this strategy are:

7. Measurable Accomplishment
Choose an accomplishment which
• is catalytic
• is realistic
• will have a substantial impact
• will inspire commitment and action.

Taking all the above into consideration, we are committed to the following measurable accomplishment by_____ (date):

_____

_____

_____

_____

FIGURE 20. Action planning template A

A sample of the documentation of results

Figure 21 shows a typical action plan with a timeline to accomplish two strategies, with assignments and estimated budgets.

8. Strategy Write the name of the strategy on this line.	
9. Measurable Accomplishment Write the measurable accomplishment that you are committed to on this line (from step 7).	
10. Specific Actions List the specific actions needed to complete the measurable accomplishment indicated above. 11. If there are more than ten actions listed in step 10 organize them into clusters that are similar in their action focus. Each cluster should represent a distinct action step. 12. Number the actions in each cluster in the sequence that you will do them.	**13. Image/Slogan** Create a motivating image or slogan for this action campaign

FIGURE 21. Action planning template B

14. Strategy Write the name of the strategy on this line.	15.Measurable Accomplishment Copy from Step 7.
16. Action Timeline Divide the timeline into the appropriate number of time blocks and write the actions (from Step 12) that you have selected in the appropriate time block on this timeline. _____	
17. Implementing Team Who will be responsible for implementing this action plan? (at least one person in the planning group; name, not roles)	**18. Costs** Write the costs (time and money) of implementing this action plan on lines below: Money Time

FIGURE 22. Action planning template C

Action plan

Strategies	Implementing steps	6-month strategic objectives	Implementing steps	12-month strategic objectives	Implementing steps	2-year strategic objectives	Team and budget
Create a culture of appreciation for staff.	Select editorial team. Create newsletter template. Brainstorm article options. Create online submissions.	Newsletter includes key updates and accomplishments. General staff meeting every quarter.	Study all related policies. Find staff reps. Determine best recognition method. Find space options. Get space input.	Policy on Staff Recognition Program. Staff room designated.	Create budgets for functions. Generate theme options. Study on computer upgrades needed. Build in training for computer useage.	Education function per year. Two social events per year. All staff can access computer, email and Internet.	*Kyla, Greg, Sophie, Jerome $30,000
Develop systemic assessment tools for several programs across the Health Center.	Complete a tools inventory. Do best practice interviews for tools. Create an assessment schedule. Get manager suggestions for teams.	Working group formed. Assessment tool designed. Sample group chosen.	Prioritize the inventory and tools by program. Generate budgets for complete rollout. Create funding proposals.	Funding in place. Data collated by working group.	Roll out the assessment. Create support system for program help. Build in multi-year functionality. Get communication department involved.	Report written. Feedback from stakeholders. Information disseminated.	*Robert, Meredith, James, Helen $120,000

FIGURE 23. An example of action plan results for two strategies

Part D

Embedding Transformation
with Enhanced ToP Methods

12
Inspiring commitment
through supplemental tools

The spiral process is designed to assist participants in their own transformation through strategic planning. But participants can lose their courage and backtrack, especially if they do not see others participating in the transformational process. For this reason there are other ToP methods and tools that can engage participants at Stages I, II and IV that will deepen their understanding of change and make it more interesting and even fun. So far these other tools for engaging group creativity have been only briefly described. This section explores these tools further and explains how to use them.

This presentation of tools is arranged in order of stages in the overall framework of participation. These stages of the process, as covered in earlier parts of the book, include:
Stage I: Preparing for participation (page 74)
Stage II: Developing the planning context (page 75)
Stage III: Creating the strategies (page 75)
Stage IV: Implementing the plans (page 75)

The first stage of preparation involves mainly discussions with leaders to determine the suitability or intent of participatory planning, and this has been discussed in detail in Chapter 6. The following expanded discussions concern tools and methods for Stages II to IV, where the actual participatory planning takes place.

Stage II tools to increase participant clarity before visioning

In developing a planning context, the following menu of tools offers a variety of options for launching the process and engaging the participants. We will discuss each one in turn.

- Considering physical space for the sessions
- Analyzing stakeholders with the ToP framework-building tool
- Discerning trends with the social process triangles
- Discerning trends using a wave analysis
- Facilitating a ToP historical scan
- Clarifying a group's mandate
- Developing a statement of purpose
- Writing a mission statement
- Developing philosophy and values

Considering physical space for the sessions

Practitioners consider specific things when looking for a room to hold participatory strategic planning. They consider the size of the room; the walls, especially the front wall, where a large, well-lit surface is needed for consensus workshops; the table shapes, sizes, and moveability; the availability of electrical outlets and computer hook-ups. It is always wise to check the room ahead of time, create a room set-up plan, and arrange this with the venue managers.

The ideal space for a group of eighteen people is a large, well-lit, well-ventilated room of about 30 by 30 feet. It has a large empty front wall and an empty side wall, both neutrally painted, that can hold large charts with masking tape, adhesive putty, or a Sticky Wall. It is helpful if the floor is carpeted and the ceilings about ten feet high, because these acoustic features reduce the noise of small group work. Six movable tables, about 30 inches wide by five feet long, should be arranged to form an open square near the front, with a seventh table at the front for the practitioner. Five similar tables are set around the room for breakout discussions. If any presentation is to be made, an LCD projector can be aimed at a screen in the corner, or at a retractable front screen. For teleconference participants, a speaker phone connection is put in the center of the square.

Different size groups

The basic room layout will require some modification for larger groups as in Figure 24.

- *One to 20 people—Open U shape.* Participants are close enough to the wall to be able to see all the cards that are generated in a workshop, but can also see each other across the tables, for maximum interaction. The open space at the front allows the facilitator to move about inside the rectangle to pick up cards.

- *21 to 48 people—Round or rectangular tables of five or six participants each.* People are close enough to the front wall to see all the cards, and the tables provide ready-made groups for brainstorming. Unfortunately, some people cannot see others, which requires an instruction for everyone to speak loudly, and for you, as the facilitator, to speak loudly as well.
- *49 to 100 people—V-shaped lines of chairs with no tables.* Participants are close enough to the front wall to see cards, and for everyone to see the faces of at least half the other participants. This setup requires the ability to send breakout teams off to other rooms or locations for discussions. It might be necessary to use larger 8 x 11-inch cardstock rather than 5 x 8 cardstock, so people can see the cards.

You may have to be creative in the use of wall space for sticking up index cards during historical scans or consensus workshops, including:

- using moveable walls in rooms without useful wall space
- tipping a row of eight foot tables up on their ends to create a useable wall
- covering large windows with flipchart paper to make a useable wall

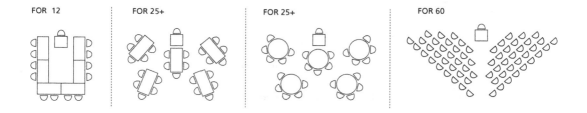

FIGURE 24. Some space setups for sessions using ToP methods

Analyzing stakeholders with the ToP framework-building tool

A **stakeholder analysis** determines who needs to be involved in the strategic planning process, and who needs to be involved in the implementation. It can be done at the very beginning of the strategic planning process, and again toward the very end for each specific measurable accomplishment. One framework can be done for each project that comes out of the strategic plan. The tool in Figure 25 gives people a visual way to reflect on what stakeholders need to be involved and how.

The **ToP framework-building tool** is a target-like diagram consisting of four concentric rings as in Figure 25. From the center moving outward, each ring represents a different level of relation-

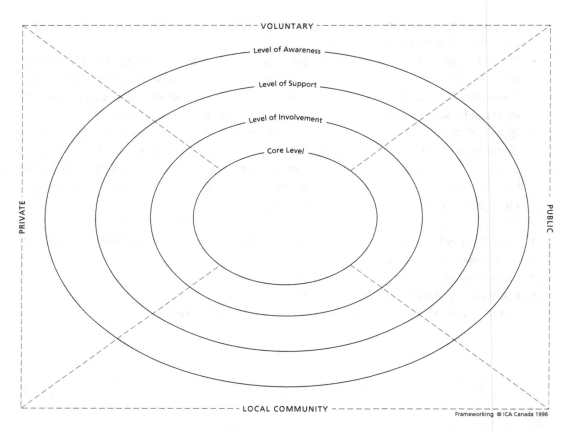

FIGURE 25. Framework-building tool

ship to the project—from "core level," to levels of "involvement," "support," or "awareness." To create the framework, the facilitator brainstorms with the steering committee about who needs to be at the "core" decision-making of the planning process, who needs to be "involved" in the planning process, who needs to "support" the process or its outcomes, and who needs to be made "aware" that planning is taking place. The sides or quadrants are generally defined in economic, political, and cultural terms—or in terms like private sector, public sector, volunteer, and local sector. Other possibilities include creating the framework according to markets, administrative areas, product specializations, or types of workers. The quadrants push the planning team to think comprehensively.

To use the tool, brainstorm responses to "Who are all the people from these different sectors who have a stake in the outcome of our strategic plan?" As they are listed, put them on the chart, discuss the roles they need to play and place them on the chart. Look for holes or gaps in the framework, and discuss who can fill those gaps. Decide what invitations or announcements will gain these people's participation.

Discerning trends with the social process triangles

Trend analysis helps participants determine the scope of the strategic planning process by revealing the external pressures that are operating on the organization and setting a context for the visioning. The social process triangles (Figure 26) can stimulate this kind of reflection.

A **ToP trend analysis workshop** is a variation of the consensus workshop method. This analysis develops a consensus on main trends in society, some of which will have an effect on the organization, and may drive its transformation. The focus question is "What trends do you see emerging as you look at the world today?" or "What are new activities you have seen people trying, because old ways aren't working anymore?"

FIGURE 26. Social process triangles for trend analysis: third level

1. Brainstorm

Brainstorm in the three main arenas of economic, political, and cultural activity. Participants share what they have seen of new developments, innovations, or attitudes. Brainstorm lots of new activities or ways of operating. Get the data on cards, and start sharing them by posting some onto the wall.

2. Cluster

Cluster the data into economic, political, and cultural clusters. If there is lots of data, cluster it further into the nine areas of the social process triangles.

3. Name

Discern groupings of data, and name a potential trend for each grouping of activities. A name will look like this: "A trend toward localized marketing," or "A trend toward cultural diversity in the workplace."

4. List positive and negative aspects

Discuss the positive and negative aspects of each trend.

Discerning trends using a wave analysis

Wave analysis is a tool for analyzing trends, and is a powerful image that helps participants understand the evolution of a trend and generate insight and dialogue. The image, shown in Figure 27, is a large ocean wave moving from the horizon toward the shore. At first, you can spot something far on the distant horizon that looks like it might become a trend. Some of these items begin to gain energy and complexity as an emerging trend. Eventually, some of these items surge into full-blown trends on the crest of a wave, clearly visible to everyone and forceful. At this point, the creativity peaks. Finally the crest passes, and what was once a powerful force moves into a trough of the wave, depleted of energy. There can even be some confusion over its value.

After a short context on the wave image, ask participants to individually brainstorm their own ideas about trends. Then they can share their ideas with another person. Have them write each idea on an index card or large post-it note, and post each on the wave image, according to where they feel that trend is on the wave. When all ideas have been posted, read out all the "emerging" ideas, asking for comments about similarities and highlighting any common ideas visually. Continue for each of the "swell," "cresting," "trough," and "undertow" trends. These trends often suggest background research that could be done using a SWOT analysis prior to visioning.

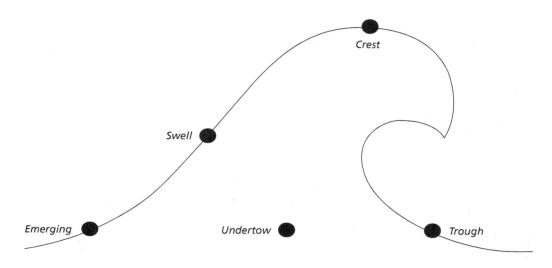

FIGURE 27. Wave trend analysis tool. *Courtesy of Larry Philbrook.*

Facilitating a ToP historical scan

An ***historical scan*** is used to help a group build a common story about its past, in preparation for visioning. The historical scan effectively provides the group with an enlarged perspective from which to examine its current situation, and therefore serves as a contextual session for the entire planning process. It can also be used for trend analysis.

Context
Explain the purpose of an historical scan, and of the wall chart for the workshop. The chart features an empty timeline that begins on the left with the year the organization began, and ends with the current year on the right. There are divisions on the timeline for each year or decade of the organization's history. And down the left side of the chart are three categories, for events in the "organization," the "field," and the "world." A typical historical scan chart will, after the workshop is finished, look something like Figure 28:

Objective level—Posting events
Ask participants first individually, and then as pairs, to write down as many events as they can think of that have had an impact on the organization, the field of endeavor, and the related world. Have them print each event on an index card with its related year. Events can include expansions, new product launches, downturns, traumatic world events, awards, staff changes, or anything else, as long as a particular year can be attributed to it. Collect these cards in bunches, by year, and read them out loud while posting them on the timeline.

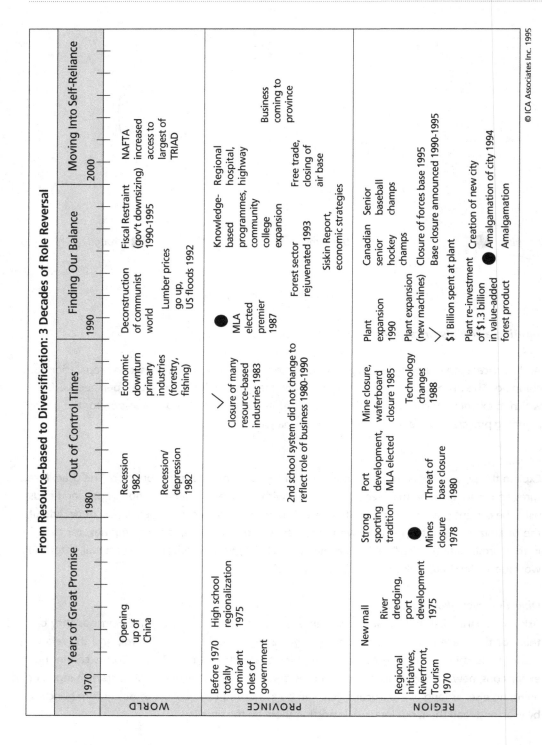

FIGURE 28. Example of a historical scan from 1998 showing regional events

Reflective level—High and low points

Invite participants to talk about any events that are high points or low points for them person-ally or for the group. No one has to agree with these evaluations of high and low, since they are purely personal perspectives. As each card is mentioned as a high or low point, mark it with an arrow pointing up or down.

Interpretive level—Turning points

Then ask participants to suggest major turning points in the organization's history. Where sev-eral people agree on a turning point, mark that shift on the timeline by drawing a vertical line upwards from that point on the timeline. As more important turning points are named, the his-tory of the organization is divided into perhaps four or five sections or periods.

Decisional level—Naming the periods

Ask the group, "As you look at the time periods delineated by the shifts we just identified, what name would you give to each period? Finish the phrase, 'This was a time of …'" Write these names on the chart above each time period, as with the title "Years of Great Promise" on the chart in Figure 26. The names can be functional, metaphoric, or highly poetic.

Extending an historical scan for trend analysis

To use the finished historical scan as a trend analysis tool, add an extension on the chart, of sev-eral feet of space to the right of the current date, with divisions for several extra years. At the far right of the chart, add an extra column for future trends. Ask participants to add as many known events as they can onto the future-forecast timeline. Shift the group's attention to trends, asking "If we look at the timeline from left to right, what trends do you see emerging in the world? In our industry? In our organization?" List these trends on the chart at the far right in the future trends column. The facilitator then probes for relevance, asking, "What are the implications of these trends for our organization?"

Clarifying a group's mandate

Mandate clarification is especially useful for multi-stakeholder groups who intend to work together over the long term and want to create a participatory strategic plan, but are unclear on their respective roles or levels of authority. This exercise helps clarify the mandates of stakeholder groups in very plain and basic terms.

The following example of a mandate discussion comes from a group of parents at a school board conference.

1. In small groups at each table briefly discuss answers to the following questions: What is our group's name, and what do we do? Why do we do it? For whom? To what end? How? What is our role and responsibility in the school district? Ask for responses from the whole group. Collect the responses on a single flipchart.

2. Validate some of the flipchart notes using some test examples.
   a. A new principal is invited to your meeting and asks, "Who are you?" What do you say?
   b. A principal from another board bumps into you at a federation meeting and asks, "So what's your group like?" What do you say?
   c. An elected school board trustee asks you in the middle of a public presentation, "Who do you represent?" You understand from the tone of voice that the question is more like, "What gives you the right to speak?" What do you say?

3. Given the words we are using to explain this, how would you string together the components of this statement on the flipchart, so that it flows better? Somebody write it neatly on a new sheet.

Developing a statement of purpose

A *statement of purpose* answers the question, "Why are we in existence?" The ToP consensus workshop method can develop a consensus on the major points of purpose, which can then be drafted by a team at a later date.

Context
The session pulls together the group's wisdom to identify the key elements of the organization's purpose and mission. The end product is a new or revised statement of purpose or mission statement. Before the session, participants might want to read Roger Harrison's *Strategies for a New Age*, for its insights into purpose, mission, and concepts of alignment and attunement. Of course, the main source of insight is the group's own wealth of experience.

Brainstorm
Read this series of questions, and ask the participants to write down their responses:
- An extra-terrestrial comes to Earth. It points to various buildings—a bus station, a power plant, and to your company or organization. It asks what your company is for. What will you tell it?
- Your son or daughter asks you why you work for your company rather than another. What is your answer?
- 1,000 years from now, archeologists find a history book from the twenty-first century. It has a

section on your company's contribution to society. What does it say?

- If you were to spend the rest of your life working with your company, and the only thing you would be remembered for is what you do there, what would you want your company to be known for?
- What would the world lose if your company quit operating tomorrow?

In teams of two or three, the participants share their answers with each other. They list the words, images, or concepts that come up more than once. Each team selects the three things that were mentioned most often or seem most important and writes them on cards.

Cluster
Ask people to pass their cards forward and cluster cards together according to similar content.

Name
Title each cluster by completing the sentence "The purpose of this organization is ..."

Resolve
Lead a short focused conversation to evaluate the data:
- Which cluster has the most cards? The least?
- Did you hear anything that surprised you?
- Which cluster would you throw away?
- Which one would you defend with your life?

Save this data bcause it provides good grist for a writing team.

Writing a mission statement

The *mission statement* of an organization brings clarity to its role and function. It answers the question, "What do we do to fulfill our purpose?" The procedures are based on the consensus workshop method, and they work for a group of 15 to 30 people. The *rational aim* is to create a consensus on the main points of a mission statement, which can then be handed over to a small writing team to draft a more polished mission statement. The *experiential aim* is to generate confidence that the writing team can express their colleagues' common will.

Brainstorm the stakeholders
Ask the participants to list all of the stakeholders in their organization, prompted by questions like these:
1. To what people, organizations, or institutions is this organization related?

2. Who has a stake in this organization?
3. Who is the organization dependent upon?
4. Who is dependent upon the organization?
5. Who would miss this organization if it ceased to exist?
6. Who would be pleased to see it succeed?

To determine the categories of stakeholders, ask, "What is the biggest category of stakeholders on your list?" As people give their answers, ask each respondent to write down their answer on a card, and send it forward, one for each category of stakeholder. These are placed in columns on the wall. After several major stakeholders are identified, the facilitator asks, "Who has a stakeholder on their list that they think no one else has thought of?" Again, these answers are shared, written on cards, and added to the list on the wall.

Cluster the stakeholders
When the group is satisfied that all the stakeholders have been named, review the categories to eliminate redundancy. For example, several types of customers might be grouped into one category called "customers."

Brainstorm the obligations
Divide the group into three or four teams of five to eight members each. Each member lists responsibilities or obligations the organization has toward each group of stakeholders. Team members then select the one or two most critical obligations toward each stakeholder. The team shares its selected items, and selects two or three per stakeholder. These are written on cards for the plenary, marking the stakeholder category on the back of each card.

Cluster the obligations
The cards are placed on the wall, under the name of the stakeholder category indicated on the back of each card.

Name the responsibilities
The facilitator reads through the responsibilities under each stakeholder category, and asks for questions of clarity from the group. Then the facilitator asks which words or phrases from the cards most aptly describe the organization's responsibility to that stakeholder. These are underlined for use by a team writing the mission statement.

Resolve
A scribe is asked to take notes on the evaluation conversation, so that insights gained can be added to the data for the writing team. Tailor the questions for this conversation roughly like this:

1. Which are the most critical relationships for our future?
2. Which relationship has the most to say about our deep purpose?
3. From all of this, what should definitely be included in our purpose and mission statement?
4. Who are the most important stakeholders for our future?

Carefully collect all the data from this workshop, including notes on the evaluation conversation, and save it for a writing team.

Developing philosophy and values

Stating the *philosophy* of an organization helps articulate the *values* it holds in carrying out its mission and fulfilling its purpose. This kind of workshop answers the question, *"How* do we do things here?"

Context
The facilitator might find it helpful to set a context by screening a 15-minute segment of the videotape, *In Search of Excellence*. This segment illustrates how Disney World goes to extremes to ensure that all of its employees understand and embody the values and philosophy of the company in everything they do. Then a focused conversation might follow the video, so participants can reflect on implications for their own organization.

If you do not use a video or reading, simply remind the participants that the organization's philosophy is a set of values that defines how things are done within an organization. This includes:
- how the organization relates to its customers
- how it relates to its product or service
- how members of the organization relate to each other
- what is valued (this may include attitudes, behavior, style of dress, etc.)
- what is discouraged

The more clearly the organization's philosophy is articulated and communicated, the better all employees are able to understand it and act accordingly.

Brainstorm
Each participant lists the values they believe the organization holds in each of the following arenas:
- Leadership
- Teamwork
- Communication

- Recognition
- Accountability
- Planning
- Problem solving
- Coordination
- Innovation
- Organization's image to project
- Things we always do
- Things we never do
- Things we look for in recruits
- Things we show to visitors
- One thing we should change
- The last thing we should ever give up
- Our story about why people come to our organization, and why they leave it

Each participant marks the five values from their entire list that they believe are most critical for the future of the organization. In teams, individuals discuss their marked values, and each team selects ten to twelve to share with the entire group. These are written on cards.

Cluster
When the whole group reconvenes, ask each team to select what it believes are the three most critical values from among its cards, and to number those three. Each team then sends forward their first card, one that represents their most important value for the organization's future. Then ask the teams to send forward any remaining important values that are not already represented by other cards on the board. As the cards are put up, similar cards are grouped into columns. The facilitator asks for any remaining cards (from among their three most important ones) that do not fit into any of the columns. These cards are sent forward and plotted on the board. Each column is then given a holding title, describing the value it represents. Ascribe a neutral graphic symbol to each column. The teams are asked to mark all cards remaining from the brainstorm with the symbol of the column into which they fit.

Name
After all the cards have been passed forward and placed in their appropriate columns, read all the cards in the first column. The group discusses and chooses a name for the value described in each column.

Resolve
A brief focused conversation helps people evaluate their work, reflecting upon the values that

have been articulated, and what they say about the organization now and in the future. Again, collect the data and save it for a writing team.

Stage III tools to strengthen commitment before action planning

Occasions were outlined in Chapter 11 on action planning, when additional tools or methods are needed between developing the strategy and planning the actions. The desired impact or type of change from participatory strategic planning may indicate which of these specialized tools will be most helpful. But it does no harm to develop the strategies first, before deciding whether or not to use these tools. Each tool empowers both strategic and tactical thinking. These "preparation for action" tools include:

- Prioritizing strategies
- Phasing the strategies
- Creating a tactical system
- Structural solutions

The table in Figure 29 outlines the situations where each tool may prove useful. Each of these tools is explained in the following pages.

Prioritizing strategies

When the implementation team is small, it may be necessary to prioritize the strategies. All strategies should be implemented, but prioritization can determine which action plans should be created first, which strategies need quick successes, and which strategies need more energy and resources. Prioritization of strategies can be done intuitively, using the focused conversation method.

For this discussion, it is assumed that a strategy workshop has been held, and that a set of six to nine strategies has been developed. The *rational aim* of the focused conversation is to determine the priorities among the strategies. The *experiential aim* is create confidence, focus, and urgency in launching the plan.

Have the group survey the chart of strategies from their strategy workshop. Then lead them in the following conversation.

Objective questions can include:
- Which of these strategies is dealing with which contradiction? How?
- Which of these strategies will have a specific effect on vision? How?
- Which strategies are clear, and which are rather vague?

Type of change or outcome	When to use the tool or method	Appropriate tools
Enhancing or changing current operating structures	If the implementation team is very small, it can be useful to prioritize strategies before doing action planning.	Prioritizing strategies (page 217)
Creating new initiatives	If the team is unfamiliar with the focus of the new initiative, and needs a process to bring a strategy online over time, phase the strategies.	Phasing strategies (page 219)
Formalizing organizational structural changes	If the team is ready to create and formalize the new structure during the strategic planning session itself, use the developing structural solutions session. If the final structure is not yet known, but will involve substantial change, phase the strategies. If the final structure is known, proceed with normal ToP action planning.	Structural solutions Phasing strategies (page 219)
Transforming whole systems	For unfamiliar strategies, the phasing strategies session can be helpful. If the large size of the organization requires implementation by a large number of people, create a tactical system. Sometimes a structural solutions session can also help.	Phasing strategies Structural solutions Creating a tactical system (page 220)
Value-based behavioral change	If the future vision is very different than the past vision, and not a simple extension of the past, create a tactical system. The careful application of ToP action planning for each main element of the tactical system helps embed participatory behaviors. If the staff is small, phase the strategies.	Creating a tactical system ToP action planning Phasing strategies

FIGURE 29. Tools between strategy and action planning

Then ask *reflective questions*, such as:
- Which strategies will be fun to work on, or not so much fun?
- Which strategies are likely to be easy, hard?

Move to *interpretive questions*:
- Which will have an immediate, motivating impact? A longer term, lasting impact?

Choose a strategy that has been mentioned a lot. Concerning the chosen strategy, ask:
- What are the implications of making this strategy a priority for implementation?
- Who has a different point of view on this?

Choose a strategy that has not been mentioned much at all. Concerning the chosen strategy, ask
- Which strategies relate to a particular department, and will happen anyway?
- Which strategies need a focus from all of us to be successful?

- What criteria can we use to decide about which strategies to focus on first?

Last, move to asking *decisional questions* such as:
- What are we saying are our top four priorities?
- Are these priorities chosen for the speed of getting something accomplished, or rather for the scope of resources or personnel needed to do them?

A different way to select priorities is multi-voting with dots. After a shortened focused conversation, you can use colored dots as visual indicators of priority. If there are eight strategies and fifteen participants, for instance, you could give each person three colored dots, and ask them to spread them across the eight strategies according to their personal sense of priority. When everyone is done, ask what the distribution indicates about priority. The group might pick the top four strategies first to start building action plans. Action plans for the other strategies can be scheduled later. It will be clear to everyone why those four strategies were selected, and every participant will be thinking about what actions they consider important. You can add interest to the analysis by handing out red dots for the strategies people are most passionate about, yellow dots for the easiest strategy to implement, green dots for the strategy that will cost the least, and blue dots for the strategy that will have the most impact.

While both the focused conversation and multi-voting are intuitive in nature, they work for getting the team to recommend a set of priorities.

The phasing of strategies

Occasionally, a strategy developed during participatory strategic planning is something so new and unknown that research has to be done on how it might be implemented. The group might need focused thinking on what goals and objectives might be relevant for that strategy. Or, the strategy might clearly require a major shift of workloads across the organization, which need to be rationalized before any implementation occurs. These are conditions in which it is useful to have a session to phase strategies.

Phasing of strategies lays out a process by which the strategies will be implemented, without knowing the actual work that will be need to be done, or the goals or strategic objectives that need to be set. The case study of the industry association (page 111) is one such example. In this situation, the strategy was to "invigorate the committee structure." But association leaders knew they couldn't plan this without more research, study, and input. In this case, a phasing exercise helped them determine "process milestones" for developing the strategy. Such process timelines can be set to cover months, quarters or, years. The result might look like Figure 30.

Strategy	First quarter process milestone	Second quarter process milestones	Third quarter process milestones	Budget	Team
A. Invigorate committee structure	Suggest a structure. Define roles and number or members for each committee.	Determine basic responsibilities. Populate committees with members.	Succession plan for each committee.	$2,000	H, I
B. Transfer workload to staff	Fill role of administrator. Create guideline for conduct. Pass on duties.	Define and fill other contract roles. Refine role of committees versus administration duties.	Re-evaluate needs for administrator. Full communication strategy in place with contract components.	$45,000	F, G

FIGURE 30. Phasing strategies

Creating a tactical system

A *tactical system* can be important when a group anticipates a major transformation within an organization, or when a very large number of people will be involved in implementing the plan. A tactical system is a methodical way of implementing a lot of strategies, while embedding behavioral change into the organization at the same time. Instead of using a SWOT analysis or a SMART screen to select measurable accomplishments for each strategy (as in action planning), a tactical system uses the ToP vision elements to help determine the focus for each strategy. The result is a highly rational system of tactics and implementation steps that not only deal with contradictions and implement strategies, but also show movement toward the vision at the same time. A tactical system names many small goals and actions over a long period of time. Since these are all generated from the strategies, each small goal and action is focused on the contradictions and the unhelpful behaviors targeted in the contradictions session.

Creating tactical systems can lead to transformation of an organization's values and behaviors. If a group chooses to create a tactical system before action planning, the focus question for developing strategies can differ slightly from when you move from strategies directly to action planning. The question is "What approaches or new directions do we need to take to deal with the contradictions and move toward our vision?" instead of "What do we need to do to...?" Brainstorming approaches and new directions leads easily to developing strategies.

Tactical System for a City Recreation Department				
Vision Elements Strategic Directions	1. Community Recreation for All	2. Facilitative Leadership	3. Integrated Outdoor Places	4. Accessible Community Facilities
Strategy A Increasing internal/external Communication	1. Establish community interest group partnerships	2. Engage research and information sharing networks	3. Develop a robust com-munication infrastructure	4. Prepare internal communication plans 5. Hire external consultant
Strategy B Soliciting broad based Input	6. Engage networks for input 7. Hold regular surveys	8. Conduct interviews with community leaders	9. Conduct formal evaluations	10. Request input from facility boards
Strategy C Partnering our resources and expertise	11. Maintain constant communi-cation	12. Identify partners 13. Activate youth	14. Sustain partners 15. Coordinate maintenance plans	16. Involve community members 17. Coordinate maintenance plans
Strategy D Training in cooperative working relationships	18. Establish a departmental training team	19. Create professional affiliations 20. Research other jurisdictions	21. Hold public forums 22. Promote community development	23. Create a partnership bulletin board 24. Conduct feedback questionnaires

FIGURE 31. Example of a tactical system for a recreation department

To create a tactical system, you populate a matrix with ideas to show how to implement each strategy and realize each component of the vision. The previously named strategies already deal with underlying obstacles, but they operate on the vision elements in different ways. In the tacti-cal systems session, each major tactic will require an action plan, with measurable accomplish-ments, timelines and assignments, as shown in Figure 31.

Whether you create a tactical system or an action plan, there is little necessity to worry about the vision or the strategies anymore. The group only has to do its tactics, and the strategies will be implemented and the vision will unfold as they should.

Designing an organizational structure

If the participants intend their strategic plan to create a *new organizational structure*, members of the leadership team may have already proposed ideas for a new structure. These ideas will require confirmation, or the group's strategic thinking might indicate modifications. Some participants might have radically different ideas on organizational structure, and others may be happy with things just as they are. These people need a safe environment to talk about potential changes and the value of the existing structures. In participatory strategic planning, this discussion occurs in the open, with everyone listening and participating, rather than behind closed doors.

Participatory strategic planning provides several built-in opportunities for safe dialogue about an organizational structure. This topic does not have to highjack the agenda, but can be done productively as side conversations during the internal environmental scan, trend analysis, historical scan, visioning, contradictions, or strategy sessions. A new structure can sometimes be proposed and resolved before action planning begins. In other cases, enough clarity emerges to allow an action plan to be developed for the new structure. Reflection on a new structure can be enabled with slight modifications to the process in each of the following workshops.

Internal environmental scan

During an *internal environmental scan*, while participants are brainstorming the internal strengths and weaknesses in their organization, some questions can focus on structure. You can ask, "What are some of the strengths of the current structure? What are some of the weaknesses?" These questions do not presuppose a specific answer, but they safely open the door to discussion in a way that anyone can answer. The scan also safely reveals different viewpoints about the current structure. For example, someone might say that the director of a department is close to retirement, and no one is ready to fill that role, so a structural change may be needed. For some participants, such discussions may be their first indication that structural changes are under consideration.

Trend analysis

During **trend analysis**, ask "What are external trends or forces that have an effect on how we structure ourselves? Which of these forces will be operative for a long time, and which are short-term? What are other positive and negative aspects of these trends and forces?" People might respond, for example, by noting shifts in technology which will render a product line or department non-viable.

Historical scan

While brainstorming events in the history of their organization, the participants can specify when different departments or committees were formed, and put these events on the timeline. You can ask about accomplishments or victories in various departments. This type of question releases people to discuss the high or low points in the history of various departments or committees. It might allow everyone to appreciate the way things have been, as a precursor to looking at how they need to change. An *historical scan conversation* can bring closure to reflection on a disintegrating or superfluous structure, and open the door for discussion of something new. When discussing what might occur over the next few years, participants might mention changes in organizational structure. In the context of the scan conversation, such suggestions will appear to build on past efforts. The participants will have heard about the highs and lows associated with the current structure, so be ready to consider where constructive change is needed.

Visioning

In response to the focus question ("What do we want to see in place for this organization in three to five years?"), some ideas might emerge that reflect components of a new structure. Cards might include dreams of "a new research department," a "highly productive sales wing," or a "new nursing division." These are intuitions about the desired future, and a direct question about structure or funding need not be asked or answered at this point. If certain participants push for a conversation about a new structure, you can say that the strategic directions part of the planning process deals with structure directly. If such cards come up more than once, ask someone to describe the new structure they see in their personal vision. The purpose of this is only to seed people's imaginations. Simply note down these comments about a new structure, within the context of the other visions for the future.

Contradictions

The topic of a new organizational change may start to become very real during the contradictions workshop. At each level of discernment, in response to the focus question of "What is blocking us from moving toward our vision?" comments related to the present structure may appear. For example:

Irritation ....I get upset when I can't get any support from my department.
Blame.............................The leadership doesn't know what is happening in the organization.
Lack of ....There is a lack of communication between departments.
Issues.............................We have specific organizational issues.
Blocks............................The current structure is causing the following problems.

Underlying blocks........These two departments are working at cross-purposes.

Contradiction ....Departmental competition undermines our important research focus.

The potential need for an organizational change may be determined by structural problems that have been experienced in the past. But those structural obstacles are not the only ones on the table for discussion, so this approach keeps one topic from highjacking all the discussion. Simply by acknowledging these concerns, without prescribing any solution, everyone grows aware that something needs to be done, if the practical vision is to be unblocked. There are occasions when a structural change becomes an obvious necessity during a contradictions workshop.

Strategy

The strategies workshop is the time for the group to propose direct ideas about a new organizational structure. The focus question for the strategies workshop is "What do we need to do to deal with the blocks and move toward our vision?" If the old structure has not been named as an underlying block, a few structure-related ideas might still come forward, like "open a new research division," or "give research its own budget and mandate." If, on the other hand, the old structure is an actual underlying block or contradiction, then you can ask for specific suggestions on how the new structure needs to change. The various cards and ideas participants produce may suggest different alternatives for structure, or a general agreement might emerge on the direction of the new structure. The topic is now fully on the table, and strategies might emerge such as "reorganizing for research autonomy." Now that a restructuring strategy is on the table, it might be dealt with in the action planning session by a team whose members will now have a very good context for their work.

As an alternative, the whole group might do more work to create an actual structural scenario, before going on to the action planning stage. Record brainstorm items on a flipchart, in response to the question "What are the key values we need to hold when considering a new structure?" This kind of open-ended and indirect question allows people to talk about the important organizational insights in a way that puts people at ease. Another question to consider is "What do we want to be able to accomplish with a new structure?"

At this point, three small groups can be convened for a short session on the question "What is a workable scenario for the new structure?" Each group can flesh out a scenario within about an hour. After each team's short report, facilitate a reflective conversation.

- What are the most important values held by each scenario?
- What is unique or different about the scenarios?
- What are the similarities between the three scenarios?

Ask a small subgroup to pull all the participants' insights together, and put flesh onto the bones for a proposed structure.

When the process moves on to action planning, the crystallization and consolidation of the proposed structure might become one of the measurable accomplishments. The implementing actions will include analysis of risks and other factors before rolling out the new structure.

Stage IV tools to empower participants for implementation

With the ToP approach there is a definite move to less hierarchical structures and decision making, and with it, a greater desire for maximizing participation and ownership.
—*Penny McDaniel, ToP practitioner, Denver, Colorado*

A number of additional participatory tools can strengthen the motivation and context. Some of these tools are very appropriate to use just after the action planning stage. They are also useful earlier in the process, just after strategy development in Stage III, or just after developing mission, purpose, or philosophy in Stage II. These tools empower the implementation of the plan, and will remain in participants' memories long after the planning session is over.

Creating a song, symbol, and story

Song, symbol, and story are expressions of a group's culture, which can convey its shared purpose and the sense of what it means to "belong."

A workshop to create a song, symbol, and story can be held after an especially expressive historical scan, after an illuminating visioning session, just after strategy development, or at the same time as action planning. Most groups will find it helpful to create a symbol to help create momentum for new initiatives. Community, not-for-profit, and civil society groups may like a song and story as well. Government and private sector groups may find only a symbol workshop relevant, unless they show an interest in the high motivation and empowerment value of song and story.

Writing a song

Surprisingly, this type of song can be written in about 20 minutes, and requires no formal musical training or ability. Writing songs comes naturally during community development planning, and is energizing during any transformational planning. It is best done by a small group of three or four uninhibited people, who have a private place to work during the planning session. These are the basic instructions for a song-writing team:

1. Pull descriptive or visual words from the vision title and brainstorm, or from the historical scan titles. Positive images and metaphors are especially powerful.
2. Select the mood that best suits the group and the song. Clap out some beats or a tempo that suits that mood.
3. Match some of the words or phrases with particular beats.
4. Try out some well-known simple tunes that hold the beat. Popular or classic are best.
5. Develop phrases that fit the refrain.
6. Write the phrases so they fit the melody.
7. Practice it once as a team.
8. Print the words on a flipchart.
9. Sing it once in front of the group. Then get the whole group to sing it together.

Here is an example of a song that was written in 15 minutes by participants at a community meeting after the visioning.

Kingston Galloway (KGO) Song
To the tune of *Edelweiss*

KGO, KGO
Strong, natural, beautiful.
Celebrate, celebrate
Our vibrant community.

Safe and prosperous we are,
A tapestry of culture.
KGO, KGO
Let's go forward together.

Writing a story

Stories have the capacity to empower participants, validate their experience, and project a new future. Writing a short metaphoric story of the group's journey can bring closure, mirror the participants' current experience, and hold out realistic promise.

A story can be as short as three sentences, one each for the past, present, and future, or it can be several paragraphs long. A good story can combine highlights of the past from an historical scan, a present challenge from elements of an obstacles brainstorm, and empowering images of the future from the vision workshop. Any three or four people, not just writers, can write the story in

20 minutes. The story can use facts picked from workshop data, or avoid facts altogether and use only metaphor and allegory, beginning with "Once upon a time … " A story catalyzes motivation and creativity through its very simplicity. It can be a context for future discussion.

Creating a symbol

A good visual symbol can express ownership, belonging, and meaning for any initiative or team. It can project recognition for marketing and branding. A symbol created during participatory strategic planning might be used for the duration of implementation, to remind people of their decision. Or it might become an established image that outlasts the planning.

Visual symbols are conceived differently from verbal thoughts. An image is created through recognition of associations, experiences, or feelings that directly confer meaning. The best way to generate symbols is by reflection on metaphors that have surfaced during the planning, and the associations these have for individuals. The best times to create symbols are during the long-range practical vision workshop or during the action planning.

During the naming stage of a vision workshop, symbols can be created to capture the vision elements graphically. Ask the participants in each small vision-naming group:
1. to come up with a name for their cluster or column of cards
2. to draw a graphic or picture that represents the vision element or the mood of the vision element.

Give the groups two cards, one for the title and one for the graphic image. When these are all posted on the wall above the columns of cards, there might be eight titles with eight images immediately above them. During the resolve stage of the workshop, you can ask participants to comment on which of the graphics captures the spirit or energy of the vision best, and why. After this conversation, you can assign a small group of two or three people to select one image, or generate a new image that best represents the entire vision. Sometimes the elements of the vision can be "mapped" onto various parts of the graphic in a way that makes the vision elements very memorable. Sometimes the graphic stands on its own, and captures the spirit of the vision. Figure 32 is a symbol from one workshop that holds together the various elements of the group's vision.

Another good time to generate symbols is during action planning, specifically after the brainstorming of activities that will implement a measurable accomplishment. Each team that develops an action plan can create a symbol to go along with its plan (see page 198).

Leading a song, symbol, story workshop

The *song, story, and symbol workshop* can be used at the end of a session on purpose, mission or philosophy, or at the end of a ToP strategic planning process to communicate the purpose, mission and philosophy to all members of the organization. Here are specific steps to follow for this workshop.

Context
The task of this workshop is to create a song, a story, and a symbol that communicate the self-understanding (mission and philosophy) of the organization both to its members and to the world. Music, art, and storytelling are especially effective media for communicating messages. After sharing some ideas, break into three teams to create a song, story, and symbol.

Brainstorm
Previous sessions of the planning have already done much of the brainstorming for song, symbol, or story ideas. The mandate, purpose, mission, and philosophy sessions, the historical scan, and the vision workshop all provide data and images that can be used as grist to create the song, story, and symbol. A focused conversation on the data from previous sessions might refresh the group's memory of these elements. The conversation might include questions like these:
- As you listened to the mission and value statements being read, what kind of music came to your mind? If you were going to read the statements with music in the background, what tunes or genre of music would seem appropriate?
- What historical epics, movements, figures, or myths come to your mind as you listened to the statements or as you worked in your teams?
- What graphic images did you see as you worked on developing those statements, such as geometric designs, patterns, or images of animals or nature? What were some of those images?
- What pop songs came to mind, or images or slogans from popular culture?

Creative Process
Break the group into teams, generally by self-selection, to work on each product (song, story, and symbol), with one person from each team assigned to take notes on their conversation. The teams then gather and review input that seems most appropriate for their particular task.

The song team considers the types of music that people suggested. Sometimes, song titles or phrases have come up in the process of writing statements, and these can also be considered as possible tunes. The team will also consider the content and style of the song lyrics. They may choose to simply express the organization's mission and philosophy. Or they may write something of the company's past and future in a form something like a ballad. By considering the tune and the lyrics together, the group usually arrives at a consensus that seems to do justice to both.

The story team takes into consideration any previous comments that refer to mythological or historical events and figures. These can provide images, themes, or frameworks around which to write the organization's story. The team may also review the historical scan in some detail, to collect vignettes from the organization's history. They decide on the style of their story (e.g. legend, science fiction, documentary, etc.), the central theme, and characters. Then they set to writing one to several paragraphs.

The symbol team reviews comments about graphic or visual images from the previous conversation, or from any earlier working sessions. They may choose to do a visualization exercise, as one member reads the mission and philosophy statements. It is perfectly legitimate to send "spies" to the song and story groups, to find out if any of their ideas suggest images that might become part of the symbol. Once several images have been suggested, the team begins to get an intuitive sense of which ones have the most power. Individuals begin to sketch their ideas and share them. Several images can be incorporated into one symbol, or they might merge together to form a new image altogether.

Gracious TSVC Style

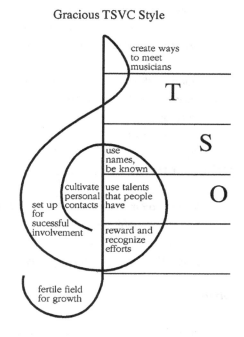

FIGURE 32. Symbol created by orchestra volunteers to express their vision

Consensus

The consensus process here is highly intuitive. Each team is engaging in cooperative art rather than planning for action. The teams may be formed voluntarily or by assignment. In either case, the individuals discover new talents in themselves and in their colleagues. The teams have fun, create meaning, and further enhance their team spirit.

Report

When each team has finished, the total group gathers, and each team presents its art form. The song team sings the song and then invites the rest of the group to join in. The story team reads the story, and may even act it out if appropriate. The symbol team presents the symbol with as much artistic flair as they can muster with any explanation that is necessary.

After the presentations, lead a focused conversation to help the group to process the art forms, so that each member identifies with all of them, not just the one they helped to create. There is typically much enthusiasm and high spirit in this plenary. Because these art forms are built from the group's experience over the past few days, the participants are usually excited to see their expenditure captured in these creative expressions.

As planning draws to a conclusion, questions might begin to emerge: "How do we communicate our work to all the members of the organization so that they, too, can share in the ownership of this mission, philosophy, and plan?" In many cases the song, story and symbol become a part of that communication.

Other methods to consider

Mixing ToP methods with others methods such as Appreciative Inquiry dialogue, Open Space, and World Café, seems to respond most honestly and creatively with more openness, flexibility and self-organization.
—Gail West, ToP practitioner, Taipei, Taiwan

Open Space

Some ToP practitioners use **Open Space technologies**, developed by Harrison Owen, as another way to involve large groups in implementation. An Open Space session is especially useful after strategies have been determined, or after a tactical system has been created. Sophisticated Open Space practitioners spend a lot of time up front working with a client to ensure that the conditions are in place for people to be open about what they want to work on during the Open Space session. Time might be spent with the client to ensure that support systems are in place for any tactics or measurable accomplishments that might arise.

Open Space participants should already be briefed about the vision, obstacles, and strategic directions. People who already know what the strategies are and why they were created will already be highly motivated to get into the tactical system phase, or action planning phase. This familiarity with the overall direction ensures that the Open Space process—of allowing people to pick any of the strategies that they want to, or create some new related strategy, or to "vote with their feet"—is very likely to produce a set of tactics or measurable accomplishments that are closely related to the strategies.

If an Open Space session is held too soon after a visioning workshop, the tendency will be for participants to organize around vision areas or vision elements, and try to implement them. This can short-change the process, because trying to implement a vision directly is a risky venture which may lead to great frustration if the underlying systemic obstacles have not yet been articulated. Use of Open Space sessions should wait until general strategies have been outlined.

ToP marketplace

The **ToP marketplace method** involves writing each of the strategies on a flipchart, and placing these on walls around the room so that participants can write comments on any strategy. This can speed up action planning, because it can get relevant input on many strategies quickly. It is helpful to put additional headers on each flipchart, such as "Possible Goals for this Strategy," or to use a "SWOT" grid on the bottom of the flipchart. There are other versions of this, including "Walkabout," which places groups of people at each flipchart, and then gives them time limits as they move sequentially to each flipchart around the room.

Appreciative Inquiry

Appreciative Inquiry, developed by David L. Cooperrider and Suresh Srivastva, can help just before the visioning stage of participatory strategic planning, to build on any previous discussions. The emphasis of Appreciative Inquiry is on building on what works. It allows people to focus on what they appreciate in their organization and develop a powerful story, which helps initiate the process of visioning. The visioning resembles the "discover" or "dream" steps of Appreciative Inquiry. And ToP methods can build on the appreciative focus through affirming all insights, without judging what is "good" or "bad."

13
Variations of the spiral process for different groups and purposes

The spiral process is successful in different size groups

Small groups of five to ten people can create participatory strategic plans, but it is necessary to determine if they all have the same reasons for wanting the plan, and how long they have known and worked with each other. If they are new to each other, the planning may perform a team building function. Visioning will play a key role, and an historical scan will help the participants share what they know about a topic. If the participants all know each other very well an historical scan plays the role of exposing any unfinished business that needs closure. They might never have openly discussed and resolved such issues before, so the contradictions workshop will be important.

For a small group, the long-range vision needs to be pushed for practicality, so that the results are as clear and do-able as possible within their time horizon. Ask "How will we know when this is achieved, and what will it actually look like in five years? Be specific."

A small group will not have a lot of data about internal contradictions, and it might be necessary to have some interviews prior to the contradictions workshop, to see if there is anything that is "raw" between people, or if there is any topic that must be broached carefully. Clarify which relationships among the participants are functional or dysfunctional, and ask what is going on there.

When working on strategies with a small group, ask individuals to unpack their language and make sure that everything is clearly spelled out for the others. People might start using buzz words, perhaps to impress each other, but such terms can means totally different things to different people around the table. Do not hesitate to push for clarity of meaning and direction. During the naming of a strategy, keep asking, "Have you tried something like this before? What happened? How can we name this strategy so that it clearly indicates the breakthrough we want to have happen this time?"

For a small group, the target dates for measureable accomplishments and launch activities can have big implications for each individual. Make sure that tactics and implementation steps have names on them, so it is clear who is responsible, what is involved, and how each person's tasks affect the other participants.

One of the main difficulties in working with small groups is the smaller pool of ideas to draw from, and the perception among some that they already know what the other person will say. You might imagine a group of five, in which two people have authority, and two are quiet people who don't talk much. If people think they know the others too well, it can limit their imagination and capacity. The facilitator must constantly draw out each individual. It will be important to take more time in individual brainstorming, making sure that everyone writes their ideas down so that there are longer lists of ideas to draw from. You might also need to do some "seeding" of brainstorm ideas, or some creativity exercises, so that new things come up that no one has heard before. During discussions it might be necessary to add some innovation to break up expected patterns, so that the same person does not always speak first, followed by the same second person, etc. Basing the order of people speaking on their month of birth could work once or twice. Writing out answers in full and reading them out will also work a couple of times. Getting people to discuss topics in pairs and report to the group, or asking whoever is wearing a certain color to report first can work once or twice. Get people to turn their answers into pictures. Change seats and seating arrangements. You can create lots of little ways to inject some interest and fun into the dialogue and enable people to get out of familiar patterns and surprise each other.

Large groups

The larger the group is, the more it depends on the practitioner to provide the logic, structure, and the discipline for moving ahead. The **participation assessment tool** (shown on page 262) can be used for preparatory discussions with a small leadership team, to help understand the assumptions and requirements of the group. The leadership team can check process recommendations and discuss pros and cons of large group participation with each step of the process. This will answer, for instance, how big the group should be for an historical scan, how many people should be involved in the visioning, and other such questions.

Project management is a useful skill for a facilitator, since there will be many meetings with different groups within the organization which must be tracked and followed up in preparing participants with notes about dates, times, locations, purposes, and agendas. A planning team will need regular meetings, and the organization's leadership team will also want an occasional session to check progress. When very large groups are involved, you might find it helpful to create an action plan for the strategic planning process itself.

With large groups there may be face-to-face gatherings for visioning, contradictions, and strategy sessions, but people can also be involved remotely by requesting brainstorm data in advance through email, online jams, or surveys. The resulting data has to be collected and put into forms that participants can use in the larger sessions, perhaps on index cards, or just lists to read from.

Generating enough raw data is not the same problem for large groups as for small groups. Logistical considerations, on the other hand, are of paramount importance, including space, walls, tables, seating arrangements, lighting, visibility, and audibility. Big sessions need small breakout spaces for subgroups, and plenary meetings for reporting and building consensus. Tables and chairs must be movable, so that the small discussion groups can be created seamlessly. Large plenary space must be arranged so that everyone can easily see the wall charts and data posted there and hear each other. It may be necessary to assign seating for each session. Otherwise, participants simply gravitate to the people they like or are most comfortable with, and old patterns of discussion will occur.

For large groups you can use LCD screens to make notes visible, or print very large on 8.5 by 11-inch cards for workshops. Use large paper templates on the walls near every discussion table, so that each group can work together on a wall during SWOT analyses, historical scans, framework analysis, trend sessions, action planning, and timelines. For instance, six large wave analysis templates around a big room, with six groups of 15 people working on each template, generates more insight and value than one big one on an LCD projector, with data coming from 90 people. In large group participatory planning, the practitioner has to ask "For which particular stages will small group discussion be vital, and how will it be fed into the large group reporting and plenary processes?"

Very large groups

For very large groups, such as 300 people, a practitioner could do 12 local focus groups of 25 people, in which each group goes through the same process of vision, obstacles, and strategies, in sessions lasting three to five hours. When the consensus workshop method is used, the outcome will perhaps be nine vision title cards, seven underlying obstacle title cards, and eight strategy title cards for each focus group. A representative "plenary" group can take the 108 vision cards, 84 obstacle cards, and 96 strategy cards to cluster and name and create a system-wide consensus. All of the hundreds of bits of individual input can be coded to give a quantitative view of the results and traceability to the system-wide consensus.

Boards

Boards of directors sometimes want to do participatory strategic planning themselves, to determine their own workplan, though sometimes they want to hand things off to the staff for implementation.

When an action-oriented board does its own participatory strategic planning, it is probably trying to gel as a team. Board members want to get some clarity on how they should operate and do some big-picture thinking. They may want to develop a consensus on how to play their oversight and governance role. Governance-oriented boards will want their staff to do some preliminary thinking in specific areas to feed into their planning process. If the board is doing participatory planning that will be implemented by staff, it will want the very best input from the staff and perhaps from other stakeholders. For this input to be most useful for a governance-oriented board, the data from staff should not come as "recommendations" or as "options," but as raw information which the board analyzes for itself. The raw information does not need to be in-depth and voluminous, but it does need to cover many perspectives.

For sessions with a board, the most relevant process includes an historical scan, a mission discussion, and then vision, contradictions and strategy workshops. The action planning will probably involve short-term goals, to be handled by standing or ad-hoc committees. The surroundings should be quiet and comfortable, with no intrusions, a hollow square table arrangement with lots of wall space up front and down one side, and with a few discussion tables around the room for groups of about three people. The process is straightforward. All brainstorming is done individually, followed by small groups of two or three, generating 40 or 50 data cards each time. Different colors of cards can be used for each workshop. Most board members are very interested in external trends, mission, values, and vision, but often less interested in contradictions, strategy, and action plans, unless an organizational restructuring is recommended.

The board members may well ask the staff to do the later stages of the planning process. However, a board is well advised to pay attention to contradictions indicated by staff, because these can point to governance problems between staff and executive that only a board can deal with. Boards also have a great interest in measurable accomplishments and in indicators of success, which are parts of action planning.

The staff can create short briefing notes after each session, to bring the board up to date on what is happening in the planning process. The CEO can show these briefing notes to the board, to see if they have any questions before a session starts. Many board members want only a high-level view.

Departmental and joint system-wide staff planning

Several departments within an organizational system can each do their own participatory strategic planning, involving the department's managers and some or all of its staff. In this case, each department creates its own long-range practical vision, which may or may not be set within the context of a larger company vision. The company vision, if there is one, may be broad and somewhat vague, with some specific references to a department's role or mandate. After practical visioning of its own desired future, a department will be much clearer about its role in relation to the company vision. Each department analyzes its own set of contradictions: some are internal to the department, and some exist at the larger system-wide level. Each department has its own set of strategies: again, some relate to its own operation, and others tie in to the larger system. Each department has its own set of measurable accomplishments and implementation timelines. Some goals may be given to the department as mandates from the larger system, while others are derived from its own participatory strategic planning.

All the departments can get together to create a system-wide participatory strategic plan, generally involving the manager and supervisor level and above, with some staff representatives. The visioning will be very straightforward, and the combined long-range practical vision will set priorities among certain elements of the overall vision. The contradictions will be very instructive, because each department encounters some underlying obstacles that are external to themselves, which they have no control over. When the departments view the underlying obstacles together, a new constellation of contradictions will appear with system-wide implications. New strategies developed at the system-wide level can resolve some of those obstacles, and the strategies will have components within each of the departments. Some strategies may be handed to particular departments to work on, but most organization-level strategies will cut across departments.

During the system-wide planning, some of the measurable accomplishments from individual departments drop away and are no longer relevant. New measurable accomplishments at the system-wide level will be created: these will need implementation plans at the departmental and system level. The practitioner will notice that the sum of all the workloads for a system-wide participatory strategic plan will be the same or less than the sum of the workload of all of the individual departmental plans done earlier. This is because the strategies at the joint enterprise level are more leveraged and effective, even though parts of each strategy may need departmental implementation.

Participatory planning at the enterprise level or joint departmental staff level has the effect of increasing horizontal and vertical communication throughout the company. Implementation teams within a department already have the authority to act. However, at the enterprise-level, implementation teams need to work across departmental lines, and these teams must also be empowered to act. Staff members on those teams need permission to coordinate with people, including managers, in the other departments. Planning in an IT department was done in this way (see page 109).

The spiral process applies to more than strategic planning

The spiral process can be applied to many situations other than traditional planning. Since the thought process is a natural one for planning, it is useful in any situation where clients want to see progress made, even if planning would not normally be considered. Here are some examples of such applications.

Conferences

Conferences can benefit from the spiral process by designing sessions which take participants through several phases. The key is to engage participants in visionary, contradictional, strategic, and tactical thinking even though they are not doing it in a planning mode. By the end of the conference, participants will feel as if they have shared deeply at several levels, and will be motivated in their own work.

To encourage visionary thinking, keynote presenters can present motivating images of what the future might hold for the topic, field, or region. A series of simultaneous sessions can be held on several dimensions of the future. The intention is to engage the participants in visionary thinking for the long-range future. In addition, a wall can be set up at the back of the conference hall on which participants write what they want to see five years into the future, posting their notes on colorful 8 x 11 card stock. These can eventually become data in a long-range practical vision brainstorm.

To engage participants in contradictional thinking, a panel discussion can explore current issues and problems faced by practitioners of the field. Alternatively, a series of concurrent sessions could be held on current issues, or the present situation. These sessions begin to set up a dialogue in the minds of participants about how the current reality differs from the desired future. While this process does not guarantee contradictional thinking, it sets up the conditions necessary for participants to do the thinking on their own.

Engaging in strategic thinking can be done through concurrent sessions or panel discussions on best practices, or on important approaches toward the future. Participants might be invited to share their own best practices and provide input on approaches to issues that many are interested in.

Through sessions like these, the thought process of each individual participant goes through a chronological thinking process of vision, contradictions, and strategies. Even though this is not a formal planning process, the conclusions and discussions at the "approaches" session will tend to be much more strategic than if the conference started with discussions on "approaches."

Conference organizers can engage participants in tactical thinking through sessions on partnerships with allied professions, through stakeholder brainstorming, or by having presentations on demonstration or pilot projects that are on a leading edge of change. Presentations on, or discussions about, best practices can also stimulate tactical thinking.

Public consultation

Public consultation is often a simple input or advice session on a given topic, which usually does not follow the logic model of the spiral process. A presenter gives some facts and some alternatives, and then participants are asked to react and give comments. The ideas given by participants usually differ little from the ideas they would give if they filled out a simple survey individually. Participants often react to other participants' reactions, and polarizations can occur, with little real thoughtfulness. The consultation is generally designed to inform people or persuade them toward a specific point of view. In most cases, the consultation's invitation list determines its outcome. Often the organizers of public consultations know this, and sometimes they take advantage of it.

There are other ways to structure public consultations, so that participants delve more deeply into the topic and undergo a transition in their own thinking during the consultation itself. By applying the spiral process to the topic and allowing open discussions at each stage of the spiral process, people come to really understand and learn from other people's points of view. This approach avoids the rabid polarization that is commonly found in public consultations, and encourages thoughtful consideration of many options. Of course, this approach only works when the client is actually looking for input on strategies.

A public consultation session using the spiral process can be done many ways. Here is one version:
1. *Welcome.* Agenda and short presentation on the topic, with factual handouts. (25 minutes)
2. *Vision brainstorm.* A quick brainstorm of 12 to 20 comments from the floor, addressing the question "What do you want to see in place in the long-range future?" Write these vision items on the front wall for all to see. A show of hands can reveal which ones are shared by

a lot of people. Do not invite debate over these items; there is no need for discussion at this point in the process. Most people want their own good ideas included. (20 minutes)

3. *Issue discussion at tables.* Participants form discussion groups to brainstorm issues and blockages, going around their table once. The facilitator then directs all participants to think on their own, write their own most important block on a card, and bring it up to post it on the front wall. This block might be one they arrived with, or one they heard in the discussion. (20 minutes)

4. *Idea clustering.* Post ideas on the front wall and cluster them quickly and intuitively, labeling them with large titles to identify the issue clusters. The facilitator guides this process with participant input from the floor. Do not push for contradictions; naming issues or obstacles is good enough. (20 minutes)

5. *Instructions and a break.* During a 15-minute break, make charts for each of the clusters of issues, and put one up near each table around the room. When the participants return from the break, they select the table dealing with the issue or topic of their choice. Also during the break, transfer the underlying obstacles to flipcharts, with one block on each flipchart, and one flipchart per discussion table. The flipchart has a large circle on it with the underlying obstacle written in the center, and six arrows around the circle pointing toward the circle. (15 minutes)

6. *Strategy discussion at tables.* Participants select their table of choice (maximum of eight people per table), and brainstorm approaches for dealing with the underlying obstacles, as the facilitator calls out instructions from the front of the room. They brainstorm their ideas directly onto the arrows. When they have six, they transfer their ideas onto cards, and bring them to the front wall. The front wall chart has been cleared of the obstacle brainstorm data, but still has the underlying obstacle title cards. Each group sticks its cards under the title for its own underlying obstacle. (30 minutes)

7. *Plenary discussion on strategies.* Ask participants to call out cards with similar actions on them. Move these quickly to form clusters, which are named as strategies or approaches. (20 minutes)

8. *Closing.* Ask participants to fill in a poll, in which they suggest which visions, issues, and actions they consider most important. They drop the poll forms in a box at the back, giving their names on the forms if they wish. Also, ask people to come and sign up to get involved in one strategy if they want, by leaving their names on the front wall.

Public consultations can quickly gather a large amount of data on vision, issues, and strategies from the workshops and closing polls, and the participants can assist in the synthesis of ideas. The synthesis of results is quantifiable, which is helpful to most government officials. The case study on regional economic development was done using this format (see page 103).

Personal change

The spiral process is not only for group process. It is also a powerful tool for transformation during periods of self-examination, reflection, and personal change. At the most general level, an individual might reflect on the questions in Figure 33 or at a more specific level, tackle questions such as "What kind of job do I really want?"

I was asked to do a participatory strategic plan to help a woman. She was strong-minded in her desire for a good environment for her son to develop in, and had strong belief in the two-parent family. In the contradictions session, she talked about her alcoholic husband and her thoughts about divorce. She talked about the great difficulty she experienced in the choice between giving her son a non-abusive environment to be brought up in, and having the two-parent environment which she strongly believed in. She had a backup plan for her life without her husband, but had not seriously considered it, always hoping the situation would change. As she talked about how her husband controlled her by making her seem as if she was a rebel against her own strongly held belief in a two-parent family, the true reality of the situation became clear and she began to recognize that her husband's control over her extended to their son, stifling his development as well. Where she had been blocked before, she now saw enough to enable her to make a firm decision and move on.
—Richard West, ToP practitioner, Taipei, Taiwan

Vision	Contradiction	Strategies	Tactics
What do I want to see happen in my own life, practically? What is that great promise that I want to fulfill?	What is blocking me from realizing that hope or dream? What is it about myself that is inhibiting my own success?	What are some new directions I can move in to deal with the obstacles and realize my hopes? What new approaches will I take?	What actions must I take in order to activate the strategies? What do I need to do today and every day?

FIGURE 33. Personal strategic planning

The spiral process can give reliable quantifiable data

During strategic planning for a city council, certain council members were predisposed not to like whatever plan was finally devised, for their own political reasons. The concrete way that they objected to the results of the strategic plan was to say, "During the public consultation we didn't get the right people to the table. If we had had other people at the public consultation we would have had different results."

On the surface this argument appears to be reasonable. For example, if a facilitator asks a group of seniors, "What you want to see in place in five years?" you'll get a very different answer than if you ask the same question to a group of parents with small kids, and a very different answer again if you ask a group of youth.

Look deeper, however, and you'll find that although the groups have different visions, the strategies that emerge will be similar because the contradictions they are dealing with are similar. The strategic planning process, and the three levels of thinking behind it, trigger a much deeper chain of thinking than a simple wish list. So, although three different groups of people might want three different sets of things, when they look at the underlying obstacles, they will likely come to a similar analysis. And when they develop strategies, their strategies are very likely to be similar. So in some cases it doesn't matter that much which individuals actually participate in the public consultation, because the strategies that will be developed from it will be similar. It is always wise, however, to have a broad base of participation, and even to get the perspectives of the opposition, which makes the discussion richer and more real.

This was fully confirmed for me, when, at the end of a planning process, councilors complained that only certain types of participants had shown up. The councilors decided to hire a professional polling firm to poll the public on the results of the strategy. The professional pollsters held a random sample telephone survey of about 500 people, which gives fairly accurate results. When the poll was done, the strategies that had been developed during the public consultation were confirmed by the poll to be the most important priority strategies. The councilors were surprised, but the survey had confirmed the validity of the strategic plan, which was then passed unanimously by the city council.

14
Examples of successful transformational strategy

A participatory strategic planning with the leaders in a midsized eastern Iowa city occurred with no great difference from many other community plans we had done, no remarkable happenings. The real learning for us came when we returned several months later for a follow-up session and re-maneuvering. One person shared this insight: "One great thing about the participatory strategic planning was the document. We have evidence that we have agreed and that these things are important to deal with. It removed the opposition from those who used to say that nothing could happen because there wasn't any consensus or agreement."
—Richard West, ToP practitioner, Taipei, Taiwan

The quality of documentation of a ToP participatory strategic plan can vary widely, depending on the intended distribution of the plan and the budget of the client. Writers, editors, and graphic designers can create documents that are beautiful and readable. If widely distributed, these can have a positive impact. They can even create websites or intranet sites for easy access.

This chapter, however, shows examples of basic documentation of the raw material from planning sessions, which can be given back to the participants for their review before any rewriting, editing, or graphic design, or before any fancier documentation is produced. A final document sent to a client might be eight to thirty pages in length, but the key insight is generally contained in the consensus generated during the spiral process. These samples reveal the clarity that can be created from the spiral process and demonstrate the insight in the results that are often achieved. We have included samples of historical scans, visioning, contradiction analysis, strategies, phased strategies, structural changes, and action plans. The samples are drawn from our case studies of transformational strategy: the professional association, the regional economic development committee, the area hospital, the international NGO, and the industry association (see page 101). The specifics have been generalized for illustrative purposes only.

Key documentation from the professional association plan

This sample documentation comes from ToP participatory strategic planning with the national board of a professional organization representing 36,000 members. Within three years the board completed almost all of its measurable accomplishments, and did another cycle of ToP strategic planning (Figure 34).

Long-range practical vision of a professional association		
Recognized practice	**Influential voice**	**Valued organization**
Strong curriculum as a vital piece of education in the field	A recognized influential voice that impacts the practice, systems, and outcomes	Appropriately resourced committee structure with an executive director
	Identifiable leadership at all levels	
A strong viable, credible, certification program with 50% of practitioners certified	Viable, effective partnerships for mutual benefit	Critical mass of active connected members who see value in the organization

FIGURE 34. Long-range practical vision of a professional association

Vision sentences

These brief statements of their three-part vision were fleshed out and written as complete sentences, as follows.

Influential voice

Within five years our association will be a recognized influential voice that impacts practice in our field, systems and outcomes. We will have identifiable leadership at all levels of society and within our field. There will be viable, effective partnerships for the mutual benefit of initiatives and of interested organizations.

Recognized practice

Within five years our curriculum will be a vital piece of practitioner education. We will have a strong, viable, credible, certification program with 50% of the country's practitioners certified.

Valued organization

Within five years we will see a critical mass of actively connected members who see value in the organization. The organization will have an appropriately resourced committee structure and an executive director.

Contradictions

The board's contradictions workshop identified the following underlying blocks to its vision.

I.   An "at-capacity" unworkable, volunteer structure

II. Triple-duty board membership: With the existing structure board members do triple duty … often on provincial boards, on a national board, as well as on all the issues and topics, all at once.

III. Tired, cynical attitudes toward change: Our members have powerful community positions but have tired, cynical, attitudes toward systemic change. Practitioners have immediate access to, and can promote change in, all parts of every community, but can be cynical about the very changes they wish to occur.

IV. Values conflict: There is a conflict between the values of practitioners in our association, and the values of practitioners from closely related associations.

V.   We often operate from a defensive philosophy.

VI. The emerging identity of professionals in our field creates difficulties because it is still only vaguely defined.

Strategic directions

The association then identified the following series of strategic directions to overcome its obstacles as in Figure 35.

Implementation plans

Following this strategic plan, the implementation plan included a new organizational structure, phased strategies for some of the strategies, and several measurable accomplishments with deadlines. The new board committees decided to create their timeline of implementation steps at a later date. But all the nine strategies were assigned to various committees, which outlined the following different approaches to implementation.

Immediate implementation

Strategy D, Formalize and implement a modified organizational structure, was implemented

A. Develop, implement and evaluate the certification process and outcomes.	B. Produce resources and mechanisms to support implementation of national standards.	C. Influence content in curricula to reflect standards.	Building our capacity as a specialty practice
D. Formalize and implement a modified organizational structure.	E. Increase capacity, profile, influence, resources, by sharing resources with appropriate partners.	F. Get an executive director.	Enhancing and sustaining an effective organization
G. Articulate uniqueness and commonality of our practitioners and related practitioners.	H. Communicate with front line and management.	I. Develop a body of expertise.	Creating an influential voice

FIGURE 35. Strategies of a professional association

immediately during the planning. They created the new organizational structure during the strategic planning session, including board standing committees and ad-hoc committees.

Sample of a phased strategy
Strategy A, Develop, implement, and evaluate the certification process and outcomes with other national groups as partners over three years.
- By June next year we will have developed, in partnership with three other associations, a research proposal to evaluate a certification process and outcomes.
- By June two years from now, we will have implemented a formative evaluation of the certification process with the three partners.
- By June three years from now, we will have implemented an outcome evaluation of the certification process with the three partners.

Sample of measurable accomplishments
Strategy H, Communicate with the front line and management, involved these steps:
- By September this year, we will have an organizational promotional package.
- In October next year, we will have the organization featured in a national professional magazine.
- By September in two years, we will have increased our membership by 200 members.

Key documentation from the regional economic development plan

This sample documentation comes from a ToP participatory strategic plan with a newly amalgamated city and its surrounding rural area. The process included 600 people in 27 community forums, and a very large action planning conference in a local gymnasium. The basic outcome was the launch of a dozen citizen action teams dealing with various arenas of the economic development plan.

The vision chart (Figure 36) is complex, because of the large number of people who participated in creating the vision. Each of the small cells in the lower half of the chart represents the comments of half a dozen to a couple of dozen people from different forums. The top half of the chart represents the weight of consensus within the entire community to shift the economy of the region in a very big way.

Six hundred people gave input to the contradictions (Figure 37), creating several levels of contradiction. The cells in the bottom half represent what large numbers of people actually said as input during the forums. Each cell represents ten to twenty comments. The cells in the top half refer to the analysis of the contradictions by the steering committee.

Regional strategies

Fifteen strategies and four strategic directions emerged from the forums (Figure 38). One hundred fifty people, most of them having participated in a forum, attended a plenary session in a college gymnasium to see the vision and strategies, and to form implementation teams. Fifteen implementation teams were launched in the afternoon, and each team created measurable accomplishments for their strategy and a simple implementation timeline.

Long-range practical vision of regional economic development

International vacation reputation			Sustainable economy allowing people to remain				Regional unity with local services		
			Decent work opportunities		*Stable base of small business*		*Unified population*	*Locally self sufficient*	
Many natural destinations	*Great river attractions*	*Enviable lifestyle*	*Youth remain*	*Higher employment*	*Industrial expansion*	*Active commerce*	*Unified population*	*Higher education*	*Local services*
Vibrant tourism	*Great river attractions*	*Enviable lifestyle*	*Youth remain*	*Higher employment*	*Industrial expansion*	*Active commerce*	*Unified population*	*Higher education*	*Local services*
Vibrant tourism	Clean, beautiful river	Bigger population	Local job opportunities	More people working	Diverse economy	Commercial entrepreneurs	Affordable city	College accessibility	Fire protection
More tourist destinations	Replenished fish stock	Cultural activities	Stay longer in school	Full-time jobs	Agricultural production	Local spending	Involved community	Educated population	Improved roads
Full range of amenities	Expanded recreation	Forward thinking	Recreation activities	More job options	Independence from forests	Neighbourhood stores	Honest politicians	Local schools	Local health resources
Well-known trails	Preserved environment	Friendly lifestyle	Practical training	Realistic wages	Light manufacturing	Regular investment	Long-term plans	Local university	Specific improvements
Year-round tourism		Local control		Skilled opportunities	Local ownership		People oriented gov't	Quality facilities	Retirement homes
Vacation-land reputation		Regional identity		Stable work	Secondary processing		Public dialogue	Relevant training	Affordable housing
Revitalized port		Safe community		Value-added work	Sustained forest industry		Unified community		Extended water & sewage
High use camps		Social services			Technology center				Lower taxes
Good signage									

FIGURE 36. Practical vision of a region

Regional contradictions

	Outside interests divide and conquer local leadership creating economic disarray		Stringent restrictions on access to capital investment for small business dampens normal entrepreneurial activity		Strong local commitments eclipse the almost non-existent regional communications linkages			Unconscious competition between regional life-style and urban values		A long dependency on forests and on government limits economic imagination	
Petty local politics creates divided interests	Fear of failure of business creates negative climate and investment difficulties	Government interferes based on outside economic interests	Hard to locate investment sources without extensive collateral or backing	Bureaucratic obstacles deter all types of micro business endeavors	Long patterns of inter-community rivalry break down effective communication	Corporate profit and government tax interests squeeze out interest in smaller development	No long term goals leave a lack of focus and a negative attitude about leadership	Existing education prepares one only for work outside the region	Centralization of services into the city has created an indifference to village life	Dependence on government grants takes away individual initiative	Long reliance on resource economy has deadened interest in diversification
Lack of cooperative, united entrepreneurial spirit	People afraid to start things because of economic insecurity	Poor communication between government and community	Inexperience in accessing capital	Abstract bureaucratic conditions block entrepreneurial activities	Long standing patterns of local and cultural self interest	High cost of production creates high competition	Inadequate leadership leads to poor focus	Lack of knowledge and information and resource people	Culturally indifferent education system robs 1st Nation identity	Overdependent on government grants and complacency	Overdependence on natural resources
Lack of community attitude and spirit	Local insecurity blocks economic risk-taking	Government dependence saps individual initiative	Blocked financial resources	Job opportunities limited by economic concentration	Individual information control	Competing political interests block development	Long term goals un-directed	Inadequate water and sewage	Caught up in assimilation, few village attractions	History of living beyond means	
Not working together well, rivalry	Negativity creates hesitance to spend	Established political practices ineffective	Internal and external image of community	Individual enterprise over-regulated	History of division between communities	Big corporations and government tied together	Lack of leadership, focus and negativity	No job development	Centralization of urban services	Grant catch-22	
Existing leadership not communicating	Lack of confidence in self and future	Politics blocks development	Weak community capital base	Ineffective policies for development	Intercommunity competition	Private ownership of river resources	Lack of vision and strategy				
Leadership and divided interests	Poorly projected image	Little clout divides efforts	Hard to locate money sources	Bureaucracy gone mad							
Petty politics	Low profit margin	Vested interests									
Self-inflicted uncooperation	Fear of failure in business	Balancing taxes with services									

FIGURE 37. Contradictions of a region

Coordinate business associations	Create local investment pools	Seek out entrepreneurial efforts	Help micro-business start-ups	**Towards encouraging local investment**
Expose hidden agendas	Encourage new leaders	Create new systems for dialogue	Launch community cooperation	**Towards overcoming old rivalries**
Build on college technology success	Promote unified planning	Increase tourist destinations	Promote region in a unified way	**Towards promoting regional attractions**
Staff needs-based social programs	Make joint submissions		Teach entrepreneurial thinking	**Towards planning for the long term**

FIGURE 38. Strategies of a region

Key documentation from the hospital and area health centre plan

This documentation (Figure 39) comes from a ToP participatory strategic plan with a hospital, in which board members, senior managers, and key stakeholders took part. The plan created a solid footing for the future, and changes happening even seven years later were anticipated by the plan.

Sample of a sentence describing a vision element:

Seamless care model for seniors
In five years we want to see local continuous access to health care and support for individuals to be able to age in this community.
This is important because:

- Seniors represent an expanding portion of our population.
- It would enhance the quality of life by augmenting support systems within familiar environments.
- It would maintain the economic viability of an area with a static senior population.

Long-range practical vision *Growing into an area health centre*		
In Business	**In Client care**	**In Staffing**
State-of-the-art equipment	Seamless care model for seniors	Competent, stable, renewable workforce
	Community partnerships	Staff education
Balanced business management	Tertiary prevention	
	Essential programs	Satisfied staff
	Philosophy of choice in client care	

FIGURE 39. Practical vision of a hospital

This would look like:

- Additional support housing units on-site at the Center, to allow for continuous access to services, and to reflect the unique life style and spirit to which we are accustomed.
- Agreed-to programs to extend independent community living.

Contradictions

The Health Center stakeholders identified four major contradictions to their vision. These are listed below, with the full contradiction statement included for the first one.

I. *Our own understanding of different types of clients.*

While our vision is of providing choice to all Health Center clients and of giving people alternatives, our past experience is of healing and of making people comfortable in their healing process. So while our clients need to be told and understand the options open to them, our own expertise is in doing things for people rather than patiently explaining and helping them to understand what they need to do for themselves.

II. *Unrealistic public expectations*

III. *Internal politics slows down several vision elements*

IV. *Competing, huge workloads*

Strategies

Seven prioritized strategies emerged from the planning (Figure 40).

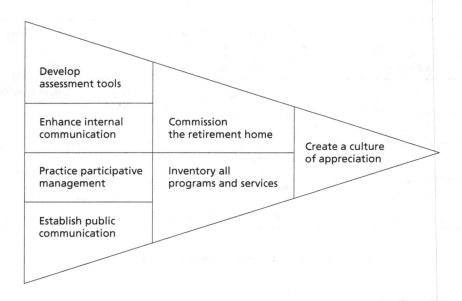

FIGURE 40. Strategies of a hospital

Action plans

During implementation planning, six-, twelve-, and twenty-four month measurable accomplishments (strategic objectives) were determined for each strategy, along with a few key actions. Later, hospital staff members were tasked with creating implementation plans and timelines (Figure 41).

Implementation plan			
Strategies	**6-month strategic objectives**	**12-month strategic objectives**	**2-year strategic objectives**
Create a culture of appreciation for staff.	• Expand newsletter to include hospital updates, financial and statistical data, sick time results, individual accomplishments. • General staff meeting every quarter.	• Formal policy on Staff Recognition Program • Designate a staff room.	• One staff function per year formalized. • Two social event staff functions formalized per year. • All staff can access computers, internet.
Practice participative management.	• Strategic plan shared with staff. • Schedule set of regular general staff meetings. • Business addendum to the Newsletter.	• Departmental financial information and info affecting the Health Center written up and shared with staff.	• Progress of strategic plan reviewed at General Meeting.
Develop systemic assessment tools across the Center.	• Working group formed. • Assessment tool designed. • Sample group chosen. • Approvals and consents obtained. • Funding sources identified.	• Funding in place. • Tool applied. • Responses received. • Data collated by working group. • Follow-through with group.	• All data collated. • Team formed for writing of report. • Feedback received from necessary stakeholders. • Information disseminated to necessary stakeholders.
Commission the retirement home.	• Complete staff orientation in May. • Complete resident admissions. • Changes to charting system. • Occupancy review passed in May. • Draft preoccupancy plan submitted in Jan. • Approval of final occupancy plan.	• Residents settled. • Period of relocation, adjustment and evaluation.	• Expanded volunteer program in May. • Audited and adjustment programs. • Completed market survey for supportive housing June.
Inventory current status of programs and services.	• Inventory of administrative, clinical and supportive services completed.	• Cost and viability analysis of new proposed programs completed.	• Required changes implemented.
Establish good communication and education system for the public.	• Staff meetings in January and March • Celebration opening. • Tours of the new building for public and staff. • Recognition of fundraising work.	• Quarterly public newsletter with volunteer coordinator. • Public focus groups. • Continued staff appreciation efforts.	• Three advisory groups in place. • Employee of the month program. • Public acknowledgement of staff
Enhance internal communications and performance management systems	• Inform staff of intentions	• Improved employee appraisals form. • New facility appraisals.	• Improved appraisals process and facility performance reviews.

FIGURE 41. Implementation plan of a hospital

Key documentation from the international NGO plan

This documentation comes from a ToP participatory strategic plan held with the staff, management, and board of a small government body that grew into an international organization. The practitioner worked with the NGO to assist with implementation of various parts of the plan over the next four years.

Long-range practical vision for an international NGO			
Practical global commitments	**Sustainable health resources**	**Long-term increased nutrition**	**Results-oriented organization**
Compelling global advocacy	Virtual elimination of the health deficiency	Multiple food programs in targeted countries	Expanded professional organization
Solid African presence	Targeted delivery of the necessary supplies	Diverse secure supplies	Results-oriented reputation
Long–term public and private commitment	Effective monitoring and evaluation systems in place	Foods integrated into broader development	International partnership network
	Global dissemination of technical information	Transfer of applicable technologies	

FIGURE 42. Practical vision of an NGO

Contradictions

I. Competing interests and agendas hamper effective cooperation.

II. Unsettled internal organizational unit structure creates unclarity.

III. Complex health solutions defy visible impacts.

IV. Health problems are not easily recognized.

V. Local priorities and weak capabilities of the beneficiaries create dependency.

VI. Donor-driven priorities divert our attention from long-term plan.

Strategy

See Figure 43.

Build capacity through training	Seek and involve partners in diverse sectors	Generate demand that leads to committed action	Enhance and expand new dialogue with partners	**Creating multi-level partnerships**
Monitor and evaluate programs and their structure		Disseminate results and success widely and routinely		**Broadcasting results of successful interventions**
Hold constraint assessments and gap analyses	Develop technologies and other initiatives		Expand long term donor base with collaboration	**Focusing targets for maximum impact**
Identify and assign priorities with a concrete schedule	Clarify roles, responsibilities and accountability		Share information systematically	**Systematizing staff interaction**

FIGURE 43. Strategies of an international NGO

Key documentation from the industry association plan

This documentation is drawn from a ToP participatory strategic plan with the board of an industry association. The plan launched several new initiatives and new hiring practices within the association. The documentation includes an historical scan, mission, vision, contradictions, strategies, phased strategies, action plan, and some organizational restructuring.

Historical scan

See Figure 44.

Mission statement

We are a national association whose members are dedicated to promoting the highest standards of products, installations, services, and ethics for the benefit of the consumer and our industry.

Industry association historical scan			
At the mercy of the manufacturer *Big companies* *Infancy* *Eastern states*	Entrepreneurial revolution *Gaining momentum* *Expansion and new chapters* *Adolescence*	What have you done for me today? Jacks of all trades! *New products* *Same folks – cliques* *Stagnation*	Searching for Purpose Questioning *Refocus* *Look in the mirror*
1980 1985	1990	1995	2000	2005
• Reduction in tax from 10 to 2% • Trade Show	• Revised standards • Apprenticeship program • The purchase group • Project of the year – 3 years running	• New logo • No significant member drives or increases • "Special" board meeting • Office moved • Workers legal benefits from 2% to 8%	• Membership apathy • Standards published • Minimal dues increases • Enforcement of bylaws in chapters • Focus on revenue instead of member services • New materials • Certification • Website established	• Office move • Other country joins • Tax discounts • Resource tariffs • Steel imports • Trade shows • Charity campaign

FIGURE 44. Historical scan of an industry association

Vision

See Figure 45.

Contradictions

I. *Unfocused undeveloped message causing waning interest.*
   Communication and messages from the national board have been unfocused and in some cases non-existent. This has resulted in many members losing interest in the organization beyond paying their annual membership dues.

II. *Protective attitude amongst members restricts recruitment and involvement.*
   At the chapter level, members can be business competitors with one another, or they can be suppliers or clients of one another, which leads to caution in recruiting new members and in involvement in the association.

III. *Inadequate staffing.*

Five-year practical vision of industry association			
Healthy finances	Continuous leadership	Industry recognition	Informed membership
Financially healthy organization	Centrally coordinated administration	More active, involved members	Comprehensive education resources
High-profile trade shows	Strong continuity of leadership	High level of recognition	Consistent informative communication

FIGURE 45. Practical vision of an industry association

IV. *Conventional face-to-face meetings not drawing us together.*

V. *Short term, past-oriented cash accounting.*

Strategy

A. *Invigorate committee structures.*

The thrust of this strategy is to create and sustain a set of committees with the potential to engage the wider membership in initiatives and projects that can get national board support. Committees will conduct business in other modalities besides face-to-face meetings, and will create succession plans.

B. *Transfer workload to staff.*

Many activities currently done by board members will be transferred to association staff to ensure the highest quality of implementation.

C. *Inform, communicate to, and educate members.*

D. *Ensure succession by training our leaders.*

E. *Upgrade the finance system.*

Phased strategies

See Figure 46.

Action plan

See Figure 47.

Three-year phased strategic objectives					
Strategy	**By September**	**By March**	**By next March**	**Budget**	**Team**
A. **Invigorate committee structure**	• Structure suggested • Define roles and number of members for each committee	• Basic responsibilities determined • Committees populated with members	• Succession plan for each committee	$	H, I
B. **Transfer workload to staff**	• Fill role of administrator • Create guideline for conduct • Pass on duties	• Other contract roles defined and filled • Refine role of committees versus administration duties	• Re-evaluate needs for administrator • Full communication strategy in place with contract components	$ Determine proper budget format	F, G
C. **Inform, communicate to, and educate, members**	• Publish newsletter • Information sent out on this meeting, chapter information, mission statement	• Publish report by trade show • Continue newsletter quarterly	• Quarterly newsletter • External communication plan created	Income covers expense. $ budget overall	A, B, C, D, E.
D. **Ensure succession by training our leaders**	• Chapter, national manuals found and accessible • Bylaws reviewed • Translation done or in works • Succession plan developed	• Future leaders scouted from full membership • Professional training course identified for national and chapter leadership • Mentors for each role	• Defined President-elect, Vice-President and past President • Mentoring working	$	J, K
E. **Finance**	• Work costed out • Committee in place • Revenue sources				C, G

FIGURE 46. Phased strategies of an industry association

Six-month action plan milestones

Strategy	April	May	June	July	August	By September	Team
A. Invigorate committee structure	Existing committee roles researched.	Roles described. Work delegated to administrator.				• Committee structure ready. • Roles and number or members for each committee defined.	H, I
B. Transfer workload to staff	Find history of work and roles.		RFP in June. New duties determined.	Consensus calls on candidates.		• Administrator role filled. • Conduct guideline created. • Duties passed on.	F, G
C. Inform, communicate to and educate members	Strategic plan report.		Chapter reports in.			• Newsletter published. • Information on this meeting, chapter information, mission statement sent out.	A, B, C, D, E,
D. Ensure succession by training leaders		Documents found.		Compilation over summer.	Succession plan submitted. Translation in fall.	• Chapter, national manuals found. • Bylaws reviewed. • French translation done or in works. • Succession plan developed.	J, K
E. Finance		Income strategy in Inc/Exp plan.	June Budget proposal.			• Work costed out • Committee members in place. • Revenues sourced	C, G.

FIGURE 47. Implementation plan of an industry association

Structure

As part of Strategy A, a new committee structure was recommended. Some of the new commit-tees became long-term standing committees. There are short-term working committees for spec-ial circumstances. Four of the strategies were implemented by several committees. In other cases there was a direct relationship between committees and strategies.

Priority urgency	Recommended committee	Status	Implementation of strategy	Strategy related to it
1.	Trade Show Committee	Newly mandated, but already operational for several years	National level .	All strategies
2.	Newsletter Committee	Newly mandated	National, with chapter level input	A. Inform, communicate to and educate members
3.	Finance Committee	Existing, but not operational	National	E. Finance strategy B. Transfer workload to staff
4.	Membership Committee	Mandated, but not operational	Chapter level	
5.	Training Committee	Newly mandated	National / Chapter	D. Ensure succession by training leaders
6.	Bylaw Committee	Mandated, but not operational	National	
7.	Legal Committee	Mandated, operational when needed	National	
8.	Advisory Board	Newly mandated	National	

FIGURE 48. Structural implementation of an industry association

Appendix

Participation assessment tool for stages of planning

The following chart can help facilitators think through the whole spiral process with leaders of a client organization. The chart provides a comprehensive checklist of questions and issues to ponder in tailoring the ToP process for the group's needs. It allows the leaders to consider each of the four phases of the spiral process.

Steps in the participatory strategic planning process	Executive Director or small Strat. Plan Team	Board involved	Staff involved	Community involved	Other key stake-holders involved
I. Preparing for strategic planning					
Assessing the reasons for strategic planning					
• internal					
• external					
Clarifying the planning objectives					
• expectations					
• results					
• scope					
• group					
Establishing the planning roles and guidelines					
• how much participation					
• steering committee					
• leadership					
• consultant / facilitator					
Designing the planning process					
• focus question					
• methods					
• time					

FIGURE 49. Overall framework of participation in strategic planning, Stage I

II. Developing the planning context					
Analyzing the external environment					
• stakeholders & constituents					
• competitors & collaborators					
• events					
• trends					
• opportunities & threats					
Analyzing the internal environment					
• history					
• accomplishments & setbacks					
• resources					
• strengths & weaknesses					
Clarifying the mandates and mission					
• basic mandate					
• purpose / mission					
• reason for being					
Objectifying the primary values					
• guiding principles					
• basic ethics					
• operating patterns					

FIGURE 50. Overall framework of participation in strategic planning, Stage II

Steps in the Participatory Strategic Planning Process	Ex. Dir. or small Strat. Plan Team	Board involved	Staff involved	Community involved	Other key Stake-holders involved
III. Creating the strategies					
Stating the vision of the future					
• hopes and dreams					
• 3 to 5 years					
• practical					
Identifying the underlying obstacles					
• obstacles, barriers, and roadblocks					
• underlying contradictions					
Creating the strategic directions					
• 1 to 2 years or more					
• practical					
• implement yourself					
Designing the implementation scheme					
• priorities					
• phasing					
• action projects					
Clients can decide later how much involvement they want from the facilitator-consultant in the next section, preparing to implement the plans.					

FIGURE 51. Overall framework of participation in strategic planning, Stage III

IV. Implementing the plans					
Preparing the action plans					
• specific, measurable accomplishments					
• catalytic actions					
• focused campaigns					
• coordinated timelines					
• budgeting					
Forming the implementing structures					
• ongoing committees					
• special taskforces					
• coordination team					
Monitoring the action and evaluating the results					
• tracking action					
• action reviews					
• breakthroughs and gaps					
• learnings and evaluation					
• recreated objectives					
• actions and campaigns					
• implementing structures					

FIGURE 52. Overall framework of participation in strategic planning, Stage IV

Note on terminology

Throughout this book, specific terminology is associated with each phase of the spiral process.

Vision	Contradiction	Strategy	Measurable Accomplishments	Actions
• Vision statement • Overall vision • Vision area • Vision elements • Long range practical vision	• Irritants • Blame • Lack of • Gaps • Issues • Block and obstacles • Underlying obstacles • Root systemic obstacles • Contradictions	• Approaches • Directions • Strategic directions	• Strategic objectives • Goals • Victory circle • Blue-sky victory • Ends • Outcomes • Ends indicators • Outcome indicators • Process indicators	• Tactical systems • Tactical arena • Tactics • Implementation steps • Action items • Timelines

FIGURE 53. Terminology chart

This chart does not include the terms "strategic vision" or "strategic issue," which are used by some consultants. A practitioner would need to ask why a particular vision or issue is considered strategic, which might shed some light on the terminology. A strategic vision might simply refer to a priority vision element, but it might refer to a long range outcome, or a goal or measurable accomplishment. A strategic issue might refer to an urgent problem, but it might refer to an underlying block, or a contradiction. For some clients and consultants, putting strategic in front of another word serves to elevate that word whether or not it is actually strategic.

Bibliography

Belden, Ginny, Marcia Hyatt, Deborah Ackley. (1993). *Towards the Learning Organization: A Guide.* Toronto: Belden, Hyatt, Ackley.

Bergdall, Terry. (1993). *Methods of Active Participation: Experiences in Rural Development from East and Central Africa.* Nairobi: Oxford University Press.

Bohm, D. (1980). *Wholeness and the Implicate Order.* New York: Routledge.

Bohm, D. (1996). *On Dialogue.* New York: Routledge.

Boulding, K. (1956). *The Image.* Ann Arbor, MI: University of Michigan Press.

Bryson, John. (1997). *Strategic Planning for Public & Nonprofit Organizations.* San Francisco: Jossey-Bass, 1989.

Burbidge, John, Editor. *Beyond Prince and Merchant.* New York: Pact Publications.

Doyle, Michael and David Straus. (1976). *How to Make Meetings Work.* New York: The Brekley Publishing Group.

Elgin, D. (1993). *Awakening Earth: Exploring the Evolution of Human Culture and Consciousness.* New York: William Morrow & Company, Inc.

Epps, John. (2011). *Bending History: Talks of Joseph Wesley Mathews Volume II - Societal Transformation, Toward a New Social Vehicle.* Lutz, FL: Resurgence Publishing Corporation.

Epps, John. (2003). The Journey of Meaning at Work. *Group Facilitation: A Research and Applications Journal, Spring 2003 (1), pp. 17-25.*

Epps, John. (2005). Facilitation from the Inside Out. *IAF Handbook of Group Facilitation.* San Francisco, CA: Jossey-Bass.

Gowan, J. C. (1979). "Creativity and the Gifted Child Movement." In J.C. Gowan, J. Khatena & E. P. Torrance (Eds.), *Educating the Ablest.* Durham, NC: F. E. Peacock Publishers, Inc.

Harman, W. (1986). "Transformed Leadership: Two Contrasting Concepts." In J. D. Adams (Ed.), *Transforming Leadership from Vision to Results*. Alexandria, VA: Miles River Press.

Harrison, Roger. (1995). *Leadership and Strategy for a New Age*. Malibu, CA: Harrison Associates Inc.

Heron, John. (1989). *The Facilitators' Handbook*. London: Kogan Page.

Jablin, F. M., & Seibold, D. R. (1978). "Implications for Problem-solving Groups of Empirical Research on 'Brainstorming': A Critical Review of the Literature." *The Southern Speech Communication Journal*, 43, pp. 327–356.

Jaques, Elliott. (1989). *Requisite Organization: A Total System for Effective Managerial Organization and Managerial Leadership for the 21st Century*. Gloucester, MA: Cason Hall.

Jenkins, Jon. (1996). *The International Facilitator's Companion*. Groningen, The Netherlands: Imaginal Training.

Kaner, Sam, with Lenny Lind, Catherine Toldi, Sarah Fisk & Duane Berger. (1996). *Facilitator's Guide to Participatory Decision-Making*. Philadelphia, PA: New Society Publishers.

Kant, I. (1950). *Critique of Pure Reason*. New York: Humanities Press.

Kierkegaard, S. (1954). *Fear and Trembling*. Garden City, NY: Doubleday & Company, Inc.

Kloepfer, J. (1990). *The Art of Formative Questioning: A Way to Foster Self-disclosure*. Ann Arbor, MI: University Microfilms International.

Lehman, R. (1997). *Our Common Work: A New Birth of Freedom*. Kalamazoo, MI: Fetzer Institute.

Lester, D. (1994). *Leadership for a Multicultural America*. Denver, CO: CERT.

Lewin, K. (1951). *Field Theory in Social Science*. New York, NY: Harper.

Mann, Clancy; Goetz, Klaus, eds. (2006). *Borderless Business: Managing the Far-Flung Enterprise*. Westport, CT: Praeger Publishing.

Mathews, Joseph Wesley. (1965). *Religious Studies I*. Chicago, IL: Ecumenical Institute.

Mintzberg, H. (2008). *Tracking Strategies: Towards a General Theory of Strategy Formation*. Cary, NC: Oxford University Press.

Mullen, B., C. Johnson, & E. Salas. (1991). "Productivity Loss in Brainstorming Groups: A Meta-analytic Integration." *Basic and Applied Social Psychology*, 12, 3–23.

Nelson, Jo. (2004). *The Art of Focused Conversation for Schools*. Toronto, ON: The Canadian Institute of Cultural Affairs.

Osborn, A. F. (1957). *Applied Imagination: Principles and Procedures of Creative Problem Solving* (Revised ed.). New York: Charles Scribner's Sons.

Palmer, P. (1995). *The Art and Craft of Formation: A Reflective Handbook for the Formation Programs of the Fetzer Institute.* Unpublished manuscript.

Rees, Fran. (1990). *How to Lead Teams: Facilitation Skills.* San Diego, CA: Pfeiffer and Co.

Ritscher, J. (1986). "Spiritual Leadership." In J. D. Adams (Ed.), *Transforming Leadership from Vision to Results.* Alexandria, VA: Miles River Press.

Russell, P. (1983). *The Global Brain: Speculations on the Evolutionary Leap to Planetary Consciousness.* Los Angeles: JP Tarcher.

Schuman, S. (2010). *The Handbook for Working with Difficult Groups.* San Francisco, CA: Jossey-Bass.

Schuman, S. (2005). *The IAF Handbook of Group Facilitation.* San Francisco, CA: Jossey-Bass

Senge, Peter M. (1990). *The Fifth Discipline: The Art and Practice of the Learning Organization.* New York: Peter M. Senge.

Shepard, K., Gray, J. L. (2007). *Organization Design, Levels of Work and Human Capability: Executive Guide.* Toronto, ON: Global Organization Design Society

Sherif, Muzafer. (1936). *The Psychology of Social Norms.* New York: Harper.

Spencer, Laura J. (1989). *Winning through Participation, Meeting the Challenge of Corporate Change with the Technology of Participation.* Dubuque, IA: Kendall/Hunt Publishing Company.

Stanfield, R. Brian, General Editor. (1997). *The Art of Focused Conversation: 100 Ways to Access Group Wisdom in the Workplace.* Toronto, ON: The Canadian Institute of Cultural Affairs.

Stanfield, R. Brian, General Editor. (2002). *The Workshop Book: From Individual Creativity to Group Action.* Toronto, ON: The Canadian Institute of Cultural Affairs.

Stanfield, R. Brian. (2000). *The Courage to Lead: Transform Self, Transform Society.* Toronto, ON: The Canadian Institute of Cultural Affairs.

Troxel, James, Editor. (1993). *Participation Works: Business Cases from Around the World.* Alexandria, VA: Miles River Press.

Troxel, James, Editor. (1995). *Government Works: Profiles of People Making a Difference.* Alexandria, VA: Miles River Press.

van Kaam, A. (1975). *In Search of Spiritual Identity.* Denville, NJ: Dimension Books.

Walter, M. George, Moore, E. Maynard. (2010). *Transform the Legacy: Volume II The Response and Future Directions.* Lutz, FL: Resurgence Publishing Corporation.

West, George. (2012). *Creating Community: Finding Meaning in the Place We Live.* Toronto, ON: The Canadian Institute of Cultural Affairs.

Wilber, Ken. (1981). *No Boundary.* Boulder, CO: New Science Library.

Wilber, Ken. (1997). *The Eye of Spirit.* Boston: Shambhala Press.

Williams, R. Bruce. (1997). *Twelve Roles of Facilitators for School Change.* Arlington Heights, IL: IRI/Skylight Training and Publishing, Inc.

Williams, R. Bruce. (1993). *More Than Fifty Ways to Build Team Consensus.* Palatine, IL: IRI/Skylight Publishing, Inc.

Wilson, P., Harnish, K., Wright. (2003). *The Facilitative Way: Leadership That Makes the Difference.* Kansas City, MO: TeamTech Press.

Index